ARTISTIC FREEDOM IN INTERNATIONAL LAW

The book examines in detail the essence, nature and scope of artistic freedom as a human right. It explains the legal problems associated with the lack of a precise definition of the term 'art' and discusses the emergence of a distinct 'right' to artistic freedom under international law. Drawing on a variety of case studies, primarily from the field of visual arts, but also performance, street art and graffiti, it examines potentially applicable 'defences' for those types of artistic expression that are perceived as inappropriate, ugly, offensive, disturbing or even obscene and transgressive. The book also offers a view on global controversies such as *Charlie Hebdo* and the Danish cartoons, attempting to explain the subtleties of offences related to religious sensibilities and beliefs. It also examines the legitimacy of restrictions on extremist expressions in the case of arts involving criminal acts such as child pornography.

Eleni Polymenopoulou is Associate Professor of Law at College of Law, Hamad Bin Khalifa University, and Adjunct Associate Professor at Edmund A. Walsh School of Foreign Service, Georgetown University. She is also practising artist, children's book author and illustrator.

Artistic Freedom in International Law

ELENI POLYMENOPOULOU
Hamad Bin Khalifa University

CAMBRIDGE
UNIVERSITY PRESS

CAMBRIDGE
UNIVERSITY PRESS

Shaftesbury Road, Cambridge CB2 8EA, United Kingdom

One Liberty Plaza, 20th Floor, New York, NY 10006, USA

477 Williamstown Road, Port Melbourne, VIC 3207, Australia

314–321, 3rd Floor, Plot 3, Splendor Forum, Jasola District Centre, New Delhi – 110025, India

103 Penang Road, #05–06/07, Visioncrest Commercial, Singapore 238467

Cambridge University Press is part of Cambridge University Press & Assessment, a department of the University of Cambridge.

We share the University's mission to contribute to society through the pursuit of education, learning and research at the highest international levels of excellence.

www.cambridge.org
Information on this title: www.cambridge.org/9781108844208

DOI: 10.1017/9781108933667

First published 2023

A catalogue record for this publication is available from the British Library.

Library of Congress Cataloging-in-Publication Data
NAMES: Polymenopoulou, Eleni, author.
TITLE: Artistic freedom in international law / Eleni Polymenopoulou.
DESCRIPTION: 1. | Cambridge, UK ; New York, NY : Cambridge University Press, 2023. | Includes bibliographical references and index.
IDENTIFIERS: LCCN 2022043094 (print) | LCCN 2022043095 (ebook) | ISBN 9781108844208 (hardback) | ISBN 9781108928427 (paperback) | ISBN 9781108933667 (epub)
SUBJECTS: LCSH: Law and art. | Copyright–Art. | Art–Censorship. | Obscenity (Law) | Freedom and art. | Art and religion. | Blasphemy–In art. | Blasphemy–Law and legislation. | Artists–Legal status, laws, etc.
CLASSIFICATION: LCC K3778 .P65 2023 (print) | LCC K3778 (ebook) | DDC 344/.097–dc23/eng/20230105
LC record available at https://lccn.loc.gov/2022043094
LC ebook record available at https://lccn.loc.gov/2022043095

ISBN 978-1-108-84420-8 Hardback

Contents

Acknowledgements

What makes art great is not only and not in the first place the high quality of what is created. Rather, art is great because it is an 'absolute need'.

—Nietzsche

The book is the fruit of many years of research on the intersections between art and the law. It incorporates findings from research conducted during my doctoral thesis in the sphere of human rights law (and specifically controversies over arts and religion) (2006–11); a year of studying art sociology (2005–06); several years of teaching (human rights law, media law and public international law, among others, as well as a course on 'art, media and cultural politics' at Georgetown University Qatar); and a short fellowship awarded by UCL Qatar in 2019 (Museum and Gallery Studies department), focusing on cultural heritage and the Islamic legal tradition. This book is also the product of personal insights and experience, including at Ornerakis School of Applied Arts in Athens (where I studied comics, illustration and 2D animation between 1997 and 2001).

A wholehearted 'thank you' to my husband for his encouragement and tremendous support, without which this book project would have never been realized. The writing process has not been easy, given that it coincided with Covid-19, partial school closures and a number of other difficulties. I would like to thank my family and close friends too, as well as my colleagues and students – present and former – for all the fruitful discussions we have had.

I would also like to thank all those artists, painters, musicians, performers, iconographers, illustrators and cartoonists whom I met during the past twenty years, many of whom I worked and developed enduring friendships with. They have contributed the most to my vision about 'artistic freedom in international law', although they may not be aware of it. This book is dedicated also to them.

Table of Cases

AFRICAN COMMISSION ON HUMAN AND PEOPLES' RIGHTS

Frente para a Libertação do Estado de Cabinda v Angola App no 328/06 (2013)

AFRICAN COURT ON HUMAN AND PEOPLES' RIGHTS

Lohé Issa Konaté v Burkina Faso App no 004/2013 (2014)

COMMITTEE ON THE ELIMINATION OF RACIAL DISCRIMINATION

Mohammed Hassan Gelle v Denmark, UN Doc CERD/C/68/D/34/2004 (2006)
Stephen Hagan v Australia, UN Doc CERD/C/62/D/26/2002 (2003)
TBB-Turkish Union in Berlin/Brandenburg, UN Doc CERD/C/82/D/48/2010 (2013)

COURT OF JUSTICE OF THE EUROPEAN UNION

Eva-Maria Painer v Standard Verlags GmbH C-145/10, ECLI:EU:C:2011:798

EUROPEAN COURT OF HUMAN RIGHTS

Abdulaziz, Cabales and Balkandali v UK (1985) 7 EHRR 471
Ahmet Yıldırım v Turkey App no 3111/10
Airey v Ireland (1980) 2 EHRR 305
Akdaş v Turkey App no 41056/04
Alekhina and Others App no 38004/12
Alınak v Turkey App no 40287/98

Alves da Silva v Portugal App no 41665/07
Appleby v United Kingdom App no 44306/98
Association Ekin v France App no 39288/98
Ben El Mahi and Others v Denmark App no 5853/06
Beyeler v Italy App no 33202/96
Bladet Tromsø and Stensaas v Norway App no 21980/93
Castells v Spain (1992) 14 EHRR 445
Chauvy and Others v France App no 64915/01
Choudhury v United Kingdom (1991) 12 HRLJ 172
Cumpǎnǎ and Mazǎre v Romania App no 33348/96
De Haes and Gijsels v Belgium App nos 7/1996/626/809
Delphi AS v Estonia App no 64669/09
Dorota Rabczewska against Poland App no 8257/13
Dubowska and Skup v Poland App nos 33490/96 and 34055/96
Ehrmann and SCI VHI v France App no 2777/10
Eon v France App no 26118/10
E.S. v Austria App no 38450/12
Faurisson v France App no 550/1993
Feldek v Slovakia App no 29032/95
Flux v Moldova no 6 App no 22824/04
Garaudy v France App no 65831/01
Handyside v United Kingdom (1979) 1 EHRR 737
Hoare v UK [2011] ECHR 722
İ.A. v Turkey App no 42571/98
Informationsverein Lentia and Others v Austria [1993] ECHR 57
Jelševar and Others v Slovenia App no 47318/07
Karademirci and Others v Turkey App nos 37096/97 and 37101/97
Karataş v Turkey App no 23168/94
Karttunen v Finland App no 1685/10
Klein v Slovakia App no 72208/01
Kuliś and Różycki v Poland App no 27209/03
Lambert and Others v France App no 46043/14
Lehideux et Isorni v France App no 24662/94
Leroy v France App no 36109/03
Lindon, Otchakovsky-Laurens and July v France (2008) 46 EHRR 35
Lingens v Austria App no 9815/82
Mandreigelya v Russia App no 34310/13
Manole and Others v Moldova App no 13936/02
Marckx v Belgium (1980) 2 EHRR 330
Mătăsaru v The Republic of Moldova App nos 69714/16 and 71685/16

HUMAN RIGHTS COMMITTEE

Rafael Marques de Morais v Angola, UN Doc N Doc CCPR/C/83/D/1128/2002 (2005)
Toonen v Australia, UN Doc CCPR/C/50/D/488/1992 (1994)

INTER-AMERICAN COMMISSION ON HUMAN RIGHTS

Francisco Martorell v Chile, Case 11.230, OEA/Ser.L/V/II.95 Doc 7 rev, 234 (1997)
Granier et al. (Radio Caracas Television – RCTV) v Venezuela (2015)
Javier Ortega Reyes, Paúl Rivas Bravo & Efraín Segarra Abril v Colombia & Ecuador, Resolution (2018)
Leaders of the 19 de Abril Carazo Movement and Others v Nicaragua (2018)
Report N° 31/98, Petition no 11.803 (1997)

INTER-AMERICAN COURT OF HUMAN RIGHTS

Canese v Paraguay, Series C no 111 (2004)
Compulsory Membership in an Association Prescribed by Law for the Practice of Journalism Advisory Opinion OC-5/85, Ser A no 5 (1985)
Hellera Ulloa v Costa Rica, Series C no 107 (2004)
Olmedo Bustos et al. v Chile, OC-73/ 2001, Ser C 73 (2001) [*Last Temptation of Christ*]

NATIONAL COURTS

Canada

Johnson v The Queen (1973) 13 C.C.C. (2d) 402
R. *v Sharpe* [2001] 1 SCR 45
R *v Verette* (1978) 2 SCR 838

Chile

Supreme Court Judgment (1997) [Last Temptation of Christ]
Santiago Court of Appeal Case, 16 September 2013 [Mapocho River Installation]

England and Wales

Attorney General v Guardian Newspapers Ltd (no 1) [1987] UKHL 13
Hensher v Restawile [1976] A.C. 64

Jefferys v Boosey (1854) 4 HLC 815
Lucasfilm Limited and Others v Ainsworth [2011] UKSC 39
Shaw v Director of Public Prosecution [1962] AC 220

France

Cass, Civil Ch.1, 85-15.044 (1987)
Cass, Civil Ch.2, 98-17.574 (2001)
Cass, Civil Ch. 2, 99-10.490 (2001)
Cass, Criminal Ch., 05-81.932 (2006)
Cass. 1 no 06-19.021 (2008)
Tribunal Grande Instance, order (2009)
Lyon Appeal Court Judgment (2004) [*Demeure du Chaos*]
Paris First Instance Judgment, 17th Chamber (2007)
Lindon, Court of Cassation (2002)
Marithé et François Girbaud (2005)

Germany

BVerfGE 119 (2007) [*Esra*]
BVerfGE 30 (1971) [*Mephisto*]
BVerfGE 75 [*Strauß-Karikatur*]
Pictures on the *Berlin Wall, Re* (Case I ZR 68/93) [1997] ECC 553

Greece

Athens First Instance Court Judgment (2003) [*Life of Christ*]
Athens First Instance Court Judgment 17115/1988 [*Last Temptation of Christ*]

India

Maqbool Fida Husain v Raj Kumar Pandey and Others (2007) 5 SCC 11
Phantom Films Pvt. Ltd. and Anr v The Central Board Of Certification (2016) SCC 3862
Sujato Bhadra v State of West Bengal, 22 September 2005, 2005 (4) CHN 601

Israel

Noah Films v Censorship Council PD 30 (1) 757
Supreme Court Judgment HC 806/88

Japan

Supreme Court of Japan, *Ichii et al. v Japan* 23 Keishu 10, 15 October 1969 [*Marquis De Sade's Prosperities of Vice*]
Supreme Court of Japan, *Koyama v Japan* (1957) 11 Keishu 997, 13 March 1957 [*Lady Chatterley's Lover*]

Korea (South)

South Korea Constitutional Court (1999) 26 November 1999
South Korea Constitutional Court, 10-1 KCCR 327, 95 Hun-Ka 16

Poland

Constitutional Court Judgment SK 54/13 (2015)

USA

Alberts v California (1957) 354 US 476
Aubin v City of Chicago (unreported)
Bantam Books, Inc. v Sullivan 372 US 58 (1963)
Barnes v Glen Theatre, Inc. 501 US 560
Beauharnais v Illinois 343 US 250 (1952)
Board of Education, Island Trees Union Free School District No 26 v Pico 457 US 853 (1982)
Boos v Barry 485 US 312 (1988)
Brandenburg v Ohio 395 US 444 (1969)
CBS Corp. v FCC no 06-3575 (3d Cir. 2 November 2011)
Chaplinsky v New Hampshire 315 US, 568 US (1942)
Cohen v California 403 US 15 (1971)
Cohen v G & M Realty (*Aerosol Art Center Inc.*) Case no 13-CV-05612(FB) (RLM) (E.D.N.Y. 13 June 2018) [5Pointz]
Constantin Brancusi v United States no 209109 (U .S. Customs Ct., 3d Div., 21 October 1927)

English v BFC&R East 11th Street LLC 97 Civ No 7446 (HB) (SDNY 1997)
FCC v Pacifica 438 US 726 (1978)
Feist Publications, Inc., v Rural Telephone Service Co. 499 US 340 (1991)
Fields v Twitter Inc. 200 F. Supp. 3d. 964, 967–68 (N.D. Cal. 2016)
Hannegan v Esquire 327 US 146 (1946)
Hoehling v Universal City Studios 449 US 841 (1980)
Hustler Magazine, Inc. v Falwell 485 US 56
Jacobellis v Ohio 378 US 184 (1964)
Joseph Burstyn, Inc. v Wilson 343 US 495 (1952)
Korematsu v United States 323 US 214 (1944)
Masterpiece Cakeshop, Ltd. v Colorado Civil Rights Commission 584 US (2018)
Memoirs v Massachusetts 383 US 413 (1966)
Miller v California 413 US 15 (1973)
Mutual Film Corporation v Industrial Commission of Ohio 236 US 230 (1915)
NAACP v Claiborne Hardware Co. 458 US 886 (1982)
Near v Minnesota 283 US 697 (1931)
New York State Club Ass'n v City of New York 487 US 1 (1988)
New York Times Co. v Sullivan 376 US at 376 US 270
New York Times Co. v United States 403 US 713 (1971)
PGA Tour Inc. v Martin (2001) 204 F.3d 994
R.A.V. v St Paul 505 US 377 (1992)
Redgrave v Boston Symphony Orchestra, Inc. 855 F.2d 888 (1st Cir.1988)
Roth v United States (1957) 354 US 476
Serra v United States General Services Administration 664 F.Supp. 798 (S.D.N.Y.1987)
Shenck v USA 249 US 47 (1919)
Snyder v Phelps 562 US 443 (2011)
Stromberg v California 283 US 359 (1931)
Texas v Johnson 491 US 397 (1989)
Verizon v FCC, US Court of Appeals for the D.C. Circuit (2014)
Walker v Sons of Confederate Veterans 115 S.Ct. 2239 (2015)

Introduction

The topic of this study might appear puzzling to creative artists and art worlds,[1] namely painters, musicians, dancers, film-makers, playwriters, composers, all those who make artworks or work with artists, museum staff, art faculty, gallerists, collectors, art buyers and art lovers. What does international law have to do with art? And why is there a need to write a legal monograph on a topic that is self-evident? From the perspective of the aforementioned stakeholders, arts are and should remain free. Freedom is a vital condition for the realization of the creative process. This is true philosophically,[2] while even psychologists have argued that creativity is generated by working in an unhindered and non-conformist manner.[3] Art exists *in* freedom, and occasionally also *for* freedom – be it as a vehicle of communication, a weapon against repression and injustice or simply a means of aesthetic expression. The motto 'To every age its art. To art its freedom!' that was once proclaimed by the Vienna Secessionists still echoes in exhibitions, museums, galleries, biennales, concerts, cinemas and theatre halls. The popularity of the actual product derived from the creative process too (i.e. the artwork, performance or song,

1 Throughout the book, I use the expression 'art worlds'. The term is borrowed from Howard Becker, who sees the creative process as a collective activity. See Howard Becker, *Art Worlds* (25th ed, University of California Press 2008) 1 ('all artistic work, like all human activity, involves the joint activity of a number, often a large number, of people. Through their cooperation, the artwork we eventually see or hear comes to be and continues to be. The [art]work always shows signs of that cooperation. The forms of cooperation may be ephemeral, but often become more or less routine, producing patterns of collective activity we can call an art world. The existence of art worlds, as well as the way their existence affects both the production and consumption of art works, suggests a sociological approach to the arts').

2 Haig Khatchadourian, 'Artistic Freedom and Social Control' (1978) 12 *Journal of Aesthetic Education* 23, 25.

3 Teresa Amabil, *Creativity in Context: Update to the Social Psychology of Creativity* (Westview Press 1996) (referring e.g. to Karl Rogers (1954); Koestler (1964); and Crutchfield (1962)).

etc.) is in principle independent of its creator. Save for the occasional psychopath labelling a murder as an 'artistic performance', the illegality of the act, or even the criminality of the author, is in principle unrelated to the actual artwork. This is why works made by the American serial killer John Wayne Gayce, the infamous 'Pogo the Clown', are available for sale at online auctions, and *Lolicons* (Japanese *anime* that involves sexualized representations of children) have thousands of dedicated fans. Artworks and performances have in fact good chances of becoming acceptable and even popular, even when initially perceived as shocking or disturbing.

These remarks are surely not very helpful for lawyers and judges, who at some point in a dispute involving artistic freedom will necessarily be confronted with the dilemma of defining the legal contours of art. Such an exercise is more challenging than it may appear. At least three stumbling blocks can be identified. First, accepting anything as 'art' (by a plaintiff, or applicant before a human rights body) cannot be automatically rejected as non-art. This is because art need not serve a particular function in society – or at least not anymore. There has been much written about the presumed function (and functionality) of the arts, including the need for art to serve a highly moral or pedagogical purpose,[4] and the highly influential Marxist approach on art being the expression of capitalist societies.[5] People write poems to express their deepest thoughts and communicate these to the public at large (as in the case of the poem *The Love that Dares to Speak Its Name* that was published in a gay magazine in the United Kingdom in the early 1990s and which gave rise to court proceedings for blasphemy),[6] or to protest against injustice and repression (as in the case of Mr Karataş, who expressed with his 'colourful imaginary' his deep-rooted discontent with the population of Kurdish origin in Turkey).[7] Yet, they also write poems that no one will ever read, simply to express themselves.

Second, 'art' cannot be subject to one universal definition, whether in law or the art worlds. Value-judgements and judgements about the function of art should in principle therefore be excluded from a definition of the arts, and be seen with suspicion even in art-funding processes. The inverse scenario (i.e. predefining what is acceptable 'art') is morally and legally impossible in the

4 Ernst Cassirer, *The Educational Value of Art* (Yale University Press 1979) (compiling Cassirer's lectures 1935–45).

5 Indicatively, Ernst Fischer, *The Necessity of the Art* (Penguin 1963) (based on the author's series of essays, written in 1949).

6 *X. Ltd and Y. v United Kingdom* App no 8710/79, Commission Report, 7 May 1982, following the House of Lords decision in *Lemon and Gay News Ltd v Whitehouse* [1979] AC 617.

7 *Karataş v Turkey* App no 23168/94, ECHR 1999-IV.

post-World War II world, as it legitimizes censorship, allowing State authorities and organs (the executive, the legislative or the judiciary) to reject dissident and otherwise unwanted art. It moreover does not resonate well with the history of art, and the fact that masterpieces revered today were rejected during their lifetime (Vincent van Gogh's paintings, Egon Schiele's drawings, Edgar Allan Poe's poems among others). The celebration of spaces once rejected by the institutional art worlds (such as the *Salon des Refusés* in Paris and the Secession Building in Vienna)[8] is proof that the next generation might cherish what its predecessors loathed. The problem is equally acute in attempting to draw the boundaries of 'art' (that remains unregulated and legitimate) as opposed to pornography or obscenity. The fine line between the two may not be immediately perceptible, and in any event is subject to subjective appreciations. It took a long time for films such as the *Realm of Senses* (1976) – and its sequel, the *Empire of Passion* (1978) – to be considered part of the 'cinematography' genre. Domestic jurisdictions have a privilege in establishing their own standards in order to differentiate between the two. Until the 1970s the Supreme Court of Japan (*Saikô saibansho*) rejected such expressions as 'shameful', holding that even high artistic value cannot preclude upholding a conviction for obscenity.[9]

In this sense, art can be intelligent, creative and powerful, as well as bad, boring and meaningless, or even cruel and shameful. Should such art then be rejected as unlawful? Framing the arts within the realm of the law raises immediate suspicion, as explained above. Yet, there must be something special about art – the distinct and 'autonomous' nature of art, that has been so well defined by the German Constitutional Court in *Mephisto*.[10] People more often than not react to works of art. Art history shows that art has the power to move, fascinate and exalt human spirit, as well as profoundly shock and disturb it. Artworks will be cherished and loved, placed in valuable positions within households, displayed in galleries and bought at astronomical prices. The mere existence of the art market, despite its fallacies, is evidence of

8 The fringe of which appears on a collectors' 100-euro golden coin, issued by the Austrian government, see <https://coinweek.com/world-coins/austria-2004-vienna-secession-100-euro-gold-coin/>.

9 *Koyama et al. v Japan* 11 Keishu 997, 13 March 1957 (DH Laurence, *Lady Chatterley's Lover*); *Ichii et al. v Japan* 23 Keishu 10, 15 October 1969 (*Marquis De Sade's Prosperities of Vice*). See generally, Shigenori Matsui, 'Freedom of Expression in Japan' (1991) 38 Osaka Law Review 13, 31; James Alexander, 'Obscenity, Pornography, and the Law in Japan: Reconsidering Oshima's "In the Realm of the Senses"' (2003) 4 Asian-Pacific Law and Policy Journal 148. Also Chapter 6 of this book.

10 *Mephisto* 1 BvR 435/68 (24 February 1971) BVerfGE 30, 173 at para 49. See Edward Eberle, 'Art as Speech' (2007–08) 11 *University of Pennsylvania Journal of Law and Social Change* 1, 7.

human attachment to artworks. The death of an artwork resembles the death of a human being. How can one explain otherwise that the day after the theft of the Mona Lisa (in August 1911) the Louvre was flocked with people – to see, not a painting, but the absence of it.[11] Hot-blooded spectators may even end up hugging and kissing artworks; although not without consequences, as in the case of the woman who left a red lipstick mark on Cy Twombly's painting during an exhibition in Avignon, France.[12]

'It happened to me', writes Leonardo da Vinci in his *A Treatise on Painting*, 'to paint a religious picture which was bought by someone who loved him so much that he would have liked to have all the sacred decoration disappear in order to be able to kiss it without remorse'.[13]

Others have attempted to take artworks with them to eternity – not that long ago a Japanese millionaire made headlines by insisting that he be buried along with Van Gogh's *Portrait of Dr. Gachet*.[14]

Akin to human beings, artworks are not only loved. They may be hated and loathed, vandalized and become objects of ferocious attacks. Creators of despicable, blasphemous, obscene or otherwise transgressive artworks have been the object of curses and aphorisms. The case of Nikos Kazantzakis, whose novels *The Last Temptation of Christ* and *Capitan Michalis* cost him an aphorism by the Greek Orthodox Church provides an apt illustration. In fact, both censorship and vandalism are quite common in the art worlds, especially in respect of works perceived as blasphemous, or offensive to religious sensibilities. Many controversial artworks that have become objects of legal disputes have been attacked, including for instance Andres Serrano's *Piss Christ*,[15] Otto Muehl's *Apocalypse*[16] and the works exhibited at the *Caution, Religion!* ('Осторожно, религия!') exhibition in the Sacharov Museum in Moscow.[17] Yet, vandalism does not necessarily involve or give

[11] Darian Leader, *Stealing the Mona Lisa: What Art Stops Us from Seeing* (Counterpoint 2004) 3.

[12] AFP, 'Le baiser au rouge à lèvres sur une toile de Cy Twombly: 1500 euros' (Libération, 16 November 2007) <www.liberation.fr/societe/2007/11/16/le-baiser-au-rouge-a-levres-sur-une-toile-de-cy-twombly-1500-euros_8379> [in French].

[13] Ernst Gombrich, *Art and Illusion: A Study in the Psychology of Pictorial Representation* (Princeton University Press 1960) 82–83.

[14] Anon, 'Ashes to Ashes, but Not with Your Van Gogh' (Newsweek, 26 May 1991) <https://www.newsweek.com/ashes-ashes-not-your-van-gogh-203950> (noting that by cremating the artworks, the heirs would avoid paying inheritance tax for the two masterpieces that were bought for more than $70 million each).

[15] See Chapters 6 and 7 of this book.

[16] *Vereinigung Bildender Künstler v Austria* App no 68354/01, Merits and Just Satisfaction, 25 January 2007, chapter 1 and 6.

[17] *Yuriy Samodurov and Lyudmila Vasilovskaya* App no 3007/06, 15 December 2009 (inadmissible).

rise to legal disputes as such. For example, in 1999, despite the sensation created by Italian artist Maurizio Cattelan's *La Nona Ora*, which depicted the Pope struck down by a meteorite, during its exhibition in Warsaw, there were no criminal charges, damage or legal dispute submitted to the courts.[18]

A discussion concerning the vandalism of artworks and the 'colourful imaginary' of poems from an international law perspective might appear paradoxical to international lawyers. 'Traditionalists' may well perceive artistic freedom as irrelevant, or at best peripheral, to the field of international law. Key arguments may suggest that although the individual (and their rights) is a concern of international law, cultural matters typically remain within the sphere of State sovereignty, and that limitations to artistic freedom, including prior restraints, are legitimate exercises of State sovereignty – especially in matters pertaining to morality and religion. These arguments would, however, not do justice to the evolution of international law during the last couple of decades – including the expansion of human rights law as an important area of law and the advent of individuals (and to some extent also communities) as subjects of international law.[19] In fact, international law sets the framework for the realization of artistic freedom in various ways.

First, artistic freedom is beyond doubt part of the international human rights edifice. Most States have undertaken obligations to respect artistic freedom with reference to treaty law, chiefly with a view to protecting both free speech and cultural rights. Universal human rights bodies have been especially proactive in striving to safeguard this freedom of the artist – as well as its limits vis-à-vis unacceptable expressions of hatred, racial superiority or religious intolerance – as discussed further in Chapters 2 and 3 of this book. To date, the European Court of Human Rights has issued over thirty judgments that are directly relevant to artistic freedom (especially with respect to satire) and elaborated a detailed methodology with respect to balancing this right against other rights and public interests. Because of the evolution of human rights law, States are or should be held accountable for the violation of artistic freedom. This is especially true in respect of States that regularly impose prior restraints and discriminate without reasonable and objective justifications against certain types of art. Most States routinely promote certain

[18] See Jean-Cristophe Claude, *Les grands scandales de l'Histoire de l'Art : cinq siècles de ruptures, de censures et de chefs d'œuvre* (Beaux Arts 2008).

[19] Indicatively, Andrew Clapham, 'The Role of the Individual in International Law' (2010) 21(1) *European Journal of International Law* 25; Rosalyn Higgins, 'Human Rights in the International Court of Justice' (2007) 20 *Leiden Journal of International Law* 745.

forms of expressions over others, including by privileging particular types of art (e.g. arts that are in line with the State's cultural or religious identity). Even this well-established State prerogative, however, has been eroded with the increased participation of communities in cultural – and artistic – governance.[20] In other words, States can no longer freely ban films, plays and songs or seize books and artworks as they please without being subjected to some type of accountability. Human rights mechanisms, intergovernmental organizations, civil society and increasingly also courts and tribunals have the power to scrutinize States' restrictions to artistic freedom; discriminatory policies that impede artistic freedom; and even those that inhibit the promotion of cultural diversity.

Second, artistic freedom is indirectly promoted by the safeguarding of artists' intellectual property (IP) rights.[21] The Berne Convention's guarantees of moral and economic rights have been also incorporated in article 15(1)(c) of the International Covenant on Economic Social and Cultural Rights (ICESCR).[22] Consequently, any prejudice against authors' IP rights also falls within the protective scrutiny of the Committee on Economic, Social and Cultural Rights (CESCR), State reporting and individual complaints (by virtue of the 2009 Optional Protocol to the ICESCR). Intellectual property rights can also be claimed before regional human rights bodies on the ground that they constitute property rights; privacy rights (with respect to moral rights); and eventually also as cultural rights. Intellectual property claims could, therefore, also be addressed by human rights bodies. The American Convention on Human Rights specifically addresses cultural rights in article 26 and the Additional Protocol of San Salvador (which in turn recognizes the right to take part in the *artistic* life of the community). Moral rights are directly relevant to the promotion of artistic freedom in the public space, as the latter is clearly of no use if any member of the public is given a right to request the government to stop or remove from the public space anything it finds controversial or offensive. These questions will be discussed in more detail in Chapter 5 of this book.

20 International Law Association, International Law Association Committee on Participation in Global Cultural Heritage Governance – Final Report (2022).

21 cf UN Human Rights Council, 'Report of the Special Rapporteur in the Field of Cultural Rights, Farida Shaheed', 14 March 2013, UN Doc A/HRC/23/34, paras 6–8.

22 Article 15 of the ICESCR contains a provision that guarantees authors' rights, both moral and copyright. For an overview on the human rights 'lens' see indicatively, Peter Yu, 'The Anatomy of the Human Rights Framework for Intellectual Property' (2016) 69 *SMU Law Review* 37–95; also UN Human Rights Council, 'Report of the Special Rapporteur in the Field of Cultural Rights, Farida Shaheed', 24 December 2014, A/HRC/28/57.

Third, various international agreements and declarations promote cooperation in cultural matters. UNESCO is mandated precisely to promote the arts, as part of its 'cultural cooperation' objective. When UNESCO was set up in 1945, the States parties to the UNESCO Constitution agreed to collaborate in the fields of culture and education, with the aim of contributing to peace and security, and 'in order to further universal respect for justice, for the rule of law and for the human rights and fundamental freedoms which are affirmed for the peoples of the world'.[23] Most UNESCO conventions, recommendations and statements equally have an impact on the realization of artistic freedom, and the work of many artists in the field, especially those whose work is engaged and politically coloured. This is even more true since the protection of the art is no longer associated with high arts alone, taken in their elitist sense. In the 1980s, UNESCO solemnly defined 'artists' extremely broadly,[24] emphasizing the role of freedom in the creative process, and in cultivating talent:

> Member States, recognizing the essential role of art in the life and development of the individual and of society, ... have a duty to protect, defend and assist artists and their freedom of creation. For this purpose, they should take all necessary steps to stimulate artistic creativity and the flowering of talent, in particular by adopting measures to secure greater freedom for artists, without which they cannot fulfil their mission ....[25]

Fourth, the actual 'product' of artistic practice is to be protected and safeguarded as part of States' cultural heritage, whether tangible or intangible, for the benefit of present and future generations. In addition, the promotion of artistic expressions are equally part of State agendas in terms of media and artistic content, and in some cases they are synonymous with the promotion of intangible cultural heritage (and also, living traditions and 'traditional cultural expressions). This is also the case with respect to indigenous and tribal arts, as well as certain types of art, such as, for instance, performance, oral arts and other arts that manifest particular know-how. In other words, a good part of cultural heritage law may at times overlap or eventually also conflict with artistic freedom. Competing claims over cultural heritage and artistic freedom may lead to conflict and impair the right of communities to enjoy their heritage. As the first UN Special Rapporteur on Cultural Rights noted, a sensible balance needs to be achieved between the protection of artistic

23 UNESCO Constitution (1945), adopted in London, United Kingdom, 16 November 1945, Preamble.

24 UNESCO, 'Recommendation concerning the Status of the Artist' (Belgrade 1980), article 1(1).

25 ibid at para 3.

freedom and the boosting of creativity on the one hand, and the protection of cultural heritage against misappropriation[26] on the other.[27] In addition, within the context of UNESCO and other intergovernmental organizations, various initiatives have been undertaken by States to promote the principle of cultural diversity in a spirit of openness to different cultures and religions. This is self-evident given that States are also increasingly interested in strategies to attract tourists by means of cultural cooperation, as well as enhancing their profile as open and culturally diverse.

Fifth, artists (as well as musicians, performers, film-makers, writers, cartoonists, etc.) working to promote the cause of human rights are protected also in their capacity as human rights defenders. The starting point is the Declaration of Human Rights Defenders (HRDs).[28] Article 2(1) of this declaration refers to the general responsibility of States to protect, promote and implement all human rights on their territory, whereas article 2(2) refers to the duty of States to take all necessary steps in order to ensure that these rights are effectively guaranteed. It is not possible to dissociate in this scenario artistic freedom from the defence and promotion of human rights.[29] One should think of the case of Tuany Nascimento, for example, the Brazilian dancer who initiated a 'favela dance school' teaching girls how to dance in slums and helping them to 'make something with their lives',[30] or Tousin Chiza (Tusse), the Congolese-Swedish singer with a refugee background who participated in the 2021 Eurovision Song Contest.[31]

[26] Misappropriation and copyright related to artistic freedom involving communities and indigenous peoples' rights are not part of this study. Chapter 5, however, is specifically dedicated to questions touching upon IP rights in the case of street art and 'urban identities', to the extent that these issues relate to artistic freedom and the values that States ultimately aim at safeguarding.

[27] UN Human Rights Council, 'Report of the Independent Expert in the Field of Cultural Rights, Farida Shaheed', 21 March 2011, UN Doc A/HRC/17/38, para 12.

[28] UN General Assembly Resolution, 'Declaration on the Right and Responsibility of Individuals, Groups and Organs of Society to Promote and Protect Universally Recognized Human Rights and Fundamental Freedoms', 8 March 1999, UN Doc A/RES/53/144, Preamble.

[29] UN Human Rights Council, 'Report of the Special Rapporteur in the Field of Cultural Rights, Karima Bennoune', 20 January 2020, A/HRC/43/50, at 3, para 8 (d) (noting that 'cultural rights defenders' include those who 'use their work in the arts or culture to defend human rights generally').

[30] Priscilla Frank, 'How One Brazilian Dancer Is Changing the Lives of Young Girls through Ballet', 10 April 2016 <www.huffpost.com/entry/tuany-nascimento-ballet-brazil-teacher_n_57f3df18e4b0703f75913e5c>.

[31] UNHCR, 'Three Performers with Refugee Backgrounds Participate in Eurovision 2021', 18 May 2021 <www.unhcr.org/news/press/2021/5/60a3f1214/three-performers-refugee-backgrounds-participate-eurovision-2021.html>.

Finally, since the end of the Cold War, the international community has witnessed the rise of religious extremism, including in particular Islamic fundamentalism. A certain manifestation of this extremism has found fertile ground in controversies related to artistic expression. The deliberate and systematic destruction of cultural heritage in many parts of the world and especially the Middle East is arguably part of the same narrative, although it has consistently been condemned by Muslim scholars and international lawyers alike,[32] and also by well-known religious figures from the Islamic world, such as Imam Qaradawi.[33] Subsequently, questions related to artistic freedom and offences to religious beliefs are broader than artistic freedom per se, touching upon sensitive issues related to the dynamics between States of different cultural and religious identities, beliefs, customs, traditions, wealth, values and ideologies.[34] States are deemed to coexist harmoniously and be able to cooperate inter alia with the aim of promoting and encouraging respect for human rights.[35] In practice, however, the symbiosis is far from easy. The variety of approaches to artistic freedom controversies, precisely reveals the need for tolerance and a better management of cultural diversity not only at the national level, but also in international law.

This book does not aim to offer a one-size-fits-all solution, nor does it intend to provide answers to all questions touching upon artistic controversies, or 'cultural conflicts'. Rather, it endeavours to contribute towards a better interpretation of the legal dimension of such controversies, the specificity of art and eventually also corroborating arguments that suggest distinctive legal treatment for artworks and artists. Artistic freedom is only the first step of the creative process and as such it should be thoroughly understood and preciously safeguarded. Imagination can never be limited – yet this should not be an excuse for intolerance, hatred or fanaticism. Many of the questions addressed in this book touch upon sensitive issues, at the heart of the cultural (and religious) sphere and way beyond the boundaries of international human rights law.

[32] Indicatively, see Francesco Francioni and Federico Lenzerini, 'The Destruction of the Buddhas of Bamiyan' (2003) 14 *European Journal of International Law* 619, 621–24; Maulana Wahiduddin Khan, 'The Preservation of Culture' in *Proceedings of the Doha Conference of 'Ulamâ on Islam and Cultural Heritage* (UNESCO, 2005) 65.

[33] Hamid Al-Ansari, 'Islam and the Preservation of the Human Heritage' in *Doha Conference supra* note 32 at 27, 31.

[34] On coexistence and divergences, see Georges Abi-Saab, 'Whither the International Community' (1998) 9 *European Journal of International Law* 248, 250.

[35] Article 1(3) of the UN Charter.

1

Defining Art

'Art' as an object of legal exploration is a fascinating topic. The first feature of this fascination is arguably law's love for rules, order and definitions. In discussing the nature of law, Joseph Bingham explained the process of advancing knowledge through definitions:

> Definitions are made of words, phrases, and other labels. Formulae are devised. Orderliness and systematization are aimed at throughout. All of these mental processes . . . are inspired by the purpose of acquiring, retaining, and communicating knowledge concerning concrete objective phenomena.[1]

There are various instances where a definition is crucial in determining the legal status of either an object or a person. Definitional imprecision is typical in legal disputes involving aesthetic judgements. Dilemmas associated with the definition of an artwork arise even in cases that are seemingly unrelated to the arts, at least in the sense that most people understand this term. A good illustration is offered by a case discussed by the US Supreme Court, whereby an expert baker and devout Christian running a bakery in Colorado refused to sell a wedding cake to a gay couple.[2] The couple subsequently filed a complaint with the Colorado Civil Rights Commission alleging discrimination on the basis of sexual orientation in violation of the Colorado Anti-Discrimination Act.[3] The baker in turn invoked not only his religious freedom, but further, his constitutional right to free speech, and the fact that he could not be compelled 'to exercise his artistic talents to express a message with which he disagreed'.[4] In the opinion delivered by Justice Kennedy for the

1 Joseph W Bingham, 'What Is the Law' (1912–13) 11 *Michigan Law Review* 1, 7.

2 *Masterpiece Cakeshop, Ltd. v Colorado Civil Rights Commission* 584 US (2018).

3 ibid at 1.

4 ibid at 7.

majority, the Court did not directly address the question of cakes being considered artworks. It confined itself to consider the case under the 'free exercise' clause of the US Constitution and the State's duty 'not to base laws or regulations on hostility to a religion or religious viewpoint'.[5] Yet, Justice Thomas did point out that this was an expressive statement (falling under the protective scope of the First Amendment) because '[using] artistic talents to create a well-recognized symbol that celebrates the beginning of a marriage clearly communicates a message – certainly more so than nude dancing . . . or flying a plain red flag'.[6]

Three options are, in principle, available to the legislator or the judge dealing with such claims. The first is a compulsion to define the term 'art' with reference to art history or a specific theory of aesthetics – including with reference to the 'art world' and by requesting an opinion from experts. The second is to allow the legislator or the judge to define the arts as they think fit in the context of a particular dispute – with reference, for instance, to some special field of national or international law (such as intellectual property [IP] law, cultural heritage law or human rights law). The third is to leave the question of definition open-ended and allow decisions to be made on a case-by-case basis at the expense of legal certainty. These three options have advantages and disadvantages, yet, for the reasons that are going to be explored in this chapter, only the last option is viable.

1.1 DEFINING ART IN THEORY OF ART

Under the theory of art there is no one single definition of 'arts'. Artists have always practised art differently and philosophers since antiquity have never stopped engaging in heated debates, expressing different views about art, artists and their potential political functions. A very rough categorization of these ideas could be based upon two diametrically different postulates. The first is that artists should represent, or even imitate, reality, regardless of the way reality is understood. The second is that art has some sort of 'inherent' legitimacy that renders it self-referential, and as such, need not, or shall not, represent reality. This understanding of art legitimizes modern, abstract or conceptual art, as well as decorative, non-iconic or non-figurative art.

5 ibid at 16.

6 Opinion of Justice Thomas at 7 (citing *Barnes v Glen Theatre, Inc.* 501 US 560, 565–66 (1991) and *Stromberg v California* 283 US 359, 369 (1931)). The latter are both protected under the First Amendment to the US Constitution as 'expressive conduct'. See also Chapter 6 of this book (on public morality).

1.1.1 *Classical Approaches to Art*

1.1.1.1 Does Art Mean Making Beautiful Things?

The term 'art' is typically associated with a set of rules concerned with beauty ('aesthetics'),[7] as well as harmony, talent, creativity and imagination. The current version of the Oxford Dictionary defines art as 'the expression or application of human creative skill and imagination, typically in a visual form such as painting or sculpture, producing works to be appreciated primarily for their beauty or emotional power'. 'Artwork', on the other hand, is defined as 'paintings, drawings, or other artistic works',[8] with 'artefact' being conceived as the broader term that includes any 'object made by a human being, typically one of cultural or historical interest'.[9] This means that the ordinary meaning of the word 'art' necessarily involves some association with beauty.

In practice, however, art, artists and artefacts are far from being subject to a single definition – or even a single art theory. 'Talent, creativity and imagination' are all far from being unique to arts – let alone beauty and harmony: 'there are beautiful ways of ploughing or trimming a hedge, just as there are beautiful mathematical solutions or beautiful rugby manoeuvres'.[10] Ernst Gombrich starts his *Story of Art* by stating that 'there is no such thing as art – only artists';[11] the *Stanford Encyclopedia of Philosophy's* entry on the 'Definition of Art' suggests seven types of arguments 'against defining art';[12] and Monroe Beardsley finds that an 'enormous and even ridiculous variety of objects, events, situations, texts, thoughts, performances ... have drawn the label "artwork" from their authors, admirers, or patient endurers'.[13]

The first reason for this difficulty in defining the arts is arguably the vagueness surrounding the 'constitutive properties' of the artistic phenomenon. As will be further analysed in the following sections, theories of art typically succumb

[7] The current version of the Oxford Dictionary defines aesthetics as 'a set of principles concerned with the nature and appreciation of beauty' <https://en.oxforddictionaries.com/definition/aesthetics>.

[8] <https://en.oxforddictionaries.com/definition/artwork>.

[9] <https://en.oxforddictionaries.com/definition/artefact>.

[10] Dominic McIver Lopes, *Beyond Art* (Oxford University Press 2014) 65–66 (attributing this to Bourdieu).

[11] Ernst Gombrich, *The Story of Art* (16th ed, Phaidon 1995) 15. 'Arts' here is understood primarily with reference to the visual arts.

[12] Thomas Adajian, 'Definition of Art' in *The Stanford Encyclopedia of Philosophy* (2018) <https://plato.stanford.edu/archives/fall2018/entries/art-definition>.

[13] McIver Lopes *supra* note 10 at 36 (citing Monroe Beardsley, *Aesthetics: Problems in the Philosophy of Criticism* (Hackett 1981) 298).

to predefining these properties. In other words, it will never be clear whether art theory studies presuppose the existence of artwork or, conversely, whether a work of art presupposes an artistic theory to be considered as such. Anyone who makes a judgement about art – including art critics and art historians[14] – falls into this category; he or she must have at least some predisposed idea as to what art *should* look like.

The second reason is the fact that ideas and expressions are always framed within a given society – or even a certain 'generation', as a US judge once put it while deciding on the obscenity of a 'men's magazine' publication in the early 1940s.[15] By implication, arts are heavily influenced by societies' cultural, political, moral and religious precepts and may only be appreciated in the particular context they were created. In this sense, definitions of 'art' cannot be dissociated from the subjective experiences of the artists and their political (or apolitical) role, as well as those of art critics and philosophers.

1.1.1.2 Does Art Mean Imitating Reality?

Views on art and the artists have ranged from considering the artist as wholly *ignoramus* to absolute geniuses or masters of some absolute truth. A good starting point on the matter is arguably Plato's *Republic*, authored in the fourth century BC. In Plato's worldview, artists appear only slightly more than clueless.[16] Just like poets[17] (including tragedians and arguably Homer),[18] they should be evicted from his fictitious republic. In one of the well-known dialogues of the *Republic* (Book X), Socrates discusses with Glaukon about the meaning and function of the artist as 'creator' (*ποιητής*), arguing that art's function is nothing but a second-class imitation.[19] The argument is as follows:

- In everyday language, all those who make things (such as beds or tables)[20] are 'makers' or 'creators' of things.

[14] See McIver Lopes *supra* note 10 at 65.
[15] cf *Hannegan v Esquire* 327 US 146, 157 (1946).
[16] Plato, *Republic*, Book X at 603, and Stephen David Ross (ed), *Art and Its Significance: An Anthology of Aesthetic Theory* (3rd ed, SUNY Press 1987) (providing the English translation of that passage of the *Republic*) at 39.
[17] Plato *supra* note 16 at 596b. On this passage, Kenji Yoshino, 'The City and the Poet' (2005) 114 *Yale Law Journal* 1835, 1841 (fn 32).
[18] Plato *supra* note 16 at 606e; Yoshino *supra* note 17 at 1852 (fn 129); Carleton Brownson, 'Reasons for Plato's Hostility to the Poets' (1897) 28 *Transactions and Proceedings of the American Philological Association* 5, 6 (reviewing Plato's 'condemnatory utterances').
[19] Plato *supra* note 16 at 596–97.
[20] ibid 596.

- In reality, however, neither artisans nor artists are true creators but merely imitators (*μίμησῃ*). They do not create the *ideas* of those things, as the original ideas exist only in the world of ideas.
- The only true creator of *ideas* is God; he forms the original ideas.
- The artisans are only imitating those ideas, and artists in turn are imitating the artisans.
- While artisans are already removed from the original ideas – 'from the King and from the Truth', in the wording of Socrates[21] – artists are removed even further.

Following Plato, other philosophers discussed the possibility (and utility) of arts and the artists. Different parameters have been brought forward, especially the exaltation of the human soul, or the quest of 'truth'. Kant, in particular, elaborated a theory of aesthetics based on ethics, associating it with the human soul and finding that art must promote 'the cultivation of the mental powers for sociable communication';[22] Tolstoy believed that 'art [must] communicate a morally good emotion to its audience' and dissociated arts from pure aesthetics;[23] Nietzsche presupposed that the ultimate goal of art is truth;[24] Hegel suggested that true art may only be associated with the 'unconditional and absolute' in the art, as a means of exaltation of the spirit (this resulting in the so-called Great Art as the only form of true art, as well as the 'death of art');[25] and Heidegger accepted that 'the mere reception of an artwork by a certain culture is sufficient to establish its greatness'.[26]

1.1.2 *Modern Theories of Art*

Most art theories were formulated in mid-twentieth-century Europe and focus on the definition of the *work of art*. Despite the predominance of some of these theories (especially the so-called institutional theories of art), there has been no philosophical agreement as to what renders a particular creation 'art'.

[21] ibid 601ff and Ross (tr) 39ff.

[22] Richard Eldridge, *An Introduction to the Philosophy of Art* (2nd ed, Cambridge University Press 2014) 57ff (discussing Kant's views 'on natural and artistic beauty').

[23] Leo Tolstoy, *What Is Art?* (1898, republished by Penguin 1996) and also Eldridge *supra* note 22 at 20–21.

[24] David Farrell Krell, 'Art and Truth in Raging Discord: Heidegger and Nietzsche on the Will to Power' (1976) 36 *boundary 2* 378, 380.

[25] Julian Young, *Heidegger's Philosophy of Art* (Cambridge University Press 2001) 7 (discussing Hegel's admiration of 'the magnificent days of [Ancient] Greek art').

[26] ibid; also Farrell Krell *supra* note 24 at 378, 381ff.

1.1.2.1 Modern Artistic Practice and Its Influence on Modern Artistic Theories

In the first half of twentieth-century Europe, the practice of the arts was already much different from what it had been in the eighteenth and nineteenth centuries. Artists could no longer be indifferent to world wars, economic crises and great diseases. On the one hand, the invention of photography had drastically affected the idea of 'perfection' in imitation, making the purpose of representing reality futile.[27] On the other hand, the arts gradually became secular and rationalized, with new things being added to the list of possible creations.

The scholarship of the time on psychoanalysis and the sciences of the mind had an impact on artistic practice, serving to 'explain man's alienation in a frightening but free world, and to expose the irrational basis of extreme political options such as Fascism and communism'.[28] The publication of Freud's *Leonardo da Vinci's Childhood Memories* (1910) in particular, in which Freud analysed da Vinci's work alongside his elaboration of the unconscious self (*id*), became popular among certain circles of artists, especially abstract expressionists and surrealists. Leonardo da Vinci henceforth used the concept of *id* as an unlimited source of inspiration, drawing pictures inspired from dreams or trying to write while half-asleep ('automated writing'). In his *Manifesto of Surrealism* (1924), André Breton pays particular emphasis to dreams and their function,[29] defining 'surrealism' as 'psychic automatism in its pure state, by which one proposes to express ... the actual functioning of thought ... in the absence of any control exercised by reason, exempt from any aesthetic or moral concern'.[30] Hence, for the surrealists, the experience of 'art' would legitimately include not only aesthetic contemplation but also a good deal of shock, pain and disgust. An illustrative example is Luis Buñuel and Salvador Dali's (silent) short film *Un Chien Andalu* (1927). The opening of the film includes a scene wherein Buñuel wields a straight razor, cutting through a person's eyeballs. This is a highly symbolic scene. As Julius explains, 'according to some authors, Buñuel symbolically destroys the eyes of the spectator ... in order to disturb stereotypical perceptions and prepare us for

[27] By way of indication, see Régis Debrary, *Vie et mort de l'image* (Gallimard 1992) 283ff [in French] (discussing 'the shock of photos').

[28] David Hopkins, *Oxford History of Art 1945–2000* (Oxford University Press 2000) 11.

[29] Hal Foster, Rosalind E Krauss, Yve-Alain Bois, Benjamin HD Buchloh and David Joselit, *Art since 1900* (Thames & Hudson 2019) 196–97 (reproducing Breton's *Manifesto*).

[30] ibid 197 *in fine*.

the disturbing images and follow this sequence.... If the response of the audience is that the horror is in the work alone and not in the world itself, then the work has failed'.[31]

Subsequent artistic movements based on experimentation with traditional concepts and materials also found support among artistic circles. Dadaism and the avant-garde, in particular, became popular in Paris and other European cities, progressively leading to the emergence of conceptual art, installation art and pop art. A cutting point in the history of modern art is arguably Duchamp's *Fountain* (a male urinal made of porcelain), which was submitted to the first annual exhibition of the American Society of Independent Artists in 1917. This was Duchamp's first attempt to expose a so-called 'ready-made' (i.e. 'an ordinary object elevated to the dignity of a work of art by the mere choice of an artist') in an avant-garde artistic space (and in fact among Duchamp's first ready-mades, following his *Bicycle Wheel*, made earlier in 1913).[32] The impact of this work on art theory has been nothing short of colossal. As Carroll remarks,

> A work like *Fountain* ... problematized aesthetic theories of art, while, on the other hand, it also alerted philosophers to the importance that context, including institutional frameworks and art history, might bear on art status.... In its role as a counterexample or provocation, Fountain made a contribution to the evolution of the project of the self-definition of art and it did so in a way that did not necessarily rely on words.... Therefore, it is not the case that art must be verbal for art history to continue to move forward philosophically.[33]

From then on, other ready-mades followed – such as Schamberg's *God* (1918), consisting of a piece of plumbing; Andy Warhol's *Big Torn Campbell's Soup Can* (1962); and Manzoni's *Merda d'Artista* (1963), consisting of a can with the inscription 'Artist's Shit Contents 30 gr net Freshly preserved Produced and tinned in May 1961'. The underlying idea would be to dissociate the object from its usual context and associate it with a concept,[34] as well as to mock the art market and the elitist 'salons' of the time. Ready-mades were borderline cases of artwork and, as such, tested the limits of art: would objects

[31] Antony Julius, *Transgressions of the Arts: Art That Offends* (University of Chicago Press 2002) at 35. cf Amy Adler, 'Post-Modern Art and the Death of Obscenity Law' 99 (1990) *Yale Law Journal* 1359, 1368, fn 66, also Marci Hamilton, 'Art Speech' (1996) 49 *Vanderbilt Law Review* 73, 94.

[32] Lois Fichner-Rathus, *Understanding Art* (Wadsworth-Cengage 2013) 22 and 188 (citing the *Dictionnaire abregé du Surrealism*); Julius *supra* note 31 at 16–28; Hamilton *supra* note 31 at 94–95; Louise Harnon, 'Art, and the Killing Jar' (1994) 79 *Iowa Law Review* 367, 403. On the influence of women artists and performers on the history of Dada, see also Irene Gammel, *Baroness Elsa: Gender, Dada, and Everyday Modernity – A Cultural Biography* (MIT Press 2003).

[33] Noël Carroll, 'The End of Art?' (1998) 37 *History and Theory* 17, 24–25.

[34] Fichner-Rathus *supra* note 32 at 188; Hopkins *supra* note 28 at 84–85; Julius *supra* note 31 at 28.

such as urinals, plumbing material and the artist's *merda* find their way to a museum collection on an equal footing with *Mona Lisa* and other masterpieces of the Renaissance? Art theorists and philosophers of the mid-1950s not only replied in the affirmative, but indeed did their best to accommodate these ready-mades in art theory by inventing new definitions of the concept of 'art' – or, in other words, by requiring the fulfillment of new conditions for works to achieve the status of 'art'.

1.1.2.2 Art as an Open Concept

In the 1950s and 1960s, discussions on the meaning and value of the arts became more intense and more elaborate. Weitz's art theory was perhaps the most influential in the perception of modern art. He proposed that concepts can be divided into 'open' and 'closed',[35] arguing that classical aesthetic theories until then had never managed to provide a valid definition of art, maintaining a rather 'evaluative' function.[36] Weitz largely followed Wittgenstein's ideas, who had suggested, first, that art is a phenomenon too diverse in nature to be unified and, second, that philosophy should abandon the practice of defining notions in favour of the search for common elements (what he describes as 'family similarities').[37] Weitz's argument about art being an 'open concept' is as follows:

> 'Art' itself, is an open concept. New conditions (cases) have constantly arisen and will undoubtedly constantly arise; new art forms, new movements will emerge, which will demand decisions on the part of those interested, usually professional critics, as to whether the concept should be extended or not. Aestheticians may lay down similarity conditions but never necessary and sufficient ones for the correct application of the concept. With "art" its conditions of application can never be exhaustively enumerated since new cases can always be envisaged or created by artists, which would call for a decision on someone's part to extend or to close the old or to invent a new concept.[38]

By implication, in Weitz's view, arts did not attribute to expressions such as painting, novels or tragedy 'necessary and sufficient properties' for them to be

35 Morris Weitz, 'Open Concepts' (1972) 26 *Revue Internationale de Philosophie* 86, 87.

36 Morris Weitz, 'The Role of Theory in Aesthetics' (1956) 15 *Journal of Aesthetics and Art Criticism* 27, 27 (arguing that some theories emphasize 'too few properties', whereas others omitted inclusion of 'very important features', or were simply 'too general and cover[ed] objects that are not art as well as works of art').

37 Weitz *supra* note 35 at 98ff (analysing Ludwich Wittgenstein's *Philosophical Investigations* [1953], according to which there are no philosophical problems, only 'language games' and 'misunderstandings of language').

38 Weitz *supra* note 38 at 32.

characterized as 'art'; it merely specified some random 'criteria of recognition'.[39] This in turn entails that art includes also non-art, making any possibility for definition of art a *non-lieu*.

1.1.2.3 Danto and the Institutional Theory of the Arts

As a counterbalance to Weitz's arguments, other theories were developed, contesting the open concept argument.[40] In the mid-1970s, the 'institutional theory' of the arts made its appearance. Its leading figure was the American philosopher Arthur Danto. In his early scholarship, Danto strives to find what makes the difference between reality and the arts. According to Danto, art is intrinsically metaphoric and highly contextual – necessarily influenced by the author's experience. Taking pop art as an example, and with reference to Warhol's soup cans and *Brillo Boxes* (1964), he explains that when we look at a modern art painting that represents an ordinary object such as a can of soup or a box of Brillo what matters is not really the representation of the work, but rather the particular standpoint of the artist – that is, what the artist had in mind when he represented that object and the associations the artist made. In this way, the 'art viewer' or simply the public acquires an equally important role. They are implicitly requested to put themselves in the shoes of the artist and think metaphorically – think of those soup cans and Brillo boxes in a different way than how they would normally do.[41] This, in turn, has an important consequence, as it implies that art can only exist if it is recognized as such by the art worlds.[42] According to Danto, 'what in the end makes the difference between a Brillo Box and a work of art consisting of a Brillo Box is a certain theory of art'.[43] Danto writes,

[39] ibid 35.

[40] Joseph Margolis, 'Open Concepts' (1979) 10 *Metaphilosophy* 330, 337 (citing Morris Weitz, *The Opening Mind: A Philosophical Study of Humanistic Concepts* (University of Chicago Press 1977) xi and arguing that Weitz 'avoids to provide a general theory of open and closed concepts' and that 'there are concepts other than closed ones, of varying degrees of openness'); also Lewis Zerby, 'A Reconsideration of the Role of Theory in Aesthetics. A Reply to Morris Weitz' (1957) 16 *The Journal of Aesthetics and Art Criticism* 253; Raymond Hoekstra, 'Art and Truth, in Reply to Mr. Weitz' (1945) 5 *Philosophy and Phenomenological Research* 365.

[41] Jeff Mitchell, 'Danto, Dewey and the Historical End of Art' (1989) 25 *Transactions of the Charles S. Peirce Society* 469, 471.

[42] Arthur Danto, 'The Artworld' (1964) 61 *The Journal of Philosophy* 571, 577–80 (explaining that 'art . . . requires something the eye cannot decry – an atmosphere of artistic theory, a knowledge of the history of art: an artworld'); W. E. Kennick, 'Theories of Art and the Artworld: Comments' (1964) 61 *The Journal of Philosophy* 585, 586.

[43] Danto *supra* note 42 at 580.

> ... It is as if a work of art were like an externalization of the artist's consciousness, as if we could see his way of seeing and not merely what he saw.[44]

Some philosophers aligned themselves with the institutional theory and attempted to elaborate and systematize its requirements even further. According to George Dickie, for instance, the conditions for something to be characterized as art are both objective and subjective. First, the artwork needs to be a reproduction of an object (and this, even if it consists only of a simple intervention such as that of the displacement of an object – i.e. an *artefact*). Second, if it is indeed an artefact, it must be received by a circle of scholars (*artworld*) as a work of art.[45] This explains why ready-mades such as Fountain can be classified as artworks,[46] whereas others that are not perceived as such by the art worlds cannot – fake paintings for instance or student copies of masterpieces are according to Danto and Dickie 'non-art'[*sic*].[47]

These debates did not come to a particular conclusion, nor did they provide a single solution as to the definition of the work of art. Other philosophers contested and debated these classifications, as well as the institutional theory underlying them as a whole. Clement Greenberg, in particular, an art critic close to abstract expressionists has been arguably the most influential. Greenberg's theory differed in that he maintained the self-referential role of the arts, finding that each artistic discipline serves a particular goal – purity for instance in the case of visual arts.[48] Others, yet, virtually dissociated the object of the art and its qualities (such as its aesthetic standing) from the artistic experience, insisting on the self-referential role of the arts and finding that art should be disengaged from politics and social realities or highlighted the personal experience and the intent of the artist.[49] Wolheim, for example, found the institutional theory to be ill-founded, simply shifting the problem

44 Mitchell *supra* note 41 at 471 (citing Danto's *The Transfiguration of the Commonplace* (Harvard University Press 1981) 147–48).

45 George Dickie, 'What Is Art' in *Art and the Aesthetic: An Institutional Analysis* (Cornell University Press 1974) 426, 427; also Eldridge *supra* note 22 at 78–79.

46 Dickie *supra* note 45 at 430 (referring to 'urinals, hatracks, snow shovels and the like').

47 ibid 435; Arthur Danto, 'Art works and real things' (1973) 39 *Theoria* 1, 1.

48 Harnon *supra* note 32 at 400 (explaining that this purity 'would be pursued by a maniacal preoccupation with the inherent qualities of the medium of painting itself – its materials, its color, its application, its optical flatness').

49 Hans Belting, Andrea Buddensieg and Peter Weibel (eds) *The Global Contemporary: The Rise of New Art Worlds after 1989* (MIT Press 2013) 1–2; Mitchell *supra* note 41 at 481 (citing Dewey: 'By common consent, the Parthenon is a great work of art. Yet it has aesthetic standing only as the work becomes an experience for a human being').

to academics and the elite, as the aesthetic element is entirely disregarded,[50] noting that it 'can ill-afford to confirm the social facts that it postulates by appeal to mere explanatory force'.[51] According to Wolheim, Dickie's classification is a misconception, as 'it's hard to see how there could be reasons putatively for making an *artifact* which were better thought of as reasons for being one'.[52] Yet, the debate on the nature, value and meaning of art has expanded, allowing a plethora of artistic expressions to gain the status of 'art', even as borderline cases. In essence, artists were warranted a much higher degree of freedom in creating – if freedom can ever be classified into degrees – and with this, the blessing of the (high influential) art circles.

1.1.3 *Contemporary Art Theories*

The period that follows the late 1960s to date is generally named 'contemporary art'. This period is marked by a proclamation of the 'end of art' in the mid-1990s by Danto and other philosophers.[53]

Contemporary art is not governed by a single predominating art theory. Rather, it is characterized by a large degree of 'hybridity', appropriation of various techniques and dialogue between Western and non-Western concepts of art in the post-colonial context.[54] The various theories of art formulated until then have contributed to some extent in shaping and informing contemporary artistic practice, thus allowing a variety of artistic trends to coexist.[55] Conversely, various artistic movements that appeared in the second half of the twentieth century, both short- and long-lived ('85 New Wave art; neo-aboriginal art; Young British Artists' art; Relational art), have informed contemporary artistic practice. A good example is arguably 'postmodern art' (or 'Postart'), a short-lived movement that appeared in the 1970s and which questioned the 'purely aesthetic considerations of the art'.[56] Post-modernism

[50] Richard Wolheim, *Art and Its Objects* (2nd ed, Cambridge University Press 2015) 109.

[51] ibid 108–09.

[52] ibid.

[53] Arthur Danto, 'The End of Art' in *The Philosophical Disenfranchisement of Art* (Columbia University Press 1986); Carroll *supra* note 33 at 17–29. Also Arthur Danto, *After the End of Art: Contemporary Art and the Pale of History* (Princeton 1996) 11.

[54] Fichner-Rathus *supra* note 32 at 538–39 and also generally Belting et al *supra* note 49.

[55] McIver Lopes *supra* note 10 at 46. cf Belting et al *supra* note 49 at 390–91.

[56] The editors of Phaidon Press, *Art in Time, a World History of Art Movements* (Phaidon 2013) 29–30; Danto *supra* note 42 at 11 (noting that contemporary art is sometimes wrongly associated *only* with that movement). On the failure of 'postmodern' art, Kristine Stiles (ed) *Theories and Documents of Contemporary Art: A Sourcebook of Artists' Writings* (2nd ed, University of California Press 2012).

was a 'rebellious movement that attack[ed] any standard used to judge it',[57] and had a great influence on art theory, dissolving the very last threshold of the definition of 'art' – that is, art as being entirely self-defined. Yet, it would be wrong to associate contemporary art with that particular movement alone. The former does not follow a particular rule, while classic art and painting in particular have never stopped finding their way into galleries and art schools.

Contemporary art varies from merely aesthetic concerns to philosophical interrogations and political 'statements'. More often than not it is presented in a way that often blurs the boundaries between art and non-art. In terms of form, the advent of the new media and the acceptance of installations and performances as genuine artistic forms are perhaps its main characteristic.[58] Anything can be a performance: in *Washing/Tracks/Maintenance: Outside* for instance, Mierle Laderman Ukeles scrubbed the steps and mopped the floor of the museum for several hours as if she was a cleaner, only to question the relations between female artists and feminism, and to address the importance of routine in daily life.[59] Likewise, anything can be presented as an installation – Damien Hirst's shark-tank sculpture for instance titled *Physical Impossibility of Death in the Mind of Someone Living* consists of an old shark, well preserved in formaldehyde but 'smelly, and with a fallen off fin' pushing the spectators to wonder about their own vulnerability and relation to death.[60] In terms of substance too, artistic works may be apolitical or politically engaged (*art engagé*). The feminist movement, the hippy movement, gay rights, ecological concerns and other political considerations have all been reflected in contemporary art.

Political engagement and artistic experimentation therefore, even at purely aesthetic level, will often result in challenging the limits set by the law. A good illustration is the case of the artist Dread Scott, who, as a fine art student preparing for a student exhibition in the Chicago Art Institute in 1989, placed a US flag on the floor and allowed spectators to walk over it. The work was titled *What Is the Proper Way to Display a US Flag?* and was displayed along with similar works of other local artists. A few months earlier, the US Supreme

57 Adler *supra* note 31 at 1378 and 1368–69.

58 Hopkins *supra* note 28 at 239ff.

59 Michael Willson, *How to Read Contemporary Art: Experiencing Art of the 21st Century* (Abrams 2013) 43–45; Hilary Robinson (ed) *Feminism Art Theory: An Anthology 1968–2014* (Blackwell 2015) 88–90.

60 Julius *supra* note 31 at 214; Willson *supra* note 59 at 191; see also Chapters 4 and 6 of this book, and, Steven Gay, 'Deconceptualizing Artists' Rights' (2012) 49 *San Diego Law Review* 37, 43 (noting that it was later sold at Saatchi for an astronomical price of seven million dollars).

Court, in *Texas v Johnson*,[61] had invalidated various States' prohibitions of desecration of the American flag following 'flag burning' episodes throughout the country. Shortly after Dread Scott's work was exhibited, therefore, an ordinance was passed banning flag desecration and the work was seized. In the ruling that followed the same year the County court judge followed *Texas v Johnson*, finding that 'when the flag is displayed in a way to convey ideas, such display is protected by the First Amendment.... For every artist who paints our flag into a corner, there are others who can paint it flying high'.[62] Aesthetic judgement pervades the law. In the tax code and tariff system, in obscenity cases and public-funding choices, in connection with zoning, land use and eminent domain and throughout IP law, judges and other government officials are constantly deciding what is art, or what counts as artistically or aesthetically valuable.

1.2 DEFINING ART IN LAW

The question that naturally arises is the following: why should law define the arts, if both artists and the art worlds are unwilling, or incapable of offering a plausible definition? And further, wouldn't there be any occasions where such definition is needed – at least for the sake of legal certainty? These questions will be addressed in the following sections discussing the various theories of art in law.

1.2.1 *Why the Law Should Not Provide a Definition of the Arts*

Art is free and should remain free. Far from being a *legal lacuna*, this 'avoidance' to define, or describe the arts is an indispensable feature of democratic societies. Constitutional provisions on the 'freedom of the arts' are born out of the sore experiences of repression and propaganda emanating from totalitarian regimes of the nineteenth and twentieth centuries. Attempts to define the arts by any State organ (be it the executive, legislature, judiciary or any other State authorities) effectively constitute prior restraints (i.e. *stricto sensu* censorship).[63] A definition of the arts is in substance an effort to control what is acceptable as 'art' within a given society and by implication preventing 'non acceptable' art from being disseminated. A non-definitional conception

[61] *Texas v Johnson* 491 US 397, 404 (1989); also Hamilton *supra* note 31 at 85ff.

[62] Cook County Circuit Court, *Aubin v City of Chicago*, cited by Calvin Massey, 'Pure Symbols and the First Amendment' (1990) 17 *Hastings Constitutional Law Quarterly* 369, 377.

[63] See Chapter 3 of this book.

of art leaves sufficient discretion and flexibility to artists and creators in the case of any attempt at 'suppress[ing] in advance of publication',[64] as opposed to subsequent imposition of liability and punishment.

The same applies to the so-called aesthetic censorship of art, that is, the imposition of particular aesthetic rules in order to promote a certain style of arts or discourage others. This type of censorship, as noted by the first UN Special Rapporteur on Cultural Rights in her report on 'creative freedom' is preeminent today in relation to 'specific styles of music or visual arts deemed to be political, and/or considered to carry a foreign ideology'.[65] Rules on aesthetic representation however trace back in history, and are arguably rooted in human vices such as vanity and lust for power – if not in the Exodus and the Ten Commandments.[66]

With the advent of the eighteenth century aesthetic censorship generally was eclipsed, whereby, at least in Western art, there was less and less observance to the form.[67] Totalitarian and semi-totalitarian regimes, however, including strict religious regimes, have never been truly freed from such rules. Censorship and State propaganda go hand in hand in defining cultural policies and predefining the qualities that artworks should have. One of the most pertinent historic illustrations of the early twentieth century is the 'socialist realism' of the former Soviet Union. In particular, the Manifesto of Socialist Realism that circulated in 1920s, embodying collectivist ideals, operated as the basis of communist propaganda, condemning abstract and modern art as 'decadent and bourgeois'.[68] In 1932 the Communist Party circulated a decree calling upon all artists and writers 'supporters of the Soviets' to align to the Union and endorse 'the Statutes of the Union of Soviet Artists' (and 'Writers' respectively),[69] that imposed a vision of political aesthetics of the arts on the basis of realism.

64 LT Beman, *Selected Articles on Censorship of Speech and the Press* (Wilson 1930) 365.

65 UN Human Rights Council, 'Report of the Special Rapporteur in the Field of Cultural Rights, Farida Shaheed', 14 March 2013, UN Doc A/HRC/23/34, para 28.

66 See this book, Chapter 8.

67 See also Brent Plate, *Blasphemy; Art That Offends* (Black Dog 2006) 46 (referring to what Rancière in his *Politics of Esthetics*, 2005, named the 'aesthetic regime' of the arts).

68 Victoria Alexander and Marilyn Rueschmeyer, *Art and the State: The Visual Arts in Comparative Perspective* (Palgrave 2005); Sheldon Nahmod, 'Artistic Expression and Aesthetic Theory: The Beautiful, the Sublime and the First Amendment' (1987) *Wisconsin Law Review* 221, 225.

69 For a discussion on literature, see Gary Saul Morson, 'Socialist Realism and Literary Theory' (1979) 38 *The Journal of Aesthetics and Art Criticism* 121, 122; and generally, Henry Hardy (ed) 'The Arts in Russia under Stalin' in Isaiah Berlin, *The Soviet Mind Russian Culture under Communism* (Brookings Institute 2011) 1–27.

1.2.2 *The Law Does Not Offer a Definition of the Arts*

Domestic and international laws generally avoid providing a statutory definition of the arts. At least two categories of norms are directly relevant to the arts, namely cultural heritage law and IP law. This chapter draws on these regimes, in the aim of finding whether such norms prioritize one definition of the arts over another. Human rights law on the contrary, despite provisions concerning the protection of artistic freedom, is not relevant to this section – for the simple reason that human rights law applies to everyone and not only to artists – or artworks. It is by implication only incidentally that definitions of 'art' may be discussed in the context of a human rights claim.

1.2.2.1 Non-definition of the Arts under Cultural Heritage Law

The United Nations Educational, Scientific, and Cultural Organization (UNESCO) is the obvious candidate for providing a definition of the 'arts' at an international level. Indeed, under its constitutive Charter, the purpose of the UNESCO is, among other things, 'to encourag[e] cooperation among the nations in all branches of intellectual activity, including the international exchange of persons active in the fields of education, science and culture and the exchange of publications, objects of artistic and scientific interest'.[70] In one of the first agreements on cultural cooperation drafted under its auspices, UNESCO 'urges co-operation between nations in all branches of intellectual activity, including 'the exchange of publications, objects of artistic and scientific interest'.[71]

Yet, a definition of either 'art' or the 'artist' does not appear in any UNESCO treaty, declaration or recommendation. The best illustration of this remark is arguably the UNESCO Recommendation on the Status of the Artist (1980), which ascribes the qualification 'artist' to anyone who 'creates art' and 'considers his artistic creation to be an essential part of his life' as well as anyone 'who is, or asks to be recognized as an artist'.[72] Other recommendations provide equally good illustrations of the non-definition of the arts, typically associating the arts with abstract notions such as 'creativity', 'originality', 'authenticity', 'value' or 'interest'. For instance, in its *Recommendation on Movable Property*

70 UNESCO, Constitution (16 November 1945).

71 UNESCO, 'Agreement on the Importation of Educational, Scientific and Cultural Materials' (Florence, 17 June 1950) and additional Protocol (Nairobi, 26 November 1976), Preamble.

72 UNESCO, 'Recommendation Concerning the Status of the Artist' (Belgrade 1980), art 1(1).

(1978), UNESCO defines the term 'movable cultural property' as: 'all movable objects which are the expression and testimony of human creation or of the evolution of nature and which are of archaeological, historical, artistic, scientific or technical value and interest', specifying that this includes 'items of artistic interest, such as: paintings and drawings, produced entirely by hand on any support and in any material (excluding industrial designs and manufactured articles decorated by hand); original prints, and posters and photographs, as the media for original creativity; original artistic assemblages and montages in any material; works of statuary art and sculpture in any material; works of applied art in such materials as glass, ceramics, metal, wood, etc'.[73]

This connection between 'artistic interest', 'creativity' and 'originality' is maintained in the UNESCO Convention on Illicit Traffic (1970), where the term 'cultural property' per se however is taken to mean 'property which, on religious or secular grounds is . . . *specifically designated by each State* as being of importance for archaeology, prehistory, history, literature, art or science' and which belongs inter alia to the 'category' of 'elements of artistic or historical monuments' and 'property of artistic interest'.[74] There is nothing in the convention to explain what 'specifically designated by each State' means, and indeed article 1 'imposes no meaningful constraints'.[75] The finite list of items mentioned in article 1 of the convention defines the material scope of the 1970 convention, seeking a balance between the significance of cultural heritage on the one hand, and the recognition of national ownership of property on the other (rather than attempting to lay out criteria or qualities defining artistic works). As a matter of 'UNESCO rule', States are the ones that have discretion in defining their own cultural heritage.[76]

From the beginning of the 1980s, there has been a shift in terminology in UNESCO instruments: from 'cultural property' (which implies strict perception of ownership and tangibility of physical objects) to the broader term 'cultural heritage' (which implies the association of cultural objects with

73 UNESCO, *Recommendation for the Protection of Movable Cultural Property* (28 November 1978), art 1(1)(a)(vi).

74 UNESCO, 'Convention on the Means of Prohibiting and Preventing the Illicit Import, Export and Transfer of Ownership of Cultural Property' (1970) art 1(d) and (g)(i–k).

75 Patrick O'Keefe, *Commentary on the UNESCO 1970 Convention on Illicit Traffic* (Institute of Art and Law 2000) 36–37; PM Bator, 'An Essay on International Trade in Art' (1982) 34 *Stanford Law Review* 275, 377.

76 cf O'Keefe *supra* note 75 at 35 referring also to Guido Carducci, *La restitution internationale des biens culturels et des objets d'art volés ou illicitement exportés : droit commun, directive CEE, conventions de l'Unesco et d'Unidroit* (LGDJ 1997) 218 [in French].

humanity as a whole, rather than with a single nation).[77] This amounted overall to abandoning efforts to define either creativity or originality. The shift is clear following the 1972 World Heritage Convention that was originally conceived to protect cultural objects, sites and monuments (tangible heritage) and the 2003 Convention for the Safeguarding of Intangible Cultural Heritage (CSICH),[78] as well as the more recent UNESCO Convention on the Protection of Cultural Diversity (2005), where 'cultural expressions' are those with a 'cultural content' and which result from the 'creativity of individuals', and 'cultural content' refers to the 'symbolic meaning, artistic dimension and cultural values that originate from or express cultural identities'.[79] An exception to this is arguably the Recommendation concerning the Protection and Promotion of Museums and Collections, Their Diversity and Their Role in Society (17 November 2015), which defines the term collection as 'an assemblage of natural and cultural properties, tangible and intangible, past and present'.[80] As a result, akin to UNESCO practice in relation to its other conventions, the UNESCO leaves the definition of art in the discretion of States,[81] including therefore the art world and policy-makers.

1.2.2.2 Non-definition of the Arts under Intellectual Property Law

Intellectual property norms are central to the perception of a certain form of expression as 'art'. The transnational copyright system does not specifically protect artworks, and the 1896 Berne Convention does not provide a definition of either 'art' or the 'artist'; it merely sets forth illustrative lists.[82] The same issue appears under statutory IP laws. Rather than attempting to define the substance or meaning of 'art' (or ascribing to it abstract notions such as 'interest'

77 Indicatively, Francesco Francioni, 'Des biens culturels au patrimoine culturel: l'évolution dynamique d'un concept de son extension' in Abdulqawi Yusuf (ed), *L'action normative à l'UNESCO* (vol 1 UNESCO–Martinus Nijhoff 2007) 231, 231ff.

78 Janet Blake, *International Cultural Heritage Law* (Oxford University Press 2015) 163ff; overview, Janet Blake and Lucas Lixinski, *Intangible Cultural Heritage: A Commentary* (Oxford University Press 2020).

79 Art 4, paras 3 and 4.

80 UNESCO, 'Recommendation concerning the Protection and Promotion of Museums and Collections, Their Diversity and Their Role in Society' (17 November 2015), UNESCO Doc CLT/HER/MHM/2015/PI/H/1.

81 For instance, under the 'Recommendation concerning the Protection and Promotion of Museums and Collections, Their Diversity and Their Role in Society', art 5: 'Every Member State should define the scope of what it understands by collection in terms of its own legal framework, for the purpose of this Recommendation.'

82 Berne Convention for the Protection of Literary and Artistic Works 1886 (as amended on 28 September 1979) art 2(1).

and 'value'), the IP legal framework determines an indicative list of protected objects[83] that may or may not coincide with artworks.

Judges themselves typically feel uncomfortable in providing specific definitions – perhaps more than the legislator. In a leading UK copyright infringement case with respect to (prototypes of) furniture, for example, the House of Lords had to decide on the meaning of 'artistic craftsmanship' in the making of sofa beds meant for mass production – that is, whether the prototypes produced were indeed 'artistic', and of 'original design'. Several approaches were taken, and (contrary to Plato!) the Lords found that a particular design of sofa beds has some merit as artistic work. Yet, while one must necessarily display some skills of craftsmanship for copyright laws to be activated, it would not be possible to define the quality 'artistic' in relation to a particular theory of the arts, precisely because courts are not well-suited for this exercise, and because such definition falls outside the parliamentary mandate.[84] This is remindful of Justice Holmes' warning at the beginning of the twentieth century that 'it would be a dangerous undertaking for persons trained only to the law to constitute themselves final judges of the worth of pictorial illustrations'.[85]

1.2.3 *Challenges Arising from the Problem of Non-definition of the Concept of 'Art'*

It follows that the only possible option is to leave the question open-ended. The challenges arising from this exercise include several situations where a definition is crucial in resolving a legal dispute. Poignant examples include situations where the qualification 'art' triggers an exception to a rule of general application; situations where the mere classification of an object as 'art' activates administrative laws that provide for benefits, tax exemptions or in some cases pre-emption rights in the art market; situations where artworks

83 By way of example, section 3(1) of the UK Copyright Act 1956 – now section 4 of the Copyright, Designs and Patents Act 1988; section 101 ('Definitions') of the US Copyright Law. cf Peter Karlen, 'Art in the Law' 14 (1) *Leonardo* 1981, 51, 51.

84 *Hensher v Restawile* [1976] A.C. 64 paras 94–95: '... the court will endeavour not to be tied to a particular metaphysics of art, partly because courts are not naturally fitted to such matters, partly because Parliament can hardly have intended that the construction of its statutory phrase should turn on some recondite theory of aesthetics'. cf Karlen *supra* note 83 at 55; Paul Kearns, *Artistic Freedom* (Hart 2013) 137; J Pila, 'Copyright and Its Categories of Original Works' (2010) 30 *Oxford Journal of Legal Studies* 229.

85 *Bleistein v Donaldson Lithographing* 188 US 239 (1903), discussed also by Robert O'Neil, 'Artistic Freedom and Academic Freedom' (1990) 53 *Law and Contemporary Problems* 177, 178; Kearns *supra* note 84 at 137; Adler *supra* note 31 at 1374.

recognized as such by the 'art worlds' may not be protected by IP cases; and situations where the qualification 'art' may have an impact on the legitimacy of limitations of artistic freedom under human rights law. Each of these will be explained more fully in sequence.

1.2.3.1 Exceptions to Rules of General Application

As it is commonly said, the artist is not *legibus solutus* ('released from the law'). In the sphere of criminal law, in particular, an exception to the application of general standards cannot apply in the fictitious case of the crazy 'artist' who shoots his partner while participating in an original art performance. The same is true in respect of the serial killer who murders incessantly in order to create the perfect perfume, as in the case of Patrick Süskind's novel. In other legal spheres, however, a differentiation of standards in favour of the artist may be more tempting. A good example is a case considered by England's central criminal court at the Old Bailey, London, in 1986. The case concerned the works of an artist named Boggs, which at the time, 'focused on graphic representation and interpretation of numerals'.[86] Boggs was arrested during the opening of a show at the Young Unknowns Gallery in south-east London for displaying drawings remindful of bank notes (with the Queen of England wonderfully drawn and titles as inspiring as *How much does an idea weigh?*), and was subsequently indicted under section 18 (1) of the British Forgery and Counterfeiting Act of 1981.[87] A central argument of his defence was that the law on bank forgery should not apply in his case, since his art did not consist of a 'reproduction' of banknotes but rather his artistic 'impression' of them.[88] Several art experts were called in Boggs' defence, providing the jury with 'art-seminar sessions' as evidence of the evolution of contemporary arts. Boggs was finally discharged and as noted by Lydiate, art lawyer and member of Boggs' defence team, the Court for a while resembled an art gallery.[89]

Inversely, attacks on works of art do not absolve someone from liability. To the contrary, there are legitimate reasons to argue that vandalism of artworks is morally reprehensible and may give rise to aggravated penalties, compared to

[86] Henry Lydiate, 'The Courtroom as Gallery: The Judges as Spectators' in Daniel McClean (ed), *The Trials of the Art* (Ridinghouse 2007) 159, 159.
[87] ibid at 163.
[88] ibid at 160 and 166.
[89] ibid at 164–68.

attacks against ordinary objects.[90] Likewise, iconoclastic attacks against cultural objects, monuments and archaeological treasures not only breach international standards on cultural heritage protection, but go against the spirit of the United Nations, and especially UNESCO, whose purpose is the building of *peace* among nations through cultural collaboration.[91]

1.2.3.2 Classification of Artists and Artworks

The qualification 'art' or 'artist' in some situations enables a particular classification of either the object or the person, potentially activating benefits – as in the field of social security tax exemptions. European countries in particular, including France, Germany and the Netherlands, maintain special statutory schemes for 'artists', including exemptions from contribution duties and access to benefits.[92]

At the same time, several States maintain administrative laws that apply specifically to 'artistic works' or to works of a significant 'artistic value'. Such laws encompass for instance pre-emption rights of the State, as well as special regimes regulating artistic works' imports and exports – including to combat illicit trafficking.[93] In Italy, for instance, the Ministry of Cultural Heritage maintains a right of 'pre-emption' over foreign works of cultural and artistic interest, with the purpose of their acquisition by the State.[94] The Grand Chamber judgment of the European Court of Human Rights (ECtHR) had to decide on the compatibility of such administrative laws with property rights guaranteed under the convention in a case involving Vincent van Gogh's *Portrait of a Young Peasant*.[95] The painting was initially bought by a Swiss,

90 MJ Williams, 'Framing Art Vandalism: A Proposal to Address Violence against Art' (2009) 74 *Brooklyn Law Review* 581, 583 (arguing that 'unlike other tangible property, are valued both for their uniqueness and for their public significance'). Nonetheless, in most cases the perpetrators are found to be suffering from mental health issues, see Christopher Cordess and Maja Turcan, 'Art Vandalism' (1993) 33 *British Journal of Criminology* 95, 98 (containing an appendix, with a selected list of artworks attacked including location and year).

91 UNESCO, Constitution (16 November 1945), Preamble and art 1: 'The purpose of the Organization is to contribute to peace and security by promoting collaboration among the nations through education, science and culture'. On iconoclasm and religiously motivated destruction, see also Chapter 7.

92 On these schemes, see Bert Demarsin et al (eds) *Art and Law* (Die Keure–Hart 2008) 130–31.

93 See the aforementioned UNESCO, 'Convention on Illicit Traffic' (1970); O'Keefe *supra* note 75 at 12–13.

94 Law no 1089 of 1939, according to which the transfer of artworks must be declared to the Ministry. Within two months from the declaration, the Ministry may exercise a right of pre-emption over the work at the price indicated in the contract.

95 *Beyeler v Italy* App no 33202/96, 5 January 2000, ECHR 2000-I.

and, subsequently, by an Italian collector, Mr Beyeler, who requested authorization from the Ministry to transfer it to Venice (in view of its imminent sale to the Guggenheim Collection).[96] The Court did not deny the fact that it is legitimate for States to take measures in the name of 'the general interest of universal culture' and 'taking into account the margin of appreciation afforded to the national authorities in determining what is in the general interest of the community'[97] – even though in the case at hand the Italian government had been excessively late in exercising this right and the owner had not been rightly compensated.[98]

Other examples pertaining to the application of administrative laws include tax exemptions with respect to artists' classifications and the regulation of import-export of artworks. The International Federation of Arts Councils and Culture Agencies has established detailed criteria on potential classifications of artists for tax purposes.[99] Yet, here again, such classification cannot be but dependent upon the qualification of art as such, and in some cases its 'value' or 'interest'. For instance, under UK tax laws, one may benefit from capital gains tax relief and transfer tax exemptions if the Treasury finds that the work at hand is of a (preeminent) 'artistic interest'.[100] As a result, in some cases 'transfer tax exemptions will be granted as a matter of Treasury discretion for older, traditional works of art, while certain more recent works will be neglected. The same recent works will be accepted by public galleries under their statutory powers to receive and transfer works of art'.[101]

96 ibid para 19.

97 ibid para 112.

98 ibid para 105. For a comment on the case, see Andrzej Jakubowski, 'Cultural Heritage and the Collective Dimension of Cultural Rights in the Jurisprudence of the European Court of Human Rights' in Andrzej Jakubowski (ed), *The Impact of Collective Cultural Rights on General International Law – Relocating the Third-Generation Human Rights* (Brill 2016) 166; also MA Renold, 'A Landmark Decision in Art Law by the ECtHR' (2000) 5 *Art, Antiquity and the Law* 73.

99 Cristopher Madden, *Defining Artists for Tax and Benefit Purposes* (IFACCA March 2002) D'Art report 1 (discussing responses on 'who is an artist' by various artistic and cultural institutions).

100 UK Capital Transfer Tax Act 1984, section 26 para (2)(f), a transfer of value is exempted from taxes, if the property that is transferred is (among other things): 'picture, print, book, manuscript, work of art or scientific collection which in the opinion of the Treasury is of national, scientific, historic or artistic interest' and 30(1) on conditional exemptions, under which property 'which appear[s] to the Treasury to be of national, scientific, historic or artistic interest' may be subject to conditional exemptions).

101 Karlen *supra* note 83 at 55.

Likewise, under United States federal law, 'artists' are subject to studio deductions,[102] and artworks may benefit from both exemptions in capital gains taxes, and customs deduction. A good illustration is a case involving Constantin Brancusi's series of bronze sculptures *Birds in Space* (*Pasărea în văzduh*).[103] The *Birds* were imported for artistic exhibition in the United States; this was at a time when modern European art was blossoming, and Brancusi had established himself as one of the leading figures in modern art.[104] The impugned sculptures, originally created in Paris in the mid-1920s (and currently bought by private collectors and the MoMA) did not necessarily resemble a particular kind of 'bird' – if a bird at all. Purchased by an American photographer Steichen, they were to be shipped on a steamboat from France to the United States, accompanied by Marcel Duchamp, in order to be exhibited in New York and Chicago in 1928. The issue therefore arose as to the classification of the *Birds*, given that the US customs officers were not particularly inclined to endorse Dadaism. If the birds were to be classified as artworks they would be exempted from all custom duties, whereas in the opposite scenario they would be taxed at 40 per cent of the materials' value as 'pieces of metal' (interestingly, under the section on 'kitchen utensils and hospital supplies'). Ultimately, the sculptures were released on bond and while several conservative art critics attacked the works, a complaint was filed with the local customs court. The judges were in favour of the *Birds*, noting that they were part of 'a new school of art, whose exponents attempt to portray abstract ideas rather than to imitate natural objects'.[105]

Similar claims may arise in cases concerning IP disputes. The Berne Convention offers discretion to States regarding the physical representation of works on some tangible medium.[106] In addition, IP rights under both common and civil law systems do not apply to ideas alone, but rather to the

[102] See, for example, the current US Tax Cuts and Jobs Act (2018) (providing some exceptions in the renting of artists' studios).

[103] *Constantin Brancusi v United States* No 209109 (US Customs Ct, 3d Div, 21 October 1927). See Brian Soucek, 'Aesthetic Judgment in Law' (2017) 69 *Alabama Law Review* 381, 387–88; also Daniel McClean, 'Trials of the Title: The Trials of Brancusi and Veronese' in Daniel McClean (ed), *The Trials of the Art* (Ridinghouse 2007) 37.

[104] Fichner-Rathus *supra* note 32 at 490; Manfred Schneckenburger, 'Sculpture' in Ingo Walther (ed), *Art of the 20th Century* (Taschen 2012) 426.

[105] Soucek *supra* note 103 at 87–88; McClean *supra* note 103 at 52–53.

[106] Article 1(2) provides that: 'It shall, however, be a matter for legislation in the countries of the Union to prescribe that works in general or any specified categories of works shall not be protected unless they have been fixed in some material form'.

expression of these ideas.[107] This is in principle beneficiary for the artists, as the originality of their work is protected even when 'copying' from photographs or other media. There are several types of art however, such as minimal, conceptual, installation and performance art (i.e. forms of art that question aesthetic and sociocultural perceptions based on rhetoric and advocacy, rather than a tangible medium)[108] that are by their very nature ephemeral, and as such do not seem to be fit for any of these categories. Domestic copyright statutes generally contain exhaustive lists of protected works – either setting specifications of the works or expressly excluding some types of artworks from their protective scope.[109] The limitations as to what can fall within the scope of IP law are therefore visible. The issue has appeared for instance in photography, and the question of originality.[110] In the twenty-first century it has also appeared in relation to abstract art, especially the work of British gestural expressionists in the 1960s and 1970s (e.g. the dispute over Twombly's *24 pieces* that was initially considered as falling outside the protective scope of IP law).[111] French courts on the contrary have been traditionally sympathetic to conceptual art. By way of example, in a case decided in the early 2000s, the French Cassation Court had to decide whether the mere inscription of the word 'Paradise' (*Paradis*) written in golden letters on the toilet door of a psychiatric hospital could legitimately be qualified as an artwork within the realm of *art conceptuel*. The court replied in the affirmative, in favour of the artist, considering that what was at stake was not merely a reproduction of the term, but rather 'the conceptual approach of the artist materially expressed folklore arts and other in an original material realization'.[112] Similarly, one of

[107] By way of example see (US) *Hoehling v Universal City Studios* 449 US 841 (1980); (UK) *Jefferys v Boosey* (1854) 4 HLC 815. cf WIPO Copyright Treaty 1996, article 2: 'Copyright protection extends to expressions and not to ideas, procedures, methods of operation or mathematical concepts as such'.

[108] Hopkins *supra* note 28 at 161–62 (discussing 'the death of the object' and 'the move to conceptualism'); Fichner-Rathus *supra* note 32 at 512.

[109] For instance, the British Copyright, Designs and Patents Act 1988 defines artistic works as 'the works of authorship (literary, dramatic, musical and artistic works, works of artistic craftsmanship, films) and entrepreneurial works (sound recordings, broadcasts, published editions)' specifically setting a list of eight protected categories of works. See sections 1.1, 3 and 4.

[110] cf *Burrow-Giles Lithographic Co. v Sarony* 111 US 53 (1884) (concluding that photographs are sufficiently original to warrant copyright protection).

[111] 'Abstract expressionism' – or 'gestural abstraction' – is a movement characterized by 'an intensely personal and subjective response by artists to the medium', see Peter Selz and Kristine Stiles, 'Gestural Abstraction' in Stiles *supra* note 56 at 15. On Twombly's work, see Kearns *supra* note 84 at 138, fns 47–48.

[112] *Cass. 1re civ., 13 nov.* 2008, n° 06-19.021, 2008, p. 2933. See Philippe Gaudrat, 'De l'enfer de l'addiction au paradis des toilettes : tribulations judiciaires au purgatoire du droit d'auteur' (2009) *RIDA* 220 [in French].

the best known cases in IP history is the controversy over the design of Lucasfilm's Stormtrooper costumes for the first Star Wars film: if the Stormtrooper's helmets were to be classified as sculptures (i.e. artworks) they would be protected under US Copyright law, whereas in the opposite case they would merely fall under design law.[113]

1.2.3.3 Legitimate Limitations or Negation of the Qualification of Art?

In the context of a freedom of speech dispute, the qualification 'artistic' is of crucial relevance. A judge would need to decide on the merits of an artwork in at least two scenarios that are discussed below.

ARTISTIC MERIT AS PART OF PERSONALITY RIGHTS: THE ARTIST AS PLAINTIFF The first scenario appears when a judge is expressly granted discretion to decide on the aesthetic merits of an artwork, and the potential ability to dismiss an artwork as 'non-art'. This could happen however only in one situation, namely in those cases where an artist (as plaintiff) brings a legal action for defamation against an art critic or a journalist who has expressesed controversial views that are harmful to the artist's reputation. What is under examination here therefore is not the artist's freedom of speech, but rather, the legitimacy of restrictions to the art critic or eventually the journalist's freedom of speech – and specifically, the freedom to express judgements on the aesthetic merit of art.

Interestingly, some criminal codes provide specific defences to art critics, as part of 'defences', absolving criminal liability for defamation.[114] Yet, most of the times, the judge is entirely free to decide upon the merits of such case – that would potentially include damages for injury to one's personal feelings and commercial reputation, as in any other defamation case.

A good illustration of this scenario is a libel suit brought before the English courts at the end of the nineteenth century. The case involved the American painter James McNeil Whistler (a theoretician of the 'Art for Art's Sake' school) and the art critic John Ruskin (Professor of Art in Oxford and highly influential art critic of Victorian England), who, after viewing Whistler's *Nocturne in Black and Gold: The Falling Rocket* (exhibited in Grosvenor Gallery, in London), expressed the view that the gallery 'ought not to have admitted works … in which the ill-educated conceit of the artist so nearly

[113] *Lucasfilm Limited and* Others *v Ainsworth* 27 July 2011, UKSC 39 (ruling that artworks made for films are not protected under the UK Copyright Law).

[114] Greek Criminal Code, art 366 para 1 for example absolves defendants from liability in case of 'negative judgments for academic artistic works', save for insult and malicious falsehood.

approached the aspect of willful imposture', and that he 'never expected to hear a coxcomb ask for two hundred guineas for flinging a pot of paint in the public's face'.[115] Following the lawsuit, the case attracted a great interest from both the artistic circles and the public of Victorian England.[116] Eminent artists and art critics of the time were invited as expert witnesses – most of them testifying in favour of Ruskin rather than Whistler. Even so, however, the judges applied their discretion on the matter, ultimately finding in favour of the plaintiff. This, however, was not because the statements were found to be defamatory (so there was no 'presumption' by the judges in favour of 'artistic merit'), but rather because among other things Ruskin referred to Whistler as a 'coxcomb, or a vain conceited fool, falsely proud of his achievements'.[117]

FREEDOM OF ARTISTIC EXPRESSION VERSUS OTHER RIGHTS AND PUBLIC INTERESTS: THE ARTIST AS A DEFENDANT Cases when artistic freedom must be balanced against another right, or a public interest are equally complex. The reason is that the very scope of the right to artistic freedom is dependent upon the consideration of other rights ('the rights of others') or public interests, leaving open the question of possible 'defences' applicable to artists. From then on, a particularly complex situation appears, that is, the fact that there is no clear distinction between the acceptable limits of artistic expression and the negation of the 'artistic quality' as such. In other words, the question is, if something is particularly offensive, or obscene, or hateful, is it still art that should be limited, or is it simply 'non-art'? By way of example, the ECtHR has found that some forms of art should be legitimately restricted – for instance, exposing parts of dead foetuses as 'artworks' in an avant-garde exhibition (incidentally, also at the Young Unknowns Gallery),[118] while anti-Semitic speech[119] and to some extent pornography[120] are excluded from the

[115] Robert Lind, 'Visual Artist and the Law of Defamation' (1993) 2 *UCLA Entertainment Law Review* 63, 81 (explaining that the 'Art for Art's Sake' movement developed later in 'Abstract Art'). Also Costas Douzinas, 'The Aesthetics of Law' in Daniel McClean (ed), *The Trials of the Art* (Ridinghouse 2007) 68–70; Adams Strevens, 'Whistler v Ruskin: Libel, the Art and the Art Critic' in Daniel McClean (ed), *The Trials of the Art* (Ridinghouse 2007) 135–48.

[116] Strevens *supra* note 115 at 137.

[117] Lind *supra* note 115 at 82; Strevens *supra* note 115 at 145.

[118] See Chapter 6 (on public morality).

[119] See Chapter 3 of this book (on prior restraints).

[120] *Hoare v the United Kingdom* No 31211/96, Commission decision of 2 July 1997 (whereby no claim on artistic merit was made); see however, *Pryanishnikov v* Russia No 25047/05, 10 December 2019, at Concurring opinion of Judge Pinto de Albuquerque (who finds that creative freedom was also at stake). See also Chapter 6 of this book (on public morality).

protective scope of artistic freedom altogether. At least three types of challenges for the judge (and arguably the legislator) can be identified.

In jurisdictions that accept the unlawfulness of 'content-based restrictions' (namely, the United States), this syllogism leads to an oxymoron (as will be discussed in more detail in Chapter 6), that is, the need for art to be judged upon its artistic merit. As O'Neil notes discussing the US Supreme Court's practice, 'it may even be that when a given work is found to be "art", it cannot also be held obscene; the very notion of constitutionally unprotected art may be logically untenable – at least as far as obscenity is concerned'.[121] Other authors have formed similar arguments.[122] The alternative would be to allow all types of art, including for instance, hateful or obscene art. Yet, again this cannot happen, as it would entail allowing the 'art worlds' (rather than the legislator) to decide what should be allowed and what should be prohibited in a society. The problem becomes more acute in case of controversies involving public art – including sculptures, large installations and land art as well as situations where the public interest is in conflict with artistic freedom (such as obscenity for instance, or public morals) equally remains non-defined.[123]

A good starting point illustrating this difficulty is a case against Austria regarding Otto Mühl's *Apocalypse*, which was decided by the European Court in 2007.[124] The artist is a well-known performance artist and member of an avant-garde group that was especially active in the 1970s (the 'Vienna Actionists'), including the organization of the Art and Revolution rally in 1968 (*Kunst und Revolution*).[125] The impugned work, consisted of nine canvases combining caricature-style drawings, acrylics and photography (collage), and depicted public and religious figures in sexual positions – including Marie-Theresa, the Austrian Cardinal, as well as Mr Meischberger and Jörg Haider, former leaders of the extreme right wing party, FPÖ.[126] The nature of the artwork divided the Court. While the four judges in the majority noted with no hesitation that article 10 protects all '[t]hose who create, perform, distribute or exhibit works of art contribute to the exchange of ideas and opinions' (therefore implying that it does

[121] O'Neil *supra* note 85 at 188; cf Kearns *supra* note 84 at 9.

[122] Adler *supra* note 31 at 1366; Kearns *supra* note 84 at 10.

[123] See Chapter 5 of this book.

[124] *Vereinigung Bildender Künstler v Austria* App no 68354/01, Merits and Just Satisfaction, 25 January 2007 (the domestic courts had considered that the painting was offending to these politicians' personality rights whereas, before the court, the respondent government claimed that the main issue at stake was public morality). See also Chapter 7 of this book (on the protection of religious beliefs).

[125] Hubert Clocker, 'Viennese Waltzes: Viennese Actionism and the Law' in Daniel McClean (ed), *The Trials of the Art* (Ridinghouse 2007) 273, 279.

[126] E.g. see ibid 273–76.

not fall upon the State to define which sort of art should be protected), the three dissenting judges accorded minimal importance to the political nature of the painting.[127] The dissenting Judges Spielmann and Jebens found simply that 'where the "protection of the rights of others" is at stake, artistic freedom cannot be unlimited'.[128] Interestingly, they referred to the German case of *Strauß-Karikatur* (involving a cartoon portraying the then Bavarian minister as a pig copulating with another pig dressed in judicial robes) in which the German Federal court had found that artistic freedom as a constitutional right 'must be considered in conjunction with other constitutional rights, notably the right to the free development of personality and human dignity'.[129]

CONCLUDING REMARKS

The qualification of an object as 'art' is the defining element of a legal dispute in a variety of situations. Examples include the application of exceptions to rules of general application under criminal law (especially with respect to public morality and public order offences); the application of purchase taxes or customs exemptions; and the triggering of safeguarding mechanisms under cultural heritage law.

And yet it is arguably impossible to define what exactly art is under the history of the art, or aesthetic theories. Weitz's perception of art as an 'open concept' has been particularly influential in the field of modern art, while the institutional theory, developed by Danto and other art philosophers, is illustrative of the subjectivity of aesthetic judgements. Both these theories have counterparts in the legal sphere – for example, Adler argues that the term 'art' cannot be defined 'because contemporary art, by its very nature, will defy any definition that we assign to it',[130] and Karlen explains that a somewhat 'functional' approach to art is generally visible in statutes and courts' judgments (as opposed to defining the characteristics of art as a creative activity, which is 'largely ignored by the statutes').[131] In fact, allowing either the

[127] ibid, at Joint Dissenting Opinion of Judges Spielmann and Jebens, para 10 and separate dissenting of Judge Loucaides, para 1. cf *Lindon, Otchakovsky-Laurens and July v France* Nos 21279/02 and 36448/02, Merits and Just Satisfaction, 22 October 2007.

[128] ibid at 5.

[129] ibid at 6, referring to German Constitutional Court, BVerfGE 75, 369 (at C –I, para 2) (*Strauß-Karikatur*), see also Chapter 6 of this book (on artistic merit).

[130] Adler *supra* note 31 at 1359.

[131] cf Karlen *supra* note 83 at 51: 'in analysing whether an article is a work of art the courts and other legal authorities have refrained from giving positive definitions for art but have imposed certain negative limitations on what is art in terms of quality, quantity, physical and temporal characteristics, perceptual attributes, and other socially determined qualities'.

legislator or the judge to pronounce on what exactly constitutes 'art' is pernicious. Such definitions, even by allowing recourse to experts, may dissimulate an attempt to censor artistic freedom and predefine what is acceptable in a given society. In those legal systems that provide for preferential treatment of arts or artists, negating the qualification 'art' amounts to implied limitations of creative freedom, equating creativity to ordinary expression.

The only viable scenario therefore in the context of a legal dispute is to allow (and therefore distinguish between artworks and ordinary objects) on a case-by-case basis, at the expense of legal certainty. In case of restrictions, therefore, and a fortiori the imposition of prior restraints, any decision must be accompanied by a safeguard: a presumption that, in case of doubt, a contested work will be indeed considered art (in other words an '*in dubio pro artis*' criterion). This last question and its implications, including the potential treatment of artistic freedom as a right warranting special protection for artists, will be further analysed in Chapter 2.

2

The Nature, Scope and Protection of Artistic Freedom

Controversies over blasphemous, transgressive, obscene and otherwise scandalous artworks are countless in art history and highly intriguing. They usually also amount to an increase in popularity of both the artwork and their author – as in the case of the *Da Vinci Code*, which has sold over 80 million copies worldwide. In reality only a handful of these controversies will actually become the object of legal dispute. Even in such cases, proceedings typically end during the first steps of the pertinent procedures. In fact, artistic freedom is seldom the object of legal concern, as if a 'tacit freedom' is accorded to the art world. This is especially true in the case of those forms of arts that do not involve speech as a primary artistic medium such as instrumental music and dance, or those that typically appeal to a limited public, such as comics and science fiction movies (with the occasional exception, as in the case of the banning of a Belgian author's comic book titled *The Life of Christ* by the Athens First Instance Court).[1]

The question that arises, therefore, is whether it would be at least possible to suggest that the arts enjoy a certain presumption of 'freedom'. In other words, whether it would be plausible to suggest that, in case of conflicts between artistic freedom and other rights or values (such as privacy, public order or religion), there should be a presumption that the former should prevail. If this is so, then the very invocation of the right to artistic freedom should necessarily involve some kind of 'privileges' for artists, thereby absolving them from any criminal or other liability arising from their work.

[1] Athens First Instance Court (Criminal), 26 February 2003; see Efi Fokas, 'God's Advocates' in Joel Temperman and András Koltay (eds), *Blasphemy and Freedom of Expression: Comparative, Theoretical and Historical Reflections after the Charlie Hebdo Massacre* (Cambridge University Press 2017) 389, 389–410; Eleni Polymenopoulou, 'Arts, Censorship and the Greek Law: Blasphemy v Hate Speech' (2017) 6 *International Human Rights Law Review* 1, 11–12.

Appealing as it may be, the idea of a privileged protection for the arts (that could be embedded, for instance, in the subtlety, aesthetics and symbolism of artistic expression) is far from being established in international human rights law. At the beginning of the century, for example, precisely because of the powerful symbolic forms of art as a form of expression, the US Supreme Court accepted an *exceptio artis* to justify in fact *stricter* rather than lighter requirements for arts and artists.[2] The idea that art is different from other forms of expression and should therefore enjoy 'preferential treatment' compared to other forms is the fruit of modernity: a recent development in the West, and a battleground in the rest of the world.

In the context of disputes brought before human rights bodies, a certain balancing exercise between conflicting interests virtually always takes place. This exercise never amounts to a *carte blanche* privilege for any type of expression. Moreover, there is no universal consensus on any preferential treatment or privileges for artists (what Grüttemeier calls *exceptio artis* in the case of literature).[3] On the contrary, in some States the arts are protected and supported, while in others substantially repressed, especially by invoking moral and religious rules.[4] The root of this discrepancy in domestic practice lies in the fact that not every State or legal system assigns the same weight to artistic freedom (and freedom of expression more generally), particularly when balanced against other freedoms, rights or public interests. Even in the United States, however, where freedom of speech enjoys an extremely high standard of protection by virtue of the First Amendment, the US Supreme Court has established various 'tests' under which freedom of speech can be legitimately limited, as will be discussed below.

This chapter examines the proposition of an emerging independent right to artistic freedom in two ways. First, by looking into domestic practice, namely the practice of States in relation to potentially distinct constitutional guarantees to artistic freedom. Second, by examining the various human rights instruments as these apply to artistic freedom, and the practice of human rights bodies in deciding artistic freedom cases.

2 cf *Mutual Film Corporation v Industrial Commission of Ohio* 236 US 230 (1915), whereby the US Supreme Court held that 'movies were not entitled to the protective safeguards enjoyed by newspapers because they were not to be regarded as an organ of public opinion'; see Thomas Mulroy, 'Obscenity, Pornography and Censorship'(1963) 49 *American Bar Association Journal* 869, 869.

3 Ralf Grüttemeier, 'Literary Trials as Mirrors: An Introduction' in Ralf Grüttemeier (ed), *Literary Trials: Exceptio Artis and Theories of Literature in Court* (Bloomsbury 2016) 8ff.

4 See Chapters 6 and 7 of this book.

2.1 THE EMERGENCE OF A DISTINCT RIGHT TO ARTISTIC FREEDOM

2.1.1 *Issues of Terminology: Creation, Expression or Entertainment?*

The term 'artistic freedom' has only been consolidated in domestic laws after the Second World War – as a generic term encompassing all arts (including visual arts, music, film, theatre, performance, poetry and arguably also comics). For a long time, and at least during the 1990s, the reference to freedoms corresponding to specific *manifestations of arts* was much more common – especially in the American literature.[5] The dominant term is arguably the 'freedom to create', which Roeder defined in 1940 as 'a function of the right to individual liberty',[6] and which was initially used to indicate an artist's freedom vis-à-vis 'various sovereign powers of the State'.[7] Recently also, UNESCO has added to the list of variations the 'freedom to imagine'.[8]

Creation and expression however (and a fortiori 'freedom to create' and 'freedom of speech') are terms that are semantically different. The term 'create' stems from the Latin *creare*, which primarily means to 'bring something into existence'[9] and is closely related to the concept of 'Creation' (with a capital 'C') as a divine process.[10] The term 'expression' on the contrary is part of a different type of discourse and chiefly alludes to *thought* and *speech*. According to the current version of the Oxford Dictionary, 'expression' stems from the Latin term *exprimere* (itself a product of the ancient term *espreindre*), manifesting something primarily by way of *language* and corresponding to 'the action of making known one's thoughts or feelings'.[11]

5 See e.g. Robert O'Neil, 'Artistic Freedom and Academic Freedom' (1990) 53 *Law and Contemporary Problems* 177.

6 Martin Roeder, 'The Doctrine of Moral Right: A Study in the Law of Artists, Authors and Creators' (1940) 53 *Harvard Law Review* 554, 558; Steven Gay, 'Deconceptualizing Artists' Rights' (2012) 49 *San Diego Law Review* 37, 43.

7 Roeder *supra* note 6 at 558.

8 UNESCO, *Re|Shaping Cultural Policies* (UNESCO 2017) at 211 (hereafter UNESCO 2017 Report) (according to the report, artistic freedom is the freedom to 'imagine, create and distribute diverse cultural expressions').

9 Oxford Dictionary at <www.lexico.com/en/definition/express>.

10 ibid at <www.lexico.com/en/definition/create>. Creation is defined as 'the creating of the universe, especially when regarded as an act of God'. cf the *Dictionnaire de l'Académie Française* at <www.dictionnaire-academie.fr/article/A9C4870>.

11 ibid.

As an individual process, therefore, *creation* not only encompasses forms of expression, but further challenges the power of man vis-à-vis the divine.[12] It is arguably for this reason that artistic expression is debated in those religious traditions that do not convey any such powers to man.[13] An objection to a potential 'right to create' was raised by the Saudi delegate at the Human Rights Council, Mr Baroody, at the phase of drafting the Universal Declaration of Human Rights (UDHR). This delegate noticed that 'the majority of human beings did not possess within themselves the power to create, but everyone had within him an aesthetic sense which he should have the opportunity of satisfying'.[14] Other Muslim delegates however did not agree on this point. The Lebanese representative, for example, suggested a provision on the 'individual's right to a free choice of work and his mode of life' noting also that 'the concept of the right to a free choice of a mode of life was designed to protect persons like scientists and artist'.[15] Moreover, contrary to 'expression', freedom of creation is necessarily in some way related to *entertainment*, provided that quality standards are achieved. Similarly, it is generally accepted that the term 'culture' refers also to the intellectual freedoms that are requisite for cultural production and the creative process, as well as its final products.[16] In this sense, not only tangible cultural heritage, artworks, but also cultural popular arts and mass entertainment phenomena, cinema and the audiovisual sphere are also 'culture'.

In any event, there is no real distinction between arts and entertainment, even when the purpose of the latter is profit. In *Burstyn*, for example, a widely discussed case regarding a New York statute banning sacrilegious representations,[17] the Supreme Court affirmed that arts and motion pictures are both covered by the First Amendment.[18] This is because 'the importance of motion pictures as an organ of public opinion is not lessened by the fact they are

[12] In the Platonic discourse on the arts, the terms 'creator' ('δημιουργός) and 'maker' (ποιητής) are used interchangeably, see Chapter 1 of this book.

[13] See Chapter 7 of this book, with reference specifically to the Islamic tradition.

[14] See William Schabas, *Universal Declaration of Human Rights: The travaux préparatoires Vol 1, October 1946 to November 1947* (Cambridge University Press 2013) at 2740 (by reference to A/C.3/260).

[15] ibid.

[16] Indicatively, Yvonne Donders, 'Do Cultural Diversity and Human Rights Make a Good Match?' (2010) 61 *International Social Science Journal* 15, 19; Roger O'Keefe, 'The "Right to Take Part in Cultural Life" under Article 15 of the ICESCR' (1998) 47 *International and Comparative Law Quarterly* 904, 905.

[17] The statute resulted in censorship of Rossellini's film *The Miracle* which narrated the story of the love of a shepherdess for Jesus. See Chapter 7 of this book (on US practice).

[18] *Joseph Burstyn, Inc. v Wilson* 343 US 495 (1952). See also, on this case, O'Neil *supra* note 5 at 178.

designed to entertain as well as to inform'.[19] This said, in the large majority of other constitutional traditions (including countries like Japan that are substantially strengthening their film industry and art sector)[20] guarantees of freedom of speech are generally higher on political expression.

2.1.2 *The Input of Constitutional Traditions*

2.1.2.1 The Legacy of the Weimar Constitution

The first constitutional text containing distinct guarantees for the freedom of the arts was the Weimar Constitution of pre-war Germany (1919). Contrary to the previous constitution (1849), which only guaranteed the 'freedom of science', this constitution proclaimed that 'art, science, and the teaching thereof are free' and that 'the State provides protection and participates in its cultivation'.[21] This means not only that arts followed science historically (as Grüttemeier notes),[22] but further that constitutional developments increasingly took into account the profound changes that modern art had initiated.

These affirmations of the Weimar Constitution reflect the lively scientific and artistic life of the Weimar Republic, as well as the philosophical findings about freedom of the time, which are manifest in the motto of the Vienna Secessionists 'To the Age its Art, to the Art its Freedom'. It is also indicative that 1919 is the same year that an extremely influential artistic movement was founded in the town of Weimar: the Bauhaus school, aspiring to take art outside museums and galleries and 'integrate design principles in mass production and industrialization'.[23] When the Third Reich came to power, Hitler entirely rejected modern art and implemented in the then divided Germany a strenuously repressive policy, which included extensive prior censorship, destruction of so-called 'degenerate' art and persecution of writers and intellectuals.[24] The impact of the Weimar Constitution, however, remained

[19] ibid at 501–02 and also 505.

[20] cf Shigenori Matsui, 'Freedom of Expression in Japan' (1991) 38 *Osaka Law Review* 13, 19; James Alexander, 'Obscenity, Pornography, and the Law in Japan: Reconsidering Oshima's *In the Realm of the Senses*' (2003) 4 *Asian-Pacific Law & Policy Journal* 149, 155.

[21] Weimar Constitution, art 142.

[22] Grüttemeier *supra* note 3 at 9.

[23] Hugh Honour and John Fleming (eds), A World History of Art (7th ed, Laurence King Publishing 2005) 797–98; Lois Fichner-Rathus, *Understanding Art* (Wadsworth-Cengage 2013) 496–97.

[24] Gay *supra* note 6 at 48; Hellmut Lehmann-Haupt, *Art under a Dictatorship* (Oxford University Press 1954) in John-Henry Merryman and Albert Elsen (eds), *Law, Ethics and the Visual Arts* (5th ed, Kluwer Law International 2007) at 259.

vivid after the end of the war. It was reflected in the Basic Law for the Federal Republic of Germany, enacted shortly after the fall of the Nazi regime, which protects 'freedom of the arts' (*kunstfreiheit*) dictating that 'arts and sciences, research and teaching shall be free' (article 5, paragraph 1).

Some constitutions have gone on to follow the German paradigm, distinguishing art from other forms of expression, and providing for separate, and also unqualified, protection. Such constitutions are typically those of Germanic-speaking countries (Austria and Switzerland);[25] those with post-war dictatorial regimes that were particularly oppressive of music, literature and the arts – such as Southern European States (Spain,[26] Italy[27] and Greece);[28] Latin American States[29] and other States of the civil law tradition, where there is substantial emphasis on the proclamation of cultural rights. This is, however, despite the nuances in the judicial practice of these States, or the actual judicial practice with respect to protection of artistic freedom – for example, the Greek Constitution drafted right after the fall of the military junta in 1975 not only provides for an 'unqualified' protection of the arts but juxtaposes these against extensive restrictions, imposed on the basis of other constitutional rights (such as honour and dignity) and public interests (such as the State's official religion and the prohibition of obscenity).[30] Likewise, in Russia and other Eastern European States there is a generalized State obligation to recognize and promote 'artistic creativity' and 'cultural and artistic values',[31] yet in reality freedom guarantees are extremely weak.[32] The two cases that were decided by the German Federal Constitutional Court (GFCC) concerning literary freedom and private interests are indicative of the authority

[25] See e.g. article 17a of the Austrian Basic Law ('artistic creativity as well as the dissemination of art and its teaching shall be free'); article 16 the Federal Constitution of the Swiss Confederation ('freedom of artistic expression is guaranteed' (art 21)). cf also article 16(1)(c) of the South African Constitution.

[26] Spainish Constitution, Section 20–1b (noting also that their exercise 'may not be restricted by any form of prior censorship').

[27] Italian Constitution, art 33; also art 9 (stipulating that the State 'promotes the development of culture and of scientific and technical research' and 'safeguards the natural landscape and the historical and artistic heritage of the nation').

[28] Article 16(1) of the Greek Constitution provides that 'art and science, research and teaching shall be free' and further that 'their development and promotion shall be an obligation of the State' (art 16, para 1); also Polymenopoulou *supra* note 1 at 3; Fokas *supra* note 1 at 391.

[29] Colombian Constitution, art 71; Constitution of Peru, art 2, para 8; Chilean Constitution, art 25.

[30] Greek Constitution, art 14.

[31] The Constitution of the Russia Federation, art 44; also Bulgarian Constitution, art 54; and Romanian Constitution.

[32] See e.g. Simina Tănăsescu, 'Artistic Freedom and Its Limitations' (2011) 1 *Romanian Journal of Comparative Law* 9 at 17–18.

of this provision. In both *Mephisto*[33] and *Esra*[34] the court held that artistic freedom creates a 'new aesthetic reality', which necessarily encompasses the right to use real-life models. In *Esra* the court further elaborated a special 'art-specific' balancing test, according to which

> it [is] necessary to apply standards specific to art to determine what connection with reality the novel suggests to the reader ... in order to be able to assess on this basis the seriousness of the impairment of the general right of personality.[35]

2.1.2.2 The Legacy of the French Genre of Caricature

In France, on the contrary, despite the long-standing tradition of the protection of free speech, artistic freedom lacked the judicial guarantees against State interference – at least until 2016 when the law on 'the freedom to create' was promulgated.[36] The Law on the Freedom of the Press of 29 July 1881 in fact contains a variety of prohibitions protecting against public morality, hate speech and religious intolerance (namely, incitement to religious discrimination, hatred and violence;[37] religious defamation;[38] and religious insult).[39] Hence, lower courts have not hesitated to find in favour of restrictions and plaintiffs complaining about public morality, personality rights and even religious insult, in expense of artistic freedom, and this, despite the official proclamation of *laicité* (i.e. the full separation between Church and State

[33] *Mephisto* 1 BvR 435/68 (24 February 1971) BVerfGE 30, 173 at para 49 (concerning a novel written by Klaus Mann in which Mann depicts his brother-in-law, actor Gustaf Gründgens, as a Nazi collaborator).

[34] *Esra* BvR 1783/05 (13 June 2007) BVerfGE 119, 1 at para 81 (concerning a novel which recounts the illness of a woman and the relationship with her mother – both easily identified in real life).

[35] ibid para 82. See Ralf Grüttemeier, 'Literature Losing Legal Ground in Germany? The Case of Maxim Biller's Esra' (2003–09)' 141 in Grüttemeier *supra* note 3 at 146–47; also Tănăsescu *supra* note 32 at 42ff.

[36] Law of 7 July 2016. For a comparative study, see also the working paper for the French Sénat prior the adoption of the Law of 7 July 2016 specifically dedicated to artistic freedom at <www.senat.fr/lc/lc261/lc261_mono.html> [in French]. Also Eleni Polymenopoulou, 'Freedom of Art' in *Max Planck Encyclopedia of Comparative Constitutional Law* (Rainer Grote, Frauke Lachenmann and Rüdiger Wolfrum eds, Oxford University Press 2017).

[37] French Law of the Press of 29 July 1881 (last amended through 2004), art 24.

[38] ibid art 32.

[39] ibid art 33, and also art 29 and 48 (1) regarding associations promoting religious hatred.

since 1905).[40] The French Court of Cassation however, save for few exceptions,[41] has generally managed to maintain the balance between creativity and religious sensibilities or other private and public interests. Indicatively, the cases that have arrived before the French Court of Cassation concern bans of motion pictures (such as Marie Godard's *Ave Maria*);[42] seizure of cartoons (e.g. 'Jesus was his name' published in magazine *Grosse Bertha*[43] and 'Welcome to sh* Pope' by *Charlie Hebdo*);[44] and also, creative advertisement (e.g. a leaflet with a drawing and the 'the night of Saint Condom').[45] At one particular occasion, the Paris Court of First Instance even considered a parody of the Last Supper (in a 40-metre poster that was placed in the streets of Paris) – a 'gratuitous and aggressive act of intrusion to peoples' intimate beliefs',[46] making headlines in the *New York Times*.[47]

A rare instance where even the First Instance Court of Paris has found in favour of cartoonists is – to our knowledge – the case of the Danish cartoons (that were published in *Jyllands-Posten* in 2005 and republished by *Charlie Hebdo* magazine). The complaint, initiated against Philippe Val, the then director of the magazine, concerned three of the controversial cartoons: the first, showing a figure of the Prophet Muhammad with the caption stating *c'est dûr d'être aimé par des cons* (which translates roughly to: 'it's hard to be loved by stupid people'); the second, stating 'stop, stop we ran out of virgins'; and the third, representing the Prophet with a turban resembling a bomb.[48] This tribunal however found that there was no intention to attack deliberately, or

40 For an overview, René-Jean Dupuy, 'La protection et les limites de la liberté d'expression de l'artiste dans la société européenne' (1974) 7 *Revue des droits de l'Homme* 41 [in French]. Also Guilheme Gil, 'Blasphemy in French Law: From the Chevallier de la Barre to Charlie Hebdo' 25, 42 in Temperman and Koltay *supra* note 1.

41 French Court of Cassation, 3 April 2002 (*Lindon*), subsequently upheld by the ECtHR in *Lindon, Otchakovsky-Laurens and July v France* App nos 21279/02 and 36448/02, Merits and Just Satisfaction, 22 October 2007). cf *Leroy v France* App no 36109/03, Merits and Just Satisfaction, 2 October 2008; see Chapter 3 (on hate speech).

42 Court of Cassation, Civil Ch.1, 85-15.044, 21 July 1987; cf Gil *supra* note 40 at 43–44.

43 Court of Cassation, Civil Ch.2, 98-17.574, 8 March 2001.

44 Court of Cassation, Civil Ch.2, 99-10.490, 26 April 2001.

45 Court of Cassation, Criminal Ch., 05-81.932, 14 November 2006. See Gérard Gonzales, 'Liberté d'expression versus liberté de religion: le poids de la Convention européenne', *Gazette du palais*, 10 December 2006, 344–46 [in French].

46 First Instance Court of Paris, *Marithé et François Girbaud* (Tribute to a woman), March 2005. See Gil *supra* note 40 at 45–46; also Michel Leroy, 'La parodie religieuse n'est pas une injure' (2006) *Revue Trimestrielle des Droits de l'Homme* 875–84 [in French].

47 Hélène Fouquet, 'Arts, Briefly: French Court Bans "Last Supper" Ad', (*New York Times*, 11 March 2005) <www.nytimes.com/2005/03/11/arts/movies/arts-briefly-french-court-bans-last-supper-ad.html>.

48 First Instance Court of Paris, 17th Chamber, 22 March 2007, at 1; Gil *supra* note 40 at 46–49.

gratuitously, the entire Muslim community. Still however, it dismissed the joint complaint by two Muslim organizations against Val.[49]

Interestingly, the Paris Court referred not only to the fact that the cartoons contributed to the public debate (and specifically the question of fundamentalism)[50] but also to the unique role of the entire genre of caricature in French society (and cartoons whose content is 'voluntarily irreverent', as per the wording of the judgment).[51] This reference is crucial for the understanding of the discourse on cartoons as a problem involving values and traditions, and debates about 'French identity'. The genre of caricature was developed after the French Revolution,[52] way before the French Law of the Press in 1881. Cartoonists, along with artists and poets (as famous as Baudelaire and Marquis de Sade) were targeted by the authorities though a variety of prior censorship regimes established throughout the eighteenth and nineteenth centuries to protect moral values, the King and the Church.[53] The best known example of a caricaturist liable for blasphemy and sedition is Philippon, director of the magazine *Charivari* (with its special issue on the *Caricature morale, religieuse, littéraire et scénique*). His famous caricatures *Poires* representing Louis-Philippe pear-shaped (to show both his corruption and stupidity) 'ended up by making the pear symbol of the King so famous that it was scrawled all over the walls of Paris'.[54] As a result, repression of caricatures tightened, especially with respect to sedition and public order. Goldstein, for example, refers to a 1835 speech of the French minister of commerce to the Chamber of Deputies, aiming to impose cartoon censorship in these words:

> there is nothing more dangerous . . . than these infamous caricatures, these seditious more direct provocation to crimes that we all deplore.[55]

[49] ibid at pp. 10–11.

[50] ibid at p. 11.

[51] ibid.

[52] John Geipel, A *Short History of Graphic Comedy and Satire* (A. S. Barnes 1972) at 74–78 (noting that 'by 1830, France had already become the European centre of cartoons and caricature'); Werner Hoffman, *Caricature from Leonardo to Picasso* (Crown 1957) 16ff; Robert Justin Goldstein, 'Debate over Censorship of Caricature in Nineteenth-Century France' (1989) 48 *Art Journal* 9, 10; Jane Clapp, 'Art Censorship under French King Louis Philippe' in Merryman and Elsen *supra* note 24 at 627.

[53] Robert Justin Goldstein, 'Censorship of Caricature and the Theater in Nineteenth-Century France: An Overview' (2012) 122 *Yale French Studies* 14–36 (noting that in 1829, the French Ministry issued 'guidelines according to which religion must be protected from both direct and indirect offense' and 'attacks or allusions of whatever kind').

[54] ibid at 10.

[55] ibid at 9.

The response of Philippon, writing to his readers while imprisoned, is still pertinent today:

> In our hands, caricature is not only a grotesque picture, a coarse picture without an idea, without taste, and especially without a purpose . . . No, caricature for us is something grander . . . We use it . . . to make a mirror for the ridiculous, a whistle for the stupid, a whip for the wicked.[56]

2.2 THE NATURE OF ARTISTIC FREEDOM

Artistic freedom under human rights law is susceptible to a twofold meaning. *Stricto sensu* it may be defined as the 'right to artistic expression', that is, the right of every person to express oneself artistically – and in other words 'to create' (as well as to 'imagine and create' in UNESCO terminology),[57] while in a much broader sense, it encompasses 'the right of the artists to choose their own purposes'.[58] In this sense, freedom of the arts is primarily a civil (and political) right and is *lex specialis* in relation to freedom of expression, by virtue of which every person has the right to undisturbed creation without being subject to either State intervention or censorship.[59] Violations of the right to artistic freedom refer to specific attacks against the practice of the arts, especially professional artists.[60] *Largo sensu*, however, artistic freedom may be defined as the right to access the arts – and more specifically the right to access artistic practice and education, as well as artistic events (as a member of the public). UNESCO follows this second approach, since, according to its 2017 report, the right to artistic freedom is a right 'germane not only to the being and creative practice of artists themselves but also to the rights of all cultural producers and audiences',[61] which 'includes the right of all citizens to have access to these works and is essential for the well-being of societies'.[62]

56 ibid.

57 UNESCO 2017 Report *supra* note 8 at 212.

58 John-Henry Merryman, 'Artistic Freedom' 613 in Merryman and Elsen *supra* note 24.

59 Elissavet Stamatopoulou, *Cultural Rights in International Law: Article 27 of the UDHR and Beyond* (Brill 2007) 121ff and Chapter 3 of this book.

60 UNESCO 2017 Report *supra* note 8 at 29 and 212ff (reporting 430 attacks on artistic freedom in 2016; 340 in 2015 and 90 in 2014 – mostly against musicians); also UN Human Rights Council, 'Report of the Special Rapporteur in the Field of Cultural Rights, Farida Shaheed', 14 March 2013, UN Doc A/HRC/23/34, paras 6–8.

61 UNESCO 2017 Report *supra* note 8 at 3.

62 ibid at 29.

2.2.1 *The Free Enjoyment of the Arts in Light of Article 27 of the UDHR*

The framework to better understand the function of both provisions with respect to artistic freedom is the Universal Declaration of Human Rights (UDHR). The UDHR does not explicitly mention the arts (and, as discussed above, the right to 'free creation' was substantially debated). It nonetheless protects the right 'to seek, receive and impart information and ideas through any media and regardless of frontiers' (article 19), as well as the right of everyone to 'freely participate in the cultural life of the community, to enjoy the arts and to share in scientific advancement and its benefits' (article 27, paragraph 1).

The willingness of States to guarantee all forms of expression with the least possible degree of interference was seen at various stages of the drafting of the declaration and in relation to article 19 (then article 14 of the UDHR).[63] There was no discussion on the particular types of expression. The reference to the 'free enjoyment of the arts' on the contrary in article 27 of the UDHR[64] was arguably the success of the Peruvian delegation, and José Encinas in particular, who strongly urged that the word *freely* be inserted – specifically addressing freedom in creation.[65] Otherwise, the drafters of the UDHR seemed more concerned about guaranteeing the moral and material rights of the authors, including the right to just remuneration for their work. This is arguably why the French René Cassin, in supporting the Peruvian amendment, made the link with intellectual property (IP) rights and recalled that similar questions had been debated by the Commission on Human Rights while discussing the right to take part in scientific progress and the associated benefits.[66] In the view of the drafters, guaranteeing moral rights and pecuniary interests (including royalties) deriving from works 'was the only way to guarantee the intrinsically personal character of every creation of the human mind and the ensuing durable link between creators and their creations'.[67]

63 Schabas *supra* note 14 at 1439ff and 1497.

64 Article 27 of the UDHR reads: 'Everyone has the right *freely* to participate in the cultural life of the community, to enjoy the arts and to share in scientific advancement and its benefits'.

65 Schabas *supra* note 14, reprinting A/C.3/SR.151 (627) at 2722, 2738 and 2746. This amendment was adopted unanimously, with thirty-eight votes to none and two abstentions. According to Encinas, the freedom to participate in cultural life then falls under the 'right to do so, in that complete freedom from which is no creation worthy of man', and, since an article on freedom of thought was already adopted, 'it would seem relevant now to recognize another, on creative thinking, in order to protect it from insults far too frequent in recent history'. See also Stamatopoulou *supra* note 59 at 12.

66 ibid (reprinting A/C.3/SR.150) at 2722.

67 UN Commission on Human Rights, Second Session, 'Report of the Working Group on the Declaration on Human Rights' (10 December 1947) E/CN.4/57 page 15, cited by the UN SECR Committee, 'General Comment no 17 (article 15, paragraph 1 (c), of the covenant)', 12 January 2006, E/C.12/GC/17 at 4, para 12.

Subsequently, there was another amendment suggested jointly by Cuba, France and Mexico (to what was then article 25 of the draft UDHR) that added a second paragraph to the then article 25 on intellectual property and the right of 'everyone . . . to the protection of the moral and material interests resulting from any scientific, literary or artistic production of which he is the author'.[68] The force behind this second amendment, equally successful, was Guy François Pérez Cisneros, the Cuban delegate who was himself a well-established art critic, and an accomplished painter. He saw intellectual property as one of the preconditions of a meaningful access to arts. According to Cisneros,

> [. . .] intellectual works could not be placed in the same category as other forms of property. Men of learning and artists live in special conditions in which material considerations had only a limited importance. It was necessary to recognize that fact and to guarantee equitable protection for those persons [. . .] literary, artistic and scientific works should be made accessible to the people directly and in their original form: this could only be done if the moral rights of the creative artist were protected.

Other central and Latin American countries' delegates were also in favour of these findings. The Mexican, Campos Ortiz, in particular made an interesting point regarding the 'intellectual worker' and the absolute need for the declaration to 'proclaim the rights of the individual as an intellectual worker, scientist, or writer; in other words, the rights of all those who contributed to the progress and wellbeing of humanity', and that if the declaration did not do that it would be an omission, as in the original version of the draft American Declaration of the Rights and Duties of Man.[69] The Ecuadorian delegate on the contrary found that this provision of the UDHR was not particularly useful, as 'the State's obligation to render works of art and intellectual creations accessible to the people by granting admission without charge to all museums and libraries and, above all, by extending public education' was already covered by the right to education and the freedom of thought.[70]

2.2.2 *The Free Speech Approach to Artistic Freedom*

The International Covenant on Civil and Political Rights (ICCPR) explicitly states that '[the right to freedom of expression] shall include the freedom to

[68] Schabas *supra* note 14, reprinting A/C.3/360, 20 November 1948 (628) at 2710, citing Cuba, France, Mexico: Joint amendment to Article 25 of the Draft Declaration (E/800): 'Everyone has, likewise, the right to the protection of his moral and material interests in any inventions or literary, scientific or artistic works of which he is the author'.

[69] ibid 617 at 2720.

[70] ibid at 2721.

seek, receive and impart information and ideas of all kinds, regardless of frontiers, either orally, in writing or in print, in the form of art, or through any other media of his choice' (article 19).

Freedom of *artistic* expression therefore (rather than freedom of 'creation') is explicitly protected in the text of article 19, especially in its dimension as contribution to the public debate. Other treaties or eventually soft law are also relevant to the extent that they refer to vulnerable individuals or groups of individuals or collectives. For example, the Convention on the Elimination of All Forms of Discrimination against Women (CEDAW)[71] compels States to eliminate discrimination with respect to 'the right to participate in recreational activities, sports and all aspects of cultural life'; the Convention on the Rights of the Child (CRC) 'protects the right of the child to participate fully in cultural and artistic life';[72] and the Convention on the Rights of Persons with Disabilities (CRPD) provides that 'States Parties shall take appropriate measures to enable persons with disabilities to have the opportunity to develop and utilize their creative, artistic and intellectual potential, not only for their own benefit, but also for the enrichment of society'.[73] Also, the United Nations Declaration on the Rights of Indigenous Peoples (UNDRIP) mentions specifically the protection of indigenous cultural identities, which includes therefore also artistic expressions, as a central aspect of indigenous peoples' right to self-determination, and indeed to their existence.[74]

From the early stages of drafting of the ICCPR, the debate between State representatives focused on the extent of acceptable limitations to this right rather than the forms of speech that would be protected.[75] As evidenced by the *travaux préparatoires* on article 19, there was no particular disagreement on

[71] CEDAW, art 13.

[72] CRC, art 31.

[73] CRPD, art 30, para 2.

[74] See generally, Stephen Allen and Alexandra Xanthaki (eds), *Reflections on the UN Declaration on the Rights of Indigenous Peoples* (2011); Siegfried Wiessner, 'Culture and the Rights of Indigenous Peoples' in Ana Filipa Vrdoljak (ed), *The Cultural Dimension of Human Rights* (Oxford University Press 2013) 117–56.

[75] UN Commission on Human Rights, 'Report to ECOSOC' (23 June 1949) UN Doc E/L371 and E/CN.4/350 at 34ff. See, for instance, the fourteen possible limitations suggested by the United Nations Conference on Freedom of Information (at 36–37); also Marc Bossuyt, *Guide to the "Travaux Préparatoires" of the International Covenant on Civil and Political Rights* (Martinus Nijhoff 1987) 373ff.

the fact that all forms of expression should be equally protected,[76] while some delegates specifically mentioned artistic freedom.[77]

2.2.3 *Cultural and Collective Aspects of Artistic Freedom*

The term 'freedom' itself is impersonal. This implies that the ultimate beneficiary of the right is not only the individual, but also the broader public. This is because the public is the rights-holder of a closely related right, namely, the right to access art (and cultural life more broadly). In other words, art cannot be seen isolated from its cultural framework, and the vast ensemble of elements that are unique to a culture. In this sense, artistic expressions are part of a (collective) cultural identity. This is why artistic freedom is commonly understood not only as part of freedom of expression, but also as a cultural right.[78]

The relationship between artistic freedom and culture is in fact twofold. On the one hand, artistic freedom serves as a precondition for the right of access to culture and participation in cultural life.[79] As Symonides notes, 'legislation protecting artistic creation and performance' as well as '[available and accessible] professional education in the field of culture and art' are both requirements in the implementation of the right to access culture.[80] On the other hand, artistic freedom has a strong collective dimension, especially in the case

76 ibid UNCHR at E/800 (A) (referring to the text submitted by the French delegate: 'everyone is free to publish his ideas in any way he chooses').

77 ibid UNCHR at E/800 (B), E/CN.4/415 (referring to the amendment submitted by the Representative of the Soviet Union, that 'in the interests of democracy, everyone shall be guaranteed by law the right of free expression of opinion, and in particular freedom of speech, of the press and of artistic expression'). cf also the amendment of Yugoslavia, E/CN.4/L.125, cited by Bossuyt *supra* note 75 at 392).

78 Janusz Symonides (ed), *Human Rights: International Protection, Monitoring, Enforcement* (UNESCO 2003) (mentioning rights recognized in both article 19 (freedom of expression) and 27 (minority rights) of the UDHR); see also Stamatopoulou *supra* note 59 at 88; Rodolpho Stavenhagen, 'Cultural Rights: A Social Science Perspective' in Asbjørn Eide et al (eds), *Economic, Social and Cultural Rights: A Textbook* (2nd ed 2001) 85. cf Shaheed *supra* note 60 at 6–7.

79 cf Janet Blake, *International Cultural Heritage Law* (Cambridge University Press 2015) 305 (observing that 'the basic prerequisite for having the capability to participate in cultural life, to be involved in much cultural heritage-related creative activity, and even for appreciating and enjoying the cultural heritage').

80 Likewise, Shaheed *supra* note 60 at 11 para 49; UN Human Rights Council, 'Report of the Independent Expert in the Field of Cultural Rights, Farida Shaeed', 21 March 2011, UN Doc A/HRC/17/38, at 16 para 61 (noting that 'the right of access to and enjoyment of cultural heritage must be considered both as an individual and a collective human right').

of artists who belong to minorities or indigenous peoples.[81] The practice of arts in those cases, as well as the participation in the artistic life of *their* community, is a central element of the consolidation, preservation and strengthening of their collective cultural identity,[82] in the sense of the sentiment of a community that shares common characteristics and values. At the same time, artistic freedom is a right that challenges the static concept of culture, since part of its function is to precisely 'contest meanings and revisit culturally inherited ideas and concepts'.[83]

It is arguably for this reason that the provision which reads that 'the States Parties to the present covenant undertake to respect the freedom indispensable for scientific research and creative activity' is in fact part of article 15, which protects also the other three components of 'culture' (participation to culture; access to science and technology; protection of authorship under article).[84] This is equally corroborated by the *travaux* of the International Covenant on Economic, Social and Cultural Rights (ICESCR) and the debates on article 15 (then article 16) of the ICESCR. First, delegates maintained the word 'indispensable' in the wording of article 15, paragraph 3 of the final draft, so that States would only be able to impose those limitations that were 'strictly required by national security, public order and morality'.[85] Second, in their majority they refused to submit artistic freedom to constraints, rejecting amendments qualifying that freedom: the Czechoslovakian amendment, for instance, which added that the exercise of that freedom should be 'in the interest of maintaining peace and cooperation between nations'[86] and the Greek amendment stating that 'States should give particular encouragement to such creative activity as tends to the healthy development of the human personality'.[87] France, in addition, as noted by Bidault, considered article 15, paragraph 3 as expressly relevant to 'sculptors and painters', directing literary

81 Janusz Symonides, 'Cultural Rights: A Neglected Category of Human Rights' (1998) 158 *International Social Science Journal* 556, 559; also Blake *supra* note 79 at 304 fns 155 and 305 (referring to the 'list' of cultural rights established by Pratt).

82 cf Yvonne Donders, 'A Right to Cultural Identity in UNESCO' in Francesco Francioni and Martin Scheinin (eds), *Cultural Human Rights* (Martinus Nijhoff 2008) 317, 331.

83 Shaheed *supra* note 80, A/HRC/17/38, para 3.

84 cf Lea Shaver and Catarina Scanga, 'The Right to Take Part in Cultural Life' (2010) 27 (4) *Wisconsin International Law Journal* 637, 640–41 (arguing that it is 'best understood as recognizing a universal human right to science and culture').

85 UN General Assembly, 796th meeting of the GA Third Committee, 12th session (agenda item 33), UN Doc A/3764, 5 December 1957 (Peruvian delegate Mr Carlos Manuel Cox reporting).

86 ibid para 71 (referring to A/C.3/L.633 and L.637).

87 ibid para 79 (referring to A/C.3/L.633). Greece also noted in support of its amendment that States should not encourage artistic productions that appeal to the 'lowest instincts of man'.

and artistic activities 'towards a single goal, namely, the maintenance of peace', enhancing them '[to] exalt friendship between peoples'.[88]

2.3 THE SCOPE AND INSTITUTIONAL PROTECTION OF ARTISTIC FREEDOM

2.3.1 *The Protection of Artistic Freedom by UNESCO*

When UNESCO was created back in 1945, the origins of the term 'culture' were associated with individualistic and somewhat elitist notions of art – rather than the cultural and collective aspects of artistic freedom. As the UNESCO rapporteur at that time explains, the objectives of UNESCO itself as an institution at the time were limited in traditional domains 'such as the development of libraries and museums, the protection of monuments and the encouragement of artistic education and creation'.[89] The same point was made by the former Secretary-General of UNESCO Koichiro Matsuura, who found that this perception of arts was in detriment to the meaning of culture and a group's right 'to be different'.[90]

In 1945 the term 'culture' was arguably equivalent to colonial culture. Western 'civilization' would be therefore associated with the idea of a certain refinement, as well as *progress*. Folklore and indigenous artistic expressions, in particular, have typically been labelled by the Western art world as exotic, 'primitive' and backwards – if human at all. And indeed, the colonizers' perspective on the meaning and concept of art differed substantially from the arts and crafts encountered in the colonized lands. Around the same time that the *Salon des Refusés* (i.e. the Salon which exhibited the works rejected by the Official Paris Salon) displayed Edouard Manet and the *Le Dejeuner sur l'herbe* in Paris,[91] various colonial 'civilization exhibits' were taking place in Paris and other European capitals, exhibiting features of indigenous cultures

[88] Mylène Bidault, *La protection internationale des droits culturels* (Bruylant 2010) 510 (citing E/3764, para 36).

[89] Pierre Moulinier, *Programme de l'UNESCO en matière de développement culturel: présentation des travaux réalisés depuis* 1960 (UNESCO 1994, CLT/DEC/CD/94/10) at 1. See on this also generally, Pierre Moulinier, *UNESCO: Cultural Development Documentary* (UNESCO 1977).

[90] Koichiro Matsuura, 'L'enjeu culturel au cœur des relations internationales' (2006) 4 *Politique Étrangère* 1045, 1048.

[91] Indicatively Hugh Honour and John Fleming, *World History of Art* (7th rev ed, Taschen) 670–72.

as objects of anthropological observation.[92] Several painters and sculptors sought inspiration from these exhibitions to develop their own artistic practice. The most known example is arguably Picasso's 'African period' – especially his painting *Les Demoiselles d'Avignon*, inspired by African sculptures which he saw at his visit to the Trocadéro Museum of Ethnography.

The gap between elitist modern art and the exotic cultural expressions of the various non-Western civilizations penetrated the entire legal edifice of the twentieth century in matters related to arts and heritage. This in turn had at least two consequences. First, the then nascent system of IP rights granting 'legal rights of ownership to individuals and corporations over their creations' was built upon Western notions of art, including the individualistic approach to the sole artist-creator.[93] Second, a distinction between 'cultural property' (and subsequently arts), on the one hand, and 'civilizations' (or living cultures), on the other, marking the entire edifice of cultural heritage protection. These two approaches to culture have long followed the regime for international cultural heritage protection, crystallizing the dichotomy between tangible and intangible heritage. It is only after the end of the political controversy of the Cold War, and following the wave of decolonization and the emergence of newly independent states that culture started again being defined as *identity* and artistic freedom became part of the UNESCO agenda as a precondition for cultural development. In its 1980 Recommendation Concerning the Status of the Artist, for example, UNESCO urges UN Member States to take all necessary measures to develop artistic creation, emphasizing that States should 'protect, defend and assist artists in their freedom of creation' and that they should take all necessary measures to 'secure greater freedom for them'.[94] The Recommendation finds that

> art reflects, preserves and enriches the cultural identity and spiritual heritage of the various societies, constitutes a universal form of expression and

[92] See Cortelyou Kenney, 'Reframing Indigenous Cultural Artifacts Disputes: An Intellectual Property-Based Approach' (2011) 28 *Cardozo Arts & Entertainment Law Journal* 502, 509 (noting that these 'exhibits functioned as cultural zoos or circuses'); Ivan Karp and Steven Lavine (eds), *Exhibiting Cultures: The Politics and Poetics of Museum Display* (1991) 398, 400. Also Ana Filipa Vrodjlak, *International Law, Museums and the Return of Cultural Objects* (Cambridge University Press 2008).

[93] Tom Greaves, 'IPR: A Current Survey' in Tom Greaves (ed), *Intellectual Property Rights for Indigenous Peoples: A Source Book* (Society for Applied Anthropology 1994) 3 at 8.

[94] UNESCO, Recommendation Concerning the Status of the Artist, adopted in 1980 at 5 (III) (a) [guiding principles].

> communication and, as a common denominator in ethnic, cultural or religious differences, brings home to everyone the sense of belonging to the human community [and, therefore, UNESCO Member States] should accordingly, and for these purposes, ensure that the population as a whole has access to art.[95]

In recent years, UNESCO has undertaken considerable initiatives to bridge the gap between individual and collective perceptions of artistic expressions. The 2005 Convention on the Protection and Promotion of the Diversity of Cultural Expressions (which is now ratified by 145 States), despite all criticisms,[96] has proved to be a key instrument to 'endeavour to create an environment which encourages individuals and social groups to create, produce, disseminate, distribute and have access to their own cultural expressions [...]', as well as 'to recognize the important contribution of artists as well as all those involved in the creative process, and their central role in nurturing the diversity of cultural expressions'.[97] Moreover, it serves to promote artistic freedom at all levels, including detailed statistics, reports, monitoring and support to policy making activities in the context of UNESCO and beyond. According to the current Director-General of UNESCO, Audrey Azoulai, the UNESCO roadmap focuses now on four key areas, which include 'improving the conditions for the mobility of artists' and 'promoting human rights and fundamental freedoms'.[98] Within the framework of UNESCO, a Goodwill Ambassador for artistic freedom and creativity has been designated,[99] while substantial work is being done in terms of monitoring the implementation of the 1980 Recommendation on the Status of the Artist[100] as well as on monitoring violations.[101]

95 ibid.

96 Indicatively, Tania Voon, 'UNESCO and the WTO; A Clash of Cultures?' (2006) 55(3) *International and Comparative Law Quarterly* 637; also Eleni Polymenopoulou, '"Cultural Diversity" from the Perspective of Human Rights, Media and Trade Law: Cross-fertilization or Conflict?' (2021) 2(7) *Santander Art and Culture Law Review* 123.

97 UNESCO 2005 Convention, art 7; Shaheed *supra* note 80 at paras 21–23.

98 UNESCO 2017 Report *supra* note 8 at 3.

99 UNESCO, 'Address by Irina Bokova, Director-General of UNESCO, on the Occasion of the Designation Ceremony of Ms Deeyah Khan as a UNESCO Goodwill Ambassador for Artistic Freedom and Creativity, UNESCO Doc DG/2016/183.

100 UNESCO, 'Consolidated Report on the Implementation of the Recommendation Concerning the Status of the Artist', 38th Session, Legal Committee Fifth Report, 7 November 2015, UNESCO Doc 38 C/82 (in French). See also 'Address by Irina Bokova, Director-General of UNESCO, on the Occasion of the Special Side Event "Status of the Artist and Artistic Freedom"', 38th General Conference UNESCO, 13 November 2015, UNESCO Doc DG/2015/225.

101 UNESCO 2017 Report *supra* note 8 at 212ff.

2.3.2 *The Practice of International Human Rights Bodies*

2.3.2.1 The Practice of the UN Human Rights Committee

The Human Rights Committee (the UN body mandated to monitor the ICCPR) has discussed 'artistic freedom' in the context of both General Comments and individual communications. This body issued its first General Comment on the interpretation of article 19 in 1983.[102] This was a rather brief note consisting of only four paragraphs, in which the committee merely noted that freedom of expression also encompasses the freedom of expression in the form of art, as per the text of the ICCPR.[103]

The same self-evident finding was reiterated in the committee's more recent comment on article 19 of the ICCPR[104] – a comment much more detailed than the previous one. This comment is clearly richer in ideas (and much longer compared to the previous one), as well as written in a language more 'direct' than the usual UN language.[105] With many references to previous case law, the committee addresses in this comment almost all issues relating to freedom of expression, including 'thorny' issues such as minority access to media, cultural sensibilities, blasphemy and religious defamation, hate speech and other potential limitations.[106] The committee, however, here again did not highlight questions relevant specifically to artistic freedom, other than the fact that they are included in the protective scope of article 19.[107]

The UN Human Rights Committee has scarcely had the opportunity to examine complaints related to artistic freedom in the context of its individual communications' procedure. In fact, this committee has established an interesting case law on freedom of expression, yet, to date only two cases among these have specifically been considered artworks. The first is the case of

[102] UN Human Rights Committee, 'General Comment no 10, Freedom of Expression' (art 19), 29 June 1983. Also Nejib Bouziri, *La protection des droits civils et politiques par l'ONU; l'oeuvre du Comité des droits de l'Homme* (L'Harmattan 2003) 432–33 [in French].

[103] ibid at para 2. See indicatively, Sarah Joseph, 'Art and Human Rights Law' in Jani McCutcheon and Fiona McGaughey (eds), *Research Handbook on Art and Law* (Edward Elgar 2020) 389, 390–91 (noting the little guidance offered by the committee so far).

[104] UN Human Rights Committee, 'General Comment no 34, The right to freedoms of opinion and expression' (art 19), 12 September 2011, UN Doc CCPR/C/GC/34, para 11. See O'Flaherty, 'Freedom of Expression: Article 19 of the International Covenant on Civil and Political Rights and the Human Rights Committee's General Comment No 34' (2012) 12 *Human Rights Law Review* 627.

[105] The US delegate Mrs Ruth Wedgewood encouraged the Committee members, see the UN Press Release, UNGA DH/CT/723, 19 March 2010.

[106] General Comment no 34 *supra* note 104 at para 37ff.

[107] ibid at para 11.

censorship of a painting titled *Rice Plantation* on the grounds of breach of Korean national security law,[108] and the second, a case concerning the taking down of a large art installation on Mapocho River in Santiago, Chile,[109] which will be discussed in Chapters 3 and 4, regarding censorship and reparations, respectively. Before that, and in the context of individual communications, the committee had only incidentally mentioned that article 19, paragraph 2 also encompasses 'works of art'.[110]

2.3.2.2 The Practice of the Committee on Economic, Social and Cultural Rights

The Committee on Economic, Social and Cultural Rights (CESCR), as the main body that interprets the ICESCR, could also, potentially, play a significant role in ascertaining claims related to access of the arts. This committee, however, since its creation in 1985 and at least until the late 1990s has never been particularly dynamic, its role being confined to 'soft' remarks.[111] In its examination of periodic reports, only sporadically has it examined issues relevant to the arts, and this in the context of general repression and neglect for economic, social and cultural rights (for instance, in the examination of the periodic report of Korea, the committee had the opportunity to discuss censorship of cultural activities and inequality in access to funding).[112] At the same time, the approach to culture has been rather 'elitist', having been raised by the members of the committee themselves. The Senegalese, Samba Cor Konaté, for example, in a study published in 1992 on the role of the committee in the implementation of cultural rights, considered that the committee perceived cultural activities as a 'luxury' and that little interest was shown to their 'collective meaning'.[113]

The role of the committee has undoubtedly evolved, and several developments in the area of cultural rights protection have been partially owed to its

[108] *Hak-Chul Shin v Republic of Korea* (926/2000), Views, CPR/C/80/D/926/2000 (2004).

[109] *Claudia Andrea Marchant Reyes et al. v Chile*, 7 November 2017, UN Doc CCPR/C/121/D/2627/2015.

[110] *John Ballantyne et al. v Canada* (Communication Nos. 359/1989, 385/1989), 31 March 1993, para 11.3 (regarding a complaint by Canadian residents of Quebec that commercial signs until then could only be in French language); *Singer v Canada* UN doc CCPR/C/51/D/455/199, 15 August 1994, para 11.3. cf Joseph *supra* note 103 at 391.

[111] See Habib Gherari, 'Le Comité des droits économiques, sociaux et culturels' (1992) 96 *RGDIP* 75, 76 [in French]; also Stamatopoulou *supra* note 59 at 27.

[112] UN Committee on Economic, Social and Cultural Rights ('CESCR'), 18 May 2001, E/C.12/2001/SR.14 (Republic of Korea).

[113] Stamatopoulou *supra* note 59 at 49, citing Konaté's report E/C.12/1992/WP.4.

members. In the new millennium in particular, the committee has taken steps that emphasize the justiciable aspects of social, economic and cultural rights – including for instance issuing general comments on the application of the ICESCR clarifying the meaning of 'culture'.[114] In addition, following the adoption and entry into force of the aforementioned Optional Protocol to the ICESCR, the committee is now competent to examine individual communications emanating from individuals complaining about infringements on their artistic freedom. To date, however, the committee has not issued a comment specifically on artistic freedom. A brief reference to article 15 para 3 of the ICESCR ('the freedom indispensable for scientific research and creative activity') is included in General Comment no 25 on freedom of science.[115] The committee however did not seize the opportunity to explain the relationship between 'science', the 'process of scientific creation' and 'creative activity', although this could have been clearly brought up.

Presumably, nothing precludes this body from taking a more active role in the future in the protection of access to culture, including access to arts and artistic practice. Its work could also be enriched by the findings of other human rights treaty bodies (especially given the aforementioned 'spill-over' effect of cultural rights), but also largely the UN Special Rapporteur on Cultural Rights, including the report on artistic and creative freedom prepared by the first Special Rapporteur on Cultural Rights, Farida Shaheed, which was authored in 2013 in order to explore further the content of article 15 and especially 15 paragraph 3.[116] This report is significant in that it recognizes the elements of a separate treatment of artworks in the following terms:

> An artwork differs from non-fictional statements … interpretations given to an artwork do not necessarily coincide with the author's intended meaning … representations of the real must not be confused with the real, which means, for example, that what a character says in a novel cannot be equated with the author's personal views.[117]

[114] UN CESCR, 'General Comment no 21, Right of Everyone to Take Part in Cultural Life' (art. 15, § 1 (a) of the ICESCR), 21 December 2009, paras 8–16, UN Doc E/C.12/GC/21.

[115] UN CESCR, 'General Comment no. 25 on Science and Economic, Social and Cultural Rights' (article 15 (1) (b), (2), (3) and (4) of the International Covenant on Economic, Social and Cultural Rights), 30 April 2020, UN Doc E/C.12/GC/25, paras 13–14 and 18.

[116] Shaheed *supra* note 60 at 11 paras 9–11.

[117] ibid at para 37.

2.3.3 *The Practice of Regional Human Rights Bodies*

2.3.3.1 Artistic Freedom in the Context of the European System

In Europe, artistic freedom is protected by the relevant regional instruments, indirectly by the European Convention on Human Rights (ECHR) and directly by the EU Charter for Fundamental Rights. The latter expressly guarantees 'the freedom of arts' in a separate provision.[118] In the context of the EU, however, the right to artistic freedom has only been examined from a rather specific perspective, namely as concerns the right to freedom of movement of artworks and IP rights – including the legitimacy of sampling and looting techniques.[119] The European Court of Human Rights (ECtHR) on the contrary has developed considerable expertise on the matter as, over the past forty years, it has had the opportunity to establish a substantial case law on the acceptable 'limits' of artistic freedom.[120] Already in 1974, Dupuy observed that the freedom of the artist is 'implicitly recognized in the text of the Convention'.[121] Yet, the first relevant case of the ECtHR decided on the merits was only in 1980, in a case regarding the exhibition of paintings outraging public morals by a Swiss painter, in which the Court clarified that article 10 of the ECtHR encompasses artistic freedom.[122]

To date, this Court has adjudicated approximately thirty-five cases on artistic freedom *stricto sensu*,[123] while in the last three years, in particular, the cases on artistic freedom have multiplied. No doubt, this percentage represents a minimal portion of the Court's case law, yet it still leaves it significantly ahead of its regional counterparts. Although the ECtHR assumed a rather hesitant stance in the 1990s and the early 2000s, generally allowing for a large margin of appreciation to States.[124] In fact, negating the quality of an

[118] Article 13 of the EU Charter provides that 'arts and sciences are free from "all constraints"'). It further proclaims not only the 'freedom to receive and impart information and ideas without interference by public authority' but also respect of 'the freedom and pluralism' (art 11).

[119] See Chapter 5 of this book.

[120] Olivier de Schutter and Françoise Tulkens, 'Rights in Conflict: The European Court of Human Rights as a Pragmatic Institution' in Eva Brems (ed), *Conflicts between Fundamental Rights* (Intersentia 2008) 170, 171.

[121] Dupuy *supra* note 40 at 41.

[122] ECtHR, *Müller and Others v Switzerland* App no 10737/84, Merits, 24 May 1988, para 27, and Chapter 6 of this book.

[123] Eleni Polymenopoulou, 'Does One Swallow Make a Spring? Artistic and Literary Freedom at the European Court of Human Rights' (2016) 3 *Human Rights Law Review* 511, 514 (noting that as of 2016, the ECtHR had decided twenty-nine cases on artistic freedom out of the roughly 1,000 concerning freedom of expression).

[124] ibid at 531. See also Chapters 6 and 7 (on morality and religious beliefs).

artwork as such has been an exception throughout the case law of the ECtHR. To this author's knowledge, the existence of such a clash has been affirmed only once, when Judge Loucaides (as dissenting judge) argued that Otto Mühl's disputed painting in *Bildender* 'was not art' but rather 'a senseless, disgusting combination of lewd images whose only effect is to debase, insult and ridicule each and every person portrayed'.[125] Even in this case, however, the two other dissenting judges, Spielmann and Jebens, noted that 'the painting was not intended to portray reality' and that it is not the task of a Court to perform quality controls, 'or to differentiate between "superior" and "inferior" or "good" and "bad"'.[126]

This said, the Court has never engaged into philosophical discussions on the definition of 'art', or taken into consideration any qualifying conditions for this freedom to be invoked (such as whether the applicant is a professional artist, or whether the artwork can be qualified as an 'original creation' – as would be the case, for instance, in IP law) and rightly so. Over the last few years, the Court refers to 'artistic freedom' even when the slightest hint of creativity appears in the facts of the case. This has been evident in a series of cases. By way of example, in *Alves da Silva,* concerning a Portuguese journalist who had made a puppet to lampoon the attitude of the mayor of his native village, the Court explicitly affirmed that the applicant was covered by the protection of the freedom of satire, as a form of art, since the applicant wished to express himself in a way 'quite clearly satirical in nature'.[127] Likewise, in *Eon v France*, decided in 2013,[128] concerning an individual who raised a small placard reading 'get lost, you sad prick' when the French President Sarkozy passed nearby, once more the Court alluded to satire, noting that 'any interference with the right of an artist – or anyone else – to use this means of expression should be examined with particular care'.[129]

[125] ECtHR, *Vereinigung Bildender Künstler v Austria* App no 26986/03, 15 November 2007, at Dissenting Opinion of Judge Loucaides. Also Chapter 1, note 124, and Chapter 6, on obscenity and public morals.

[126] ibid at Joint Dissenting Opinion of Judges Spielmann and Jebens, para 3, citing (at para 10) the German Constitutional Court's decision in *Strauß-Karikatur* (see Chapter 1 of this book).

[127] ECtHR, *Alves da Silva v Portugal* App no 41665/07, Merits and Just Satisfaction, 20 October 2009, at para 27. cf *Tatár and Fáber v Hungary* App nos 26005/08 and 26160/08, Merits and Just Satisfaction, 12 June 2012, at para 41; *Welsh and Silva Canha v Portugal* App no 16812/11, Merits and Just Satisfaction, 17 September 2013 at 29; see Polymenopoulou *supra* note 123 at 536–37.

[128] ECtHR, *Eon v France* App no 26118/10, Merits and Just Satisfaction, 14 March 2013. cf also ECtHR, *Murat Vural v Turkey* App no 9540/07, Merits and Just Satisfaction, 21 October 2014, para 60.

[129] ibid at para 60.

With respect to the aforementioned defence of *fiction*, however, the approach of the Court remains ambivalent. In fact, it has never explicitly discussed fiction as a 'defence' for writers and poets – similar to privileges enjoyed by journalists and the press.[130] Rather, it has preferred to base its judgments on the traditional distinction between 'assertion of facts', and 'value judgements'.[131] The distinct function of the artwork as a product of fiction is taken into account for the first time only in 2005, in *Alınak*, concerning a novel that recounted the massacre at a Kurdish village in South-Eastern Turkey.[132] The events described in the book were based on real facts. The Court, however, recognized that there should be a privileged treatment of freedom of literature precisely because '… the medium used by the applicant was a novel, a form of artistic expression that appeals to a relatively narrow public compared to, for example, the mass media',[133] and this, despite the fact that it was 'purportedly based on real events'.[134] These findings were reiterated in *Jelševar and Others v Slovenia*,[135] concerning a self-published book that contained depictions of personalities resembling their private and family life. In that case, the Court did not confine itself to the usual balancing exercise: akin to the GFCC in *Mephisto* and *Esra*, it explicitly referred to literature as 'fiction', noting that 'the book at issue was written not as a biography but as a work of fiction and, as such, would not be understood by most readers as portraying real people'.[136]

This said, there is unfortunately to date no consistency in the Court's acceptance of a general defence on the grounds of artistic merit, or fiction. In *Lindon v France*,[137] for instance, in relation to the publication of the novel

[130] Jan Oster, *Media Freedom* (Cambridge University Press 2016) 84–91; Jan Oster, *European and International Media Law* (Cambridge University Press 2016) 5–12; David Rolph, Matt Vitins, Judith Bannister and Daniel Joyce, *Media Law* (Oxford University Press 2015) 221–67.

[131] See, for example, *Karataş v Turkey* App no 23168/94, ECHR 1999-IV, paras 50–52 (the Grand Chamber of the Court found by twelve votes to five against the censorship of a pro-Kurdish poem titled 'Martyrdom'); *Feldek v Slovakia* App no 29032/95, Merits and Just Satisfaction, 12 July 2001, at para 75. On this distinction, see *Lingens v Austria* App no 9815/82, Merits and Just Satisfaction, 8 July 1986, para 46; *Prager and Oberschlick v Austria* App no 15974/90, Merits and Just Satisfaction, 26 April 1995, at para 36.

[132] *Alınak v Turkey* App no 40287/98, Merits and Just Satisfaction, 29 March 2005.

[133] ibid at para 41.

[134] ibid at para 43. On auxiliary grounds, the Court equally recognized the contribution of artistic expression to the public debate, adding (at para 42).

[135] *Jelševar and Others v Slovenia* App no 47318/07, Admissibility, 11 March 2014 (inadmissible).

[136] ibid at para 38.

[137] *Lindon supra* note 41; Polymenopoulou *supra* note 123 at 531–33; also Wachsmann, 'Vers un affaiblissement de la protection de la liberté d'expression par la Cour européenne des droits de l'Homme?' (2009) 78 *Revue Trimestrielle des Droits de l'Homme* 491 [in French].

The Trial of Jean-Marie Le Pen, the majority of the Grand Chamber of the Court did not exhibit the same sensibility,[138] ultimately taking the novel 'to the letter' and dismissing any reference to fiction. Even the dissenting judges refused to ground their dissent on 'fiction' but rather on the contribution to political debate.[139]

2.3.3.2 Artistic Freedom in the Context of the Inter-American System

Article 13(4) of the American Convention on Human Rights (ACHR) protects artistic freedom through its broad freedom of expression provision, specifying that it 'includes, inseparably, the right to use any appropriate method to disseminate thought'. The ACHR equally contains (one and only) general provision on economic, social and cultural rights (ESCR) (article 26), complemented by the Additional Protocol of San Salvador, which guarantees that 'the States Parties to this Protocol recognize the right of everyone [. . .] to take part in the cultural and artistic life of the community'.[140] The Inter-American Commission on Human Rights (IACHR) has had several opportunities to discuss applications having freedom of expression as their main claim – typically in the context of severe media freedom repression (such as for instance, the violence against journalists during the protests in Nicaragua in 2018 and 2019)[141] and the targeted killings of journalists at the Colombian borders in 2016.[142] The Inter-American Court of Human Rights (IACtHR) has also largely discussed censorship practices and media regulation, including in *Granier* (licensing regime for broadcasting in Venezuela under President Chávez);[143] in a 1985 advisory opinion issued at the request of Costa Rica

[138] *Lindon supra* note 41 at para 55: '[T]he impugned work is not one of pure fiction but introduces real characters or facts'.

[139] ibid at Joint Partly Dissenting Opinion of Judges Rozakis, Bratza, Tulkens and Šikuta, para 4 (these judges found that 'the target of the book was a far-right politician who 'should accept an even higher degree of tolerance precisely because he is a politician who is known for the virulence of his discourse'). Interestingly, Judge Loucaides found that even this defence was not valid in the case at hand, see Concurring Opinion of Judge Loucaides.

[140] Additional Protocol to the American Convention on Human Rights in the Area of Economic, Social and Cultural Rights, 17 November 1988.

[141] For example, Inter-Am. Comm'n on H.R., *Leaders of the 19 de Abril Carazo Movement and Others*, Nicaragua, Resolution No 52/18, Precautionary Measures: 840/18, 841/18 and 779/18 (17 September 2018).

[142] For example, *Javier Ortega Reyes, Paúl Rivas Bravo and Efraín Segarra Abril, Colombia and Ecuador*, Resolution 25/18, PMs 309/18 and 310/18 (provisional measures) [in Spanish].

[143] *Granier et al. (Radio Caracas Television – RCTV) v Venezuela*, Report No 112/12, 14 April 2015.

(finding compulsory membership to a journalists' association incompatible with media freedom);[144] and in a case concerning the imposition of prior restraints on the cinematic version of the *Last Temptation of Christ* (based on a novel written by Kazantzakis) that will be discussed in detail in Chapter 3.[145] Save for this last case, however, and despite the growth in its case law, the Court has not heard other cases related specifically to arts or films.

Despite the large competence and experience of Inter-American bodies in relation to both cultural and collective rights (and particularly indigenous rights), the cultural aspects of artistic freedom have never been, to date, addressed before either the IACHR or the IACtHR. These bodies have not had the opportunity to discuss specifically the right of indigenous peoples' right to their 'artistic freedom' in the context of indigenous copyright claims. The latter have been almost exclusively discussed in relation to other rights – particularly land rights, and in the context of reparations.[146] This, however, does not entail that indigenous peoples' claims related to their traditional cultural expressions, artistic identities or heritage are not justiciable before Inter-American bodies. In fact, both the Commission and the Court have to date privileged an extended notion of 'property rights' (affirmed in articles 21 of the American Convention and 22 of the American Declaration) in order to protect the communal notion of indigenous rights, and it is on this basis that communal IP rights would be potentially addressed. In addition, the task of the IACHR and the IACtHR in relation to this matter has been largely facilitated since 2016, when the members of the Organisation of American States (OAS) finally adopted (by consensus) the American Declaration on the Rights of Indigenous Peoples (ADRIP),[147] which contains explicit affirmations

144 Advisory Opinion on Compulsory Membership in an Association Prescribed by Law for the Practice of Journalism (Arts 13 and 29 American Convention on Human Rights), Advisory Opinion OC-5/85, IACtHR Series A No 5, IHRL 3428 (IACHR 1985), 13 November 1985.

145 *Olmedo Bustos et al. v Chile*, OC-73/2001, IACtHR Series C 73, 5 February 2001 (*Last Temptation of Christ*), see Chapter 3 on prior restraints. Interestingly, the film has been banned in several States including Greece (Athens First Instance Court 17115/1988) and Israel (Israeli Supreme Court HC 806/88). See Chapter 7 of this book.

146 Indicatively, Kristina Hausler, 'Collective Cultural Rights in the Inter-American Human Rights System' in Andrzej Jakubowski (ed), *The Impact of Collective Cultural Rights on General International Law – Relocating the Third-Generation Human Rights* (Brill 2016) 241–46; Isabel Madariaga Cuneo, 'The Rights of Indigenous Peoples and the Inter-American Human Rights System' (2005) 2 *Arizona Journal on International and Comparative Law* 53, 55 and 62–63.

147 OAS, American Declaration on the Rights of Indigenous Peoples, 15 June 2016, AG/RES. 2888 (XLVI-O/16) in 'OAS Declarations and Resolutions Adopted by The General Assembly', AG/doc.5557/16, 16 June 2016, at 167.

of the right of indigenous persons to their own cultural identity and cultural heritage,[148] and 'protection of cultural heritage and intellectual property'.[149]

2.3.3.3 Artistic Freedom in the Context of the African System

The African Charter on Human and Peoples' Rights equally contains a provision on freedom of expression (article 9), from which artistic freedom may be deduced, while the Pretoria Declaration of Human Rights in Africa clarifies that 'the right to culture in articles 17 and 18 of the African Charter entail[s] among other things [...] participation at all levels in the determination of cultural policies and in cultural and artistic activities'. All three articles would therefore enable the African Commission and potentially also the Court to decide on individual and collective complaints related to artistic freedom – or access to arts via the provisions related with access to culture. For various reasons whose analysis goes way beyond the purposes of this book, the African bodies' jurisprudence on freedom of expression is to date marginal. The African Commission has been proactive in relation to specific issues related to freedom of expression, such as the safety of journalists working in Africa,[150] culminating into a Declaration of Principles on Freedom of Expression on access to information[151] and the appointment of Special Rapporteur on Freedom of Expression (since 2004). Freedom of expression in Africa, however, is by all accounts extremely frail, with a significant number of States violating freedom of expression and exercising censorship being members of the African Union. The task of the African human rights bodies, therefore, faces significant challenges, other than their workload and the lack of resources.[152]

To this author's best knowledge, the African Commission has not had, to date, the opportunity to examine communications alleging specifically violations of artistic freedom. Yet, if the opportunity were to arise, the African

[148] ibid 13 (1).
[149] ibid art 28.
[150] See by way of example, the AU Resolution on the Creation of AU Working Group on the Safety of Journalists and the Issue of Impunity in Africa, 15 November 2017, Addis Ababa, Ethiopia, at the request of Ghana; also ACHPR, Resolution no 185 on the Safety of Journalists and Media Practitioners in Africa, 12 May 2011.
[151] See e.g. the Declaration of Principles on Freedom of Expression in Africa (2002) ACHPR/Res.1 78(XLIX) (2011).
[152] Indicatively on the African human rights systems, see VO Orlu Nmehielle, *The African Human Rights System: Its Laws, Practice, and Institutions* (Martinus Nijhoff 2001) 17; Malcolm Evans and Rachel Murray (eds), *The African Charter on Human and Peoples' Rights: The System in Practice* 1986–2006 (Cambridge University Press 2011).

human rights bodies would have jurisdiction to find violations not only of the African Charter, but also, interestingly enough, 'any other human rights instrument' ratified by the State against which the application is filed.[153] Hence, for example, in one of the few cases where the Court decided on the merits, regarding the editor-in-chief of the leading journal in Burkina Faso, who was sentenced to twelve months imprisonment for writing an article accusing the State prosecutor of corruption and abuse of power, the African Court found that the defendant State breached not only article 9 of the Charter but also article 19 of the ICCPR.[154] On a handful of occasions, the African Commission has also considered collective cultural rights – primarily in the context of claims regarding peoples' oppression, as well as indigenous peoples, while in the case of the people of Cabinda, in particular (a people 'culturally and linguistically separate from Angola')[155] the question of artistic identity incidentally came up. The issue at stake was self-determination and the right of the people of Cabinda to pursue their own cultural and economic development. In their claim the applicants raised the applicability of the Angolan Constitution, which guarantees the 'right to respect, appreciation and preservation of the cultural, linguistic and artistic identity of the Angolan people'.[156] Such examples however remain sporadic – while more often than not potential applicants to the Commission complaining about severe repression of their freedom of expression have recourse to the universal system of human rights protection (including the Human Rights Committee and the UN Special Procedures, as in the case of Angolan journalist Rafael Marques de Morais – arrested, convicted and held incommunicado, for writing several articles critical of Angolan President dos Santos in independent Angolan journals and his book *Blood Diamonds*),[157] rather than the African Commission and the Court.

This notwithstanding, the Commission, in its 2010 guidelines, has seized the opportunity to highlight that artistic freedom is included among the

[153] African Charter, art 60; Protocol to the African Charter on Human and Peoples' Rights on the Establishment of the African Court on Human and Peoples' Rights, art 3.

[154] ACtHPR, *Lohé Issa Konaté v Burkina Faso* App no 004/2013, 5 December 2014, at para 49.

[155] ACHPR, *Frente para a Libertação do Estado de Cabinda v Angola* App no 328/06, 5 November 2013, para 10.

[156] ibid para 78 (and art 87 of the Angolan Constitution)

[157] UN Human Rights Committee, *Rafael Marques de Morais v Angola* App no 1128/2002, UN Doc N Doc CCPR/C/83/D/1128/2002, 29 March 2005; also 'Joint Report of the Special Rapporteur on the Promotion and Protection of the Right to Freedom of Opinion and Expression and the Special Rapporteur on the Situation of Human Rights Defenders', AL AGO 2/2018.

economic, social and cultural rights,[158] and that States should adopt policies aiming at the 'protection of the freedom of artistic creation and performance and professional education in the field of culture and art'.[159] Furthermore, freedom of expression and especially the need 'to ensure responsible free expression, inclusive of the freedom of the press' has been raised as one of the concerns of the New Partnership for Africa's Development (NEPAD) in the context of its Democracy and Political Governance Initiative.[160]

CONCLUDING REMARKS

This chapter discussed the nature and scope of artistic freedom, as well as the principal mechanisms of protection under international human rights law. It focused on two legal questions. The first was to locate artistic freedom in the human rights edifice with its various 'sets' of rights, in light of the classic distinction between civil and political rights on the one hand and economic social and cultural rights on the other (a distinction that albeit outdated, remains useful for taxonomy purposes). The right to artistic freedom may be defined both as a civil right (and *lex specialis* in relation to freedom of expression) and as a cultural right. This is because it cannot be isolated from the right to access freely artistic practice, education and events (and therefore, enjoy the arts as a member of the public) from its broader cultural framework. Its content therefore should be interpreted in light not only of freedom of speech provisions, but also provisions that are relevant to cultural rights (and which will be examined in more detail in Chapter 4). Article 27 of the UDHR is relevant in this respect as it provides for the right of everyone to 'freely participate in the cultural life of the community, to enjoy the arts and to share in scientific advancement and its benefits'. It is important that artists, and those who practice arts as part and manifestation of their culture are truly free to create without restraints. Those who engage in traditional arts and folklore in particular, and other types of collective expressions that are significant to people's heritage are the defenders of peoples' identities. They should therefore remain free to fulfil this role, while at the same time connecting past and present generations.

158 ACHPR, Principles and Guidelines on the Implementation of Economic, Social and Cultural Rights, adopted in November 2010, para 73 ('[the right to culture] is integral to the way of life of individuals and communities ... It refers not only to the enjoyment of cultural activities and access to materials but to participation, policy-making and artistic freedom').

159 ibid art 76, para d (4).

160 See NEPAD, Declaration on Democracy, Political, Economic and Corporate Governance, AHG/235(XXXVIII), Annex 1, para 15.

The second question addressed in this chapter was the (potential) 'special protection' of artists and artworks simply by virtue of their creative practice. This is because one of the most common arguments advanced in the sphere of art law is that creative expression should enjoy a privileged constitutional protection in domestic law (and subsequently also in human rights law), and eventually function as a type of 'defence' in tort and criminal law. It is often suggested that artists should be absolved from liability (in cases that ordinary persons would be), or at least that artistic freedom should weigh more in the balancing exercise that takes place following 'conflicts' of rights (between artistic freedom on the one hand and other rights and public interests on the other). This may be true for some constitutional traditions, especially those influenced by the German tradition. Suggesting, however, that artistic freedom enjoys a privileged protection under constitutional law akin to, say, freedom of the press and journalistic privileges is in fact far from being established. This is because of the different weight that States assign to values (such as aesthetics, morality, religion).

A special mention was made in this chapter to the jurisprudence of the ECtHR. This Court's contribution could have been pivotal in establishing defences for artists, and inspiring courts around the world to do the same. To date, however, the approach of the Court remains ambivalent as it has only seldom accepted the defence of 'fiction', for writers and poets in privacy and defamation cases (a noticeable exception was *Jelševar and Others v Slovenia*). The qualification 'artistic' in a freedom of expression case that arrives before does not by itself justify any preferential treatment. This conclusion is different in cases involving artistic expression that is at the same time either political or satirical, as in the case of a Kurdish poet whose poem titled 'Martyrdom' was censored by the Turkish authorities (*Karataş v Turkey*).

3

Censorship and Restrictions

In November 2017, an unusual exhibition was hosted in the President's Gallery of the John Jay College of Criminal Justice, New York. It was titled *Ode to the Sea*. The exhibits consisted of paintings, sculptures and handicrafts created by 'enemy combatants', namely, current and former detainees at the US military camp in Guantánamo Bay, Cuba. Most of the artists were detained for over ten years for their association with Al-Qaeda and bin Laden, or their involvement in the 9/11 bombings. The works were truly beautiful. They included Muhammed Ansi's eye crying over a stormy blue sea; Moath Alwi's model ships made of garbage; and Sabri al Qurashi's landscapes. A section on 'how and why was art made' (featuring examples of the difficulties associated with the practice of art in the camp and the lack of tools and supplies) was also part of the exhibition space.[1]

The decision to exhibit artworks made by prisoners from Guantánamo was largely seen as a pathway to better understand and prevent terrorism. Erin Thompson, the art crime professor who co-curated the event stated that '[she] firmly believe[s] that to prevent terrorism we need to understand the minds of terrorists and the minds of people wrongly accused of terrorism'.[2] In essence, the choice was related also to broader questions about cultural politics. Visual representations in particular play a crucial role in the formation of memories, and memories in turn are crucial in framing narratives. This is especially true in light of the 9/11 narrative, the US-led 'war against terror' and the atrocities that have taken place in both Guantánamo and Abu Ghraib. The artworks exhibited

1 See <www.artfromguantanamo.com>. Also Sarah Cascone, 'Poignant Artworks by Guantánamo Bay Prisoners Get a Show in New York' (*Artnet*, 2 October 2017) <https://news.artnet.com/art-world/guantanamo-bay-prisoners-art-1102325>.

2 Adam Reiss, 'Exhibit of Art by Guantanamo Detainees Draws Controversy' (*NBC News*, 29 November 2017) <www.nbcnews.com/news/us-news/exhibit-art-guantanamo-detainees-draws-controversy-n824726>.

were arguably milder than images directly alluding to torture and ill-treatment. The latter include not only the emblematic photograph 'Vietnam' (the terrifying picture of a hooded prisoner standing on card boxes, taken in Abu Ghraib),[3] but also works of contemporary art addressed to the larger public (such as Botero's paintings[4] and *Guantamera*, an art installation challenging the use of music as a method of sleep deprivation, displayed recently in Madrid's metro ventilators).[5] The controversy over the *Ode to the Sea* however did not focus on the cultural framing of terrorism as much as it did on the legitimacy of detainees as being worthy of the title 'artists' (a similar controversy has taken place in relation to art therapy offered to former terrorists as part of an inspired rehabilitation programme, following the airstrikes in Raqqa).[6]

Assuming that some of these works are good enough to be displayed in an exhibition, could a public cultural institution or private entity legitimately set up or fund such exhibition? Many people would not see a problem with that. They would probably argue that artworks should be dissociated from the personality of the artist. Others could even point out that great artists of the past were in fact criminals. They include Hitler (a failed painter himself) – and also, the Renaissance painter Caravaggio, who was imprisoned for murder, rape and other crimes. Yet the mere thought of the *Ode to the Sea* outraged many of those who lost relatives in the attacks. One critic, for instance, stated that it is 'like a slap in the face';[7] another that 'using taxpayer money to hang the artwork of criminals in [the] college for criminal justice makes [her] blood boil';[8] and a member of the board of the 9/11 Memorial Museum also said that 'this is disgusting and should be trashed'.[9] As a result,

3 Lene Hansen, 'How Images Make World Politics: International Icons and the Case of Abu Ghraib' (2015) 41 *Review of International Studies* 263, 278ff.

4 Daniel Trotta, 'Botero's Paintings of Abu Ghraib Shunned in U.S.' (*Reuters*, 2007) <www.reuters.com/article/us-arts-botero-abughraib-idUKN2421625220061025>. cf however, also, Laurel Fletcher, 'Let's Talk about the Boteros: Law, Memory, and the Torture Memos at Berkeley Law' (2020) 38 *Berkeley Journal of International Law* 1, 5–6.

5 See generally, Allen Feldman, 'On the Actuarial Gaze: From 9/11 to Abu Ghraib' (2005) 19(2) *Cultural Studies* 203; Susan Noyes Platt, 'Intimate Violence: Artists' Responses to Illegal Detention and Torture' (2013) 19(2) *Brown Journal of World Affairs* 163. Also David Darts et al, 'Scopic Regime Change: The War of Terror, Visual Culture, and Art Education' (2008) 49(3) *Studies in Art Education* 200.

6 Liz Sly, 'Captured ISIS Fighters Get Short Sentences and Art Therapy in Syria' (*Washington Post*, 14 August 2019).

7 Isabel Vincent, 'Pentagon Battles College Trying to Sell Art by "Terrorists"' (*NY Post*, 25 November 2017) <https://nypost.com/2017/11/25/pentagon-nyc-college-feud-over-gallery-of-artwork-made-by-suspected-terrorists/>.

8 ibid.

9 Reiss *supra* note 2.

when one of the artists took the artworks with him after his release from a Saudi prison, reactions increased, opposing the very concept of the prisoners owning the artworks (let alone selling them), and a new policy by the US Department of Defense stated that they were considered government property (which would therefore allow their incineration). Subsequently, a petition was signed by hundreds of academics and art historians, stating that 'burning art is something done by fascist and terrorist regimes – but not by the American people' and that 'this art belongs to the detainees and to the world'.[10]

There is arguably not a definitive response to the legitimacy of such choices and the rightness of one side over the other (and in fact, that particular exhibition is scheduled to reopen in 2022). Surely 'art belongs to the world', but the problem is precisely that what one world despises another world wants to see. Hard cases such as the *Ode to the Sea* are simply doomed to trigger controversy and prompt legal reactions, unavoidably contextual to a large extent. What they do illustrate however is the complexity of addressing restrictions in the field of art and the extent to which censorship in the art worlds remains contested. Which grounds of prior restraint are legitimate or necessary under international law? When can States legitimately restrict artistic freedom? And how do international bodies draw the fine line between illegitimate censorship, legitimate restrictions and regulation?

This chapter deals specifically with this prohibition of censorship in international law, which not only is seldom explicit – it is also full of ambiguities. The first section of the chapter therefore concerns the stance of the State in the artistic process – and is essentially about the prohibition of censorship. The second section concerns subsequent liability for expression that breaches other private rights or public interests.

3.1 ARTS SHOULD BE FREE: ABSTAINING FROM CENSORSHIP IN THE ARTS

3.1.1 *Legitimate or Illegitimate Censorship?*

Censorship is *in principle* prohibited for all types of expression, including also in respect of arts and creative expressions. This prohibition entails a spectrum of sub-obligations, entrenched upon the classic theory on three-part State obligations in the implementation of rights (to respect, protect and fulfil

[10] Vincent *supra* note 7.

human rights).[11] The questions of hate speech, incitement to hatred and discrimination and negationism deserve special attention given the difficulty in finding common rules among the various jurisdictions.

3.1.1.1 Lack of Clarity in International Standards

Technically speaking, censorship is not a legal term. It refers to all situations where the free flow of information and diffusion of culture or knowledge are unduly inhibited, as well as to all kinds of prior restraints. *Stricto sensu*, censorship refers to the State's power to 'suppress in advance of publication',[12] and this is why it is sometimes called *prior* censorship – as opposed to subsequent imposition of liability.[13] Censorship may involve for instance the seizure, confiscation or destruction of artworks prior to circulation and diffusion; preventing materials publicizing artistic events from being disseminated; or closing down websites containing artistic or other creative materials.[14] *Largo sensu*, however, censorship is also a generic notion that encompasses all situations where the free flow of information is unduly inhibited. As such, it involves all types of stringent restrictions to freedom of speech, including attempts by governmental authorities to 'limit, directly or indirectly, the information and variety of opinions available to the public'[15] in order to 'ensure its conformity with what the authority considers to be political, moral, aesthetic, or religious norms'.[16] In this sense, censorship is conflated with common restrictions to freedom of expression, differing only in broadness and gravity: restrictions that

11 Indicatively, Philip Alston and Gerald Quinn, 'Nature and Scope of States Parties' Obligations under the International Covenant on Economic, Social and Cultural Rights' (1987) 9(2) *Human Rights Quarterly* 156, 183–185; Maria-Magdalena Sepúlveda, *The Nature of the Obligations under the International Covenant on Economic, Social and Cultural Covenant* (Intersentia 2003) 171ff.

12 *Selected Articles on Censorship of Speech and the Press* (Beman ed, Wilson 1930) 365; D. P. Kommers and R. A. Miller, *The Constitutional Jurisprudence of the Federal Republic of Germany* (3rd ed, Duke University Press 2012) 375.

13 The difference between the two has been elaborated by the Inter-American Commission. See e.g. *Francisco Martorell v Chile*, Case 11.230, Report No 11/96, Inter-Am.C.H.R., OEA/Ser.L/V/II.95 Doc. 7 rev. at 234 (1997).

14 As pointed out by Lord Bridge in his dissenting opinion in the *Spycatcher* case it is the State's 'indispensable tool to regulate what the public may and what they may not know', see 'Spycatcher': *Attorney General* v *Guardian Newspapers Ltd* (No 1) UKHL 13 [1987] (UK); and subsequently, ECtHR, *Observer and Guardian v United Kingdom*, 26 November 1991, para 50.

15 Owen Fiss, 'The Censorship of Television' (1998–99) 93 *Northwestern University Law Review* 1215, 1218.

16 'Censorship' in David Kennedy (ed), *The Oxford Companion to Theatre and Performance* (Oxford University Press 2010); R. Darnton, 'Censors at Work: How States Shaped Literature' (2004) 44 *British Journal of Aesthetics* 361, 361.

constitute censorship, for example, could take the form of criminal punishment or disproportionate fines. This section does not deal with this second, broad concept of censorship.

There is no explicit prohibition of censorship in the freedom of expression provision of the International Covenant on Civil and Political Rights (ICCPR). The question of (prior) censorship was discussed within the Commission of Human Rights, as the ICCPR's *travaux préparatoires* reveal, and in fact some State delegates suggested that at least some reference should be included in the Covenant.[17] Yet, this proposal was not adopted since most delegates were satisfied that article 19, paragraph 2 concerning 'freedom to seek, receive and impart information and ideas', considering the restrictions mentioned in article 19, paragraph 3 sufficient.[18] Similarly, the UN Human Rights Committee has addressed the significance of 'a free, uncensored and unhindered press or other media', qualifying this, however, with a reference to the public opinion.[19]

On the contrary, article 15, paragraph 3 of the International Covenant on Economic, Social and Cultural Rights (ICESCR) is termed differently: 'the States Parties to the present Covenant undertake to respect the freedom indispensable for scientific research and creative activity'. The very formulation of this article, however, as discussed also earlier in Chapter 2, is the result of substantial debate between State representatives during the drafting of the covenant. As evidenced in the *travaux préparatoires* of the third paragraph of article 15, a substantial part of the discussion was devoted to whether additional qualifications should be added to this article, in relation to goals of scientific and cultural development, and whether such goals were compatible with the term 'freedom'.[20] In addition, the question of the word 'indispensable' was also debated, as some States found it too restrictive and requested its elimination[21] while others found that it recognized 'the right of the state to impose the

17 Marc Bossuyt, *Guide to the 'Travaux Préparatoires' of the International Covenant on Civil and Political Rights* (Martinus Nijhoff 1987) 398.

18 ibid. For a detailed discussion on the *travaux* on article 19, see also Molly Land, 'Toward an International Law of the Internet' (2013) 54(2) *Harvard International Law Journal* 393, 394–96 and 403ff.

19 See UN Human Rights Committee, 'General Comment no 34, 'Freedoms of Opinion and Expression', (art 19), CCPR/C/GC/34, 12 September 2011, para 13: 'A free, uncensored and unhindered press or other media is essential in any society to ensure freedom of opinion and expression [...] a free press and other media are able to comment on public issues without censorship or restraint and to inform public opinion'.

20 UN General Assembly, 796th Meeting of the GA Third Committee, 12th session (agenda item 33), UN Doc A/3764, 5 December 1957, at para 77.

21 ibid para 80.

limitations strictly required by national security, public order and morality'.[22] In any event, the final draft of article 15, paragraph 3 was adopted by seventy-one votes to none and one abstention, and in its last General Comment on article 15, paragraph 1, the Committee on Economic, Social and Cultural Rights (CESCR) has also clarified the need to abolish censorship in the arts.[23]

It could be argued therefore that article 15, paragraph 3 implies an absolute prohibition of censorship at the international level for creative activities. 'Creative activities' (as opposed to 'art') encompasses also forms of expression that are rejected by State authorities, such as dissident and unorthodox art, or prisoners' art (as in the aforementioned example of the Guantánamo Bay prisoners). It also encompasses 'creative advertisement'[24] (as in the case of Nadia Plesner's *Simple Living*, depicting a black boy holding a *Luis Viton* bag and a chihuahua, and aiming at raising awareness about Darfur).[25]

The generic obligation to abstain from prior restraints is translated into three sub-obligations. First, an obligation to 'exclude' the arts from legislative or judicial consideration; under this, State entities should not intervene in the creative process by predefining what art is and what it should look like, nor allow others to intervene as such.[26] As the German Federal Court has held, there is an intrinsic link between arts and freedom: 'The essence of artistic endeavour lies in the free creative process whereby the artist, in his chosen communicative medium, gives immediate perceptible form to what he has felt, learnt, or experienced'.[27] Second, public officials should not encourage, nor a fortiori advocate censorship practices.[28] This obligation could be

[22] ibid.

[23] See UN CESCR, 'General Comment no 21, Right of Everyone to Take Part in Cultural Life' (art 15, para 1 (a), of the International Covenant on Economic, Social and Cultural Rights), 21 Dec. 2009, E/C.12/GC/21 at 12, para 49 (b): '... implies that States parties must abolish censorship of cultural activities in the arts and other forms of expression, if any'.

[24] cf *New York Times Co. v Sullivan* 376 US 254, 271 (1964) (in which the Supreme Court affirmed that expression that appears in the form of paid advertisement is included in the protective purview of the First Amendment, and established the 'actual malice' test in defamation cases).

[25] <www.nadiaplesner.com/simple-living–darfurnica1> (noting that Plesner was sued by Louis Viton for trademark infringement, on the grounds of potential attack to the company's reputation); also Jani McCutcheon, 'Designs, Parody and Artistic Expression – A Comparative Perspective of Plesner *v. Louis Vuitton*' (2015) 41 *Monash University Law Review* 192, 192.

[26] See Chapter 1 (on State propaganda and predefining the arts).

[27] *Mephisto* 1 BvR 435/68 (24 February 1971) BVerfGE 30, 173 (1971). See also Chapter 1 (on the legacy of the Weimar Constitution).

[28] cf ARTICLE 19, *The Camden Principles on Freedom of Expression and Equality* (London, 2009), 'Principle 8: State responsibilities' (on the responsibilities of public officials): 'States should impose obligations on public officials at all levels, including ministers, to avoid as far as possible making statements that promote discrimination or undermine equality and intercultural understanding'.

expanded in such way as to encompass religious figures and institutions, especially in theocratic States or those adhering to, or recognizing, an official religion. Similar views were those advanced by the CESCR while discussing article 15 obligations, for example, during the periodic review of Iran and with respect to the implications of the fatwa issued against Salman Rushdie;[29] during the periodic review of Spain while discussing interference of religious authorities in cultural life;[30] during the periodic report of Netherlands Antilles with respect to interference with schooling because of religious beliefs;[31] and more recently, during the periodic review of Egypt (in relation to participation of Copts in cultural life without discrimination, including access to religious sites).[32] Third, States should also abstain from actions preventing self-help measures of the artistic community, the creative industry and NGOs working with artists, writers, musicians and other intellectuals.[33] Self-help measures, in turn, include those aiming to help victims of censorship (e.g. persons under death threats),[34] and those that encourage self-employment and entrepreneurship,[35] or even self-funding of the independent art scene in difficult circumstances, including pandemics such as the Covid-19 outbreak.[36]

Classification and rating on the other hand, as long as they are exercised by regulatory bodies with authority to do so, including censorship boards and

[29] Roger O'Keefe, 'The "Right to Take Part in Cultural Life" under Article 15 of the ICESCR' (1998) 47(4) *The International and Comparative Law Quarterly* 904, 911, fn. 52 citing E/1994/23, paras 1, 23. See also E/1990/5 and Chapter 7 of this book.

[30] ibid citing E/1992/23, para 284.

[31] ibid citing E/1989/22, para 238.

[32] UN CESCR, 'Concluding Observations on the Combined Second to Fourth Periodic Reports of Egypt', 13 December 2013, E/C.12/EGY/CO/2-4, para 23.

[33] There are today a number of NGOs and networks specifically aiming at protecting artistic freedom, e.g. PEN International (worldwide association of writers) and Freemuse (artistic freedom), while others have elaborated platforms specifically on artistic freedom (e.g. ARTICLE 19, has established an 'Artist Alert project').

[34] cf UN Human Rights Council, *The Right to Freedom of Artistic Expression and Creativity*, 'Report of the Special Rapporteur in the Field of Cultural Rights, Farida Shaheed' UN Doc A/HRC/23/34, at 2, paras 6–8 (mentioning e.g. the International Cities of Refuge Network (ICRN) 'Safe cities' project). Also Laurence Cuny, *Freedom & Creativity: Defending Art, Defending Diversity, Special Edition* at 18 (UNESCO 2020).

[35] See for example, EU Open Method of Coordination (OMC), *How Can Cultural and Creative Industries Contribute to Economic Transformation through Smart Specialisation?* <https://ec.europa.eu/culture/policy/strategic-framework/european-coop_en>.

[36] Laura Cumming, 'Self-Help Is Key for an Art World in Lockdown' (*The Observer*, 29 March 2020) <www.theguardian.com/artanddesign/2020/mar/29/self-help-is-key-for-art-world-in-lockdown> (referring e.g. to 'Artist Support Pledge' a webpage on which 'artists are invited to put works up for sale for no more than £200 on Instagram').

customs authorities, are generally not considered censorship, unless affecting arts disproportionately. States clearly have the right to protect their own interests through the regulation of broadcasting media and the audiovisual industry, as well as subject theatre plays and film production to ratings and other types of classification. Such regulation however should not be excessive, neither imposing cumbersome requirements to creators. A parallel could be drawn here with media freedom. Druzin and Li for instance, while discussing media regulation in China, refer to Chinese 'self-censorship' strategies to induce 'voluntary self-control'.[37] This is achieved by enacting extremely vague laws, blurring the boundaries of permissible speech and instilling the fear that (web users) are being watched.[38] As a result, a large percentage of the population believes that censorship is legitimate.[39] Vague laws on the authority of the judiciary (and 'contempt of court' laws) may be equally problematic. The reason is that they give the authorities discretion to grant the plaintiffs 'interlocutory [i.e. temporary] injunctions', which can also be tantamount to self-censorship, including in matters of serious public concern.[40]

In respect of public spectacles, this type of regulation is officially exercised by classification committees mandated to regulate freedom of information, the media and the arts. These bodies (or usually, boards) may grant exhibition and screening visas as well as control the content of audiovisual imports, and are typically mandated to control the information and entertainment available. Their decisions, largely aiming at protecting childhood and public morals, are frequently subject to judicial review, and usually scrutinized by relevant human rights bodies – as will be discussed below. In other cases, however, where audiovisual content is tightly regulated, these boards are extremely powerful and even publications are subject to prior authorization. Remedies in these cases may typically be unavailable, and even so, decisions are only seldom challenged effectively before administrative courts. This includes also countries with a powerful media scene. In India, for instance, the decisions of the Central Board of Film Certification are not amenable to review because of 'the high cost of litigation, delays, and the low success rate of applicants'.[41] Today, this has started to change and a number of Bollywood film-makers

37 Brian Druzin and Jessica Li, 'Censorship's Fragile Grip on the Internet: Can Online Speech Be Controlled?' (2016) 49 *Cornell International Law Journal* 369, 374.

38 ibid 375ff, 389.

39 ibid 392.

40 *Observer and Guardian supra* note 14, Judge Morenilla partly dissenting para 9. Also *Sunday Times v UK* (no 1) App no 6538/74, 26 April 1979.

41 See e.g. Arpan Banerjee, 'Political Censorship and Indian Cinematographic Laws: A Functionalist Liberal Analysis' (2010) 2 *Drexel Law Review* 561.

have been successfully appealing before the appellate body of the board (Film Certification Appellate Tribunal [FCAT]), as well as administrative courts.[42]

3.1.1.2 The Hate Speech Exception

Hate speech is a legitimate restriction to free speech, including by prior restraints under the conditions set by human rights law. Art speech is no different to this. At the international level, hate speech standards are defined not only in the ICCPR, but also in the International Convention on the Elimination of All Forms of Racial Discrimination (ICERD). Article 20 of the ICCPR, in particular, provides for restrictive grounds, prohibiting 'propaganda of war' and obliging States to impose laws banning 'any advocacy of national, racial or religious hatred that constitutes incitement to discrimination, hostility or violence'. The suggestion was in fact to include even more extensive propositions to ban hatred, but 'fears were expressed that such advocacy might lead to abuse and have a detrimental effect on freedom of speech'.[43] A similar – and equally heated – provision that compels States to legislate on the matter of hate speech exists also in article 4(a) of the ICERD that prohibits 'all dissemination of ideas based on racial superiority or hatred', as well as any 'incitement to racial discrimination' and 'all acts of violence or incitement to such acts' – and in fact compels States to legislate in order to declare punishable by law all dissemination of ideas based on racial superiority or hatred. Both provisions therefore (article 4 of the ICERD and 20 of the ICCPR) are applicable and indeed the exact relationship between them has been the subject of extensive discussions both at UN level and beyond.[44]

An additional attempt to clarify the term was undertaken in a series of workshops, expert seminars and meetings organized at the initiative of the Office of the High Commissioner for Human Rights (OHCHR), with the

[42] See e.g. *Phantom Films Pvt. Ltd. And Anr vs The Central Board Of Certification*, 13 June 2016 (regarding the movie *Udta Punjab*, classified 'Unrestricted Public Exhibition' following a decision by the Bombay High Court, which had originally granted a screening visa by the Indian Censor Board subject to eighty-nine cuts).

[43] Bossuyt *supra* note 17 at 404–05.

[44] E.g. OHCHR Expert meeting on the 'Links between Articles 19 and 20 of the ICCPR: Freedom of Expression and Advocacy of Religious Hatred that Constitutes Incitement to Discrimination, Hostility or Violence'. On international law standards in relation to the Danish cartoons, see analytically, Lorenz Langer, *Religious Offence and Human Rights: The Implications of Defamation of Religions* (Cambridge University Press 2012) 91–142, and Chapter 7 of this book.

participation of a number of NGOs.[45] In one such meeting, organized in 2009 at the initiative of the major freedom of expression NGO, ARTICLE 19, the Camden Principles on Freedom of Expression were adopted. Among other things, these principles clarify that the terms 'hatred' and 'hostility' refer to 'intense and irrational emotions of opprobrium, enmity and detestation towards the target group'.[46] Likewise, at the same meeting it was suggested that 'the term "advocacy" is to be understood as requiring an intention to promote hatred publicly…', and that 'incitement' refers to statements which create an imminent risk of discrimination, hostility or violence'.[47] This said, in its General Comment no 35, issued in 2013, the UN Committee on the Elimination of Racial Discrimination (CERD) notes that the 'lack of explicit reference [to the term hate speech in the ICERD] has not impeded the Committee from identifying and naming hate speech phenomena and exploring the relationship between speech practices and the standards of the Convention'.[48] In the same comment, the CERD also suggests various definitions, for instance, that 'incitement characteristically seeks to influence others to engage in certain forms of conduct, including the commission of crime, through advocacy or threats', taking into account also 'the intention of the speaker, and the imminent risk or likelihood' as well as other elements.[49]

While the ICERD remains one of the most widely ratified conventions, not all States have embraced hate speech standards. State representatives insisted on the reference to the Universal Declaration within the text of the ICERD – as a safeguard that the hate speech provision applies with 'due regard to the principles embodied in the Universal Declaration of Human Rights'. Even in that version of the text, various States placed declarations and reservations – to

45 In particular, the OHCHR 'Rabat Plan of Action' on the prohibition of advocacy of national, racial or religious hatred that constitutes incitement to discrimination, hostility or violence, conclusions and recommendations emanating from the four regional expert workshops organized by OHCHR and adopted by experts in Rabat, Morocco (2012).

46 ARTICLE 19 *The Camden Principles supra* note 28, section 1 (i–iv).

47 ibid. cf UN Human Rights Council, 'Joint Report of the Special Rapporteur on Freedom of Religion or Belief, Asma Jahangir, and the Special Rapporteur on Contemporary Forms of racism, Racial Discrimination, Xenophobia and Related Intolerance, Doudou Diène', A/HRC/2/3, 20 September 2006, para 47.

48 CERD, 'General Comment no 35, Combating Racist Hate Speech', 26 September 2013, CERD/C/GC/35, para 5.

49 ibid paras 15–16. See on this comment, Tarlach McGonagle, 'General Recommendation No. 35 on Combating Racist Hate Speech' in David Keane and Annapurna Waughray (eds), *Fifty Years of the International Convention on the Elimination of All Forms of Racial Discrimination: A Living Instrument* (Manchester University Press 2017).

date nineteen as regards article 4 of the ICERD (and seventeen in respect of article 20 of the ICCPR).[50] These declarations and reservations do not only emanate from States that typically refuse to accept any obligations whatsoever (such as the United States),[51] but also from States that refuse to lower their freedom of expression standards (Finland); those that consider that the limitation of speech for reasons of 'public order' are adequate (Australia and the United Kingdom); or simply that additional anti-discrimination legislation is not necessary (France).

After 9/11 several States started imposing prior restraints and blanket limitations on media and the arts through emergency counter-terrorism legislation. Restrictions to artistic freedom on these grounds, particularly cartoons, have been highly debated. By way of example, in *Leroy*, the ECtHR found that the seizure of a small cartoon mocking 9/11 (and published in a weekly newspaper in the Basque country only two days after the attacks) accompanied by a caption paraphrasing Nike's advertising slogan: '*We have all dreamt of it … Hamas did it*', was not a breach of freedom of expression standards under the ECHR.[52] The French authorities condemned the journal with a fine of 1500 euros each for having committed the offence of 'justification of terrorism' (*apologie du terrorisme*), criminalized under the French Law of the Press of 1881.[53] Unlike domestic courts, however, which had considered the cartoon a threat to France's national security because of its support for terrorism,[54] the Court attempted to assess whether a fair balance had been observed between freedom of expression and *public order*, as well as 'the legitimate right of a democratic society to protect itself against the actions of terrorist organizations'.[55] The Court did reiterate, as

[50] See UN treaty collection, 'Declarations and Reservations to the ICCPR' at <https://treaties.un.org/> (ICERD).

[51] This reservation states that the United States 'does not accept any obligation under [the ICERD], in particular under articles 4 and 7' and declares that 'article 20 does not authorize or require legislation or other action by the United States that would restrict the right of free speech and association'.

[52] ECtHR, *Leroy v France* App no 36109/03, Merits and Just Satisfaction, 2 October 2008 [in French].

[53] Article 24, paragraph 6 of the Act of 29 July 1881.

[54] *Leroy supra* note 52, paras 11–18 (the illustrator being an accomplice to *apologie du terrorisme*).

[55] ibid at para 36. The Court does not maintain the government's argument (at 24) that this form of expression negates the values of the convention under article 17, neither that it constitutes incitement to hatred or Islamophobia (at para 27).

always, the importance of satire, observing that the 'inherent language of cartoons is a form of artistic expression ... by definition provocative'.[56] It nonetheless focused on the wording of the caption, which in the view of the Court indicated that the applicant expressed his moral solidarity with the perpetrators of the 9/11 attacks, therefore 'judging favourably the violence against millions of civilians'.[57] More recently the ECtHR has called for better scrutiny in examining 'incitement to terror or extremism'. For example, in *Alekhina*, concerning the Russian punk group Pussy Riot and their song 'Punk Prayer: Virgin Mary, Drive Putin Away',[58] condemned under Russian laws inter alia on incitement to terror, the Court defined incitement to violence strictly:

> advocat[ing] recourse to violent actions or bloody revenge, justif[ying] the commission of terrorist offences in pursuit of their supporter's goals or [as susceptible of being] interpreted as likely to encourage violence by expressing deep-seated and irrational hatred towards identified persons.[59]

This is an interesting criterion that could be useful in distinguishing between hateful speech and 'incitement to terror', especially online. The latter, in fact, may justify fairly easily prior restraints, especially since terrorist organizations such as Al-Qaeda, ISIS and Al Shabab have started using social media for propaganda and recruitment.[60] Within the European Union, suspicion of terrorist offences, including incitement to terrorism may amount to prosecution and criminal liability, not only in respect of individuals but also platforms and media providers through 'notice and take-down' measures.[61] This has also been increasingly the practice of US-based platforms and intermediate service providers – despite the fact that the latter benefit from quasi-absolute immunity from

[56] ibid at para 39 (author's translation). On this, see Dirk Voorhoof, 'European Court of Human Rights: Where Is the "Chilling Effect"?' (Council of Europe, 2008) <www.coe.int/t/dghl/standardsetting/media/ConfAntiTerrorism/ECHR_en.pdf>.

[57] ibid at para 43 (author's translation).

[58] *Alekhina and Others* App no 38004/12, 11 September 2018, para 11 (lyrics included). See also Chapter 7 of this book.

[59] ibid at para 260.

[60] Indicatively, Alberto Fernandez (ed), *Here to Stay and Growing: Combating ISIS Propaganda Networks* (Brookings Papers 2015) 6ff on ISIS propaganda, and films and series produced by the ISIS Channel, *Al-Hayat* Media Center (HC). See also Section 3.2.3 of this chapter (on private actors).

[61] See in particular, Regulation (EU) 2021/784 of the European Parliament and of the Council of 29 April 2021 on addressing the dissemination of terrorist content online; EU Directive 2017/541 of the European Parliament and of the Council of 15 March 2017 on combating terrorism.

prosecution and limited liability for information posted on their platforms.[62] There are also interesting linkages with the domain of art trade and media regulation, especially since illicit art trafficking has become an important source of income for some terrorist organizations. By way of example, Facebook closed a number of accounts when ISIS started offering its artwork plunder from Syria and Iraq online.[63]

3.1.1.3 Negationism, Revisionism and Holocaust Denial

In 2002, the exhibition *Mirroring Evil: Nazi Imagery/Recent Art* was hosted at the Jewish Museum of New York. The exhibition displayed works of thirteen artists, some of them Jewish, and exhibited among other works, Alain Séchas' *Enfants Gâtés* (Spoiled kids), which consisted of an installation of sculptures (representing Hitler-like kittens holding swastikas).[64] This exhibition attracted substantial controversy and protests by Holocaust survivors, demanding its closure on the ground of offence to sensibilities. Is there an obligation under international law, however, to oblige States to close down such events (or criminalize their organizers) in order to make sure that sensibilities are respected?

The topic is a much contested one. Domestic laws clearly provide a variety of answers.[65] International law seems to be facing inherent limitations. Virtually all human rights bodies are concerned about the rise of anti-Jewish and anti-Muslim stereotypes in many parts of Europe,[66] as well as the rise in religious intolerance, especially against migrant communities.[67] This naturally entails lowering the standard of protection of free speech in favour of

62 Indicatively, *Fields v Twitter Inc.* 200 F. Supp. 3d. 964, 967–68 (N.D. Cal. 2016) on platforms immunities from prosecution). See on this, Land *supra* note 18 at 444–45; also Caitlin McKeown, 'Facebook, Defamation, and Terrorism: Who Is Responsible for Dangerous Posts on Social Media' (2017) 26 *Tulane Journal of International and Comparative Law* 163, 167ff.

63 Annellies Pawels, 'ISIS and Illicit Trafficking in Cultural Property: Funding Terrorism through Art' (2016) 11 *Freedom from Fear* 66, <www.un-ilibrary.org/content/journals/25190709/2016/11/7>; see also, generally, Peter Campbell, 'The Illicit Antiquities Trade as a Transnational Criminal Network: Characterizing and Anticipating Trafficking of Cultural Heritage' (2013) 20 *International Journal of Cultural Property* 113. Also Chapter 7 of this book (on ISIS iconoclasm).

64 <https://thejewishmuseum.org/exhibitions/mirroring-evil-nazi-imagery-recent-art>.

65 cf Israeli's Supreme Court 549/75 *Noah Films c. Censorship Council* PD 30 (1) 757 (on prohibitions of the Israeli Orchestra to play Wagner), discussed in Raphael Cohen-Almagor, *The Scope of Tolerance* (Routledge 2006) 85ff, and also Chapter 6 of this book.

66 E.g. UN Human Rights Committee, 'Concluding Observations on the Sixth Periodic Report of Hungary', 9 May 2018 CCPR/C/HUN/CO/5, para 17; 'Concluding Observations on the Seventh Periodic Report of the Russian Federation', 28 April 2015, CCPR/C/RUS/CO/7.

67 UN Human Rights Council, A/HRC/23/34, *supra* note 34 at para 28.

sensibilities, religious or other. At the same time, many European states, such as France, Belgium, Switzerland and Austria have enacted legislation on Holocaust denial and the denial (or distortion) of crimes against humanity (the so-called 'opinion-crimes' or 'memory-crimes').

The fact that cases are dealt with on a case-by-case basis however makes the distinction between hate speech and religious intolerance even more challenging. In a case that had arrived before the committee over twenty years ago, regarding opinions expressed by the French academic Professor Faurisson by which he denied the existence of gas chambers, the committee found that such statements are negationist and amount to hate speech (implicitly upholding the legality of the French Gayssot Act under which Faurisson was prosecuted).[68] At the same time, however, and while expression of negationist views is evidence of hate speech (rather than an offence to religious faith) in its General Comment no 34 on freedom of speech, the committee referred to *Faurisson* to make the point that the rights of individual members of a community defined by its *religious* faith may justify restrictions to free speech.[69] In the same comment further the committee notes that memory laws are incompatible with the obligations stemming from the covenant referring again to *Faurisson* (although in that particular case the memory laws in question had been found to be compatible with State obligations), while the statement on the alleged incompatibility is quickly qualified by noting that restrictions should never go beyond the standards set by article 19, paragraph 2, and the standards set by article 20 (on the prohibition of hate speech).[70]

Subsequently, censoring an exhibition such as *Mirroring Evil* is arguably not incompatible with these obligations. In contrast, a (fictitious) cartoon or installation that would involve, for example, gas chambers with a caption 'never happened' would clearly not be sanctioned by human rights law – in the same way that negating the Holocaust falls altogether outside the protective scope of freedom of speech. In the European context in particular, anti-Jewish sentiment in the context of negationism is considered a valid restriction

68 *Faurisson v France*, Communication no 550/1993, 8 November 1996 (referring to Law no 90-615, 13 July 1990 (Gayssot Act)); see generally, Institut suisse de droit comparé (ISDC) *Étude comparative sur la négation des génocides et des crimes contre l'humanité*, avis 06-184 (Lausanne, 19 December 2006) [in French] (providing an overview of practice in twelve European jurisdictions, United States and Canada). See analytically, David Keane, 'Attacking Hate Speech under Article 17 of the European Convention on Human Rights' (2007) 25(4) *Netherlands Quarterly of Human Rights* 641–63 (on anti-Semitic speech constituting 'abuse of rights' under article 17 of the ECHR, therefore excluding it from the protective scope of the ECHR).

69 UN Human Rights Committee *supra* note 19, para 49.

70 ibid at para 49.

to freedom of expression and of the press, and may justify prior restraints as the Council of Europe's Venice Commission has intimated.[71] This has been also the view of the European Court on the matter. In *Garaudy*, for example, the Court found inadmissible the author's freedom of speech claim regarding his book *The Founding Myths of Modern Israel* on the grounds of article 17 of the ECHR (i.e. the 'abuse of rights' clause).[72] At the same time, the ECtHR has clarified that the legitimacy of the 'exception' of negationism does not apply equally to all cases of denial of historical facts, and controversially held in *Perinçek* that the Armenian genocide can be legitimately debated, given that it could still be historically debated (as opposed to 'clearly established').[73] There is nothing that precludes the applicability of such laws in creative expressions, to the extent that artistic freedom defences are not recognized and artworks' symbolism is taken 'at the letter' (and therefore considered to be expressing an opinion). Similar extensive restrictions also apply to incitement to religious hatred. For example, the Court found inadmissible the freedom of expression claim of an openly anti-Semitic French comedian (Dieudonné) who had been prosecuted in France for 'deliberately offend[ing] the memory of a community'.[74]

3.1.2 *Challenging Prior Restraints before Human Rights Bodies*

Regional human rights bodies, as well as the UN Human Rights Committee, have dealt with a handful of artistic expression cases related to prior restraints, including seizure or destruction of paintings and sculptures and classification decisions of audiovisual material. There have been no judicial precedents of censorship in respect of comics, or music at the international level.

71 European Commission for Democracy Through Law (Venice Commission), 'On the relationship between freedom of expression and freedom of religion: the issue of regulation and prosecution of blasphemy, religious insult and incitement to religious hatred', 23 October 2008, CDL-AD(2008)026, at 20.

72 *Garaudy v France* App no 65831/01(inadmissible). cf also *Lehideux et Isorni v France* App no 24662/94, 23 September 1998 (the Court found a violation because the facts that were denied 'did not belong to category of clearly established historical facts'); Keane *supra* note 68 at 648–50.

73 *Perinçek v Switzerland* [GC] no 27510/08, 15 October 2015, paras 30–38, and 240 and 241 (especially since the statements could not be regarded as justifying 'any other crimes against humanity'). See *Lehideux et Isorni supra* note 72; Keane *supra* note 68.

74 *M'Bala M'Bala v France* App no 25239/13, 20 October 2015, paras 18 and 26 (inadmissible under article 17) (interestingly, at the end of the impugned show, Dieudonné invited Mr Faurisson on stage).

3.1.2.1 An Obligation of Most Careful Scrutiny

The European Convention does not mention censorship, nor does it prohibit prior restraints per se. On the contrary, article 10, paragraph 1 of the convention provides that 'States are not prevented from imposing restrictions on licensing upon 'broadcasting, television or cinema enterprises'. In addition, paragraph 2 of article 10 stipulates that 'the exercise of these freedoms [i.e. freedom of thought, opinion and expression] may be subject to such formalities, conditions, restrictions or penalties, as are prescribed by law and are necessary in a democratic society [...]'.

In interpreting article 10, however, the Court highlights the strict standards of scrutiny that national courts are bound to apply. Censorship is subject to the usual tests expounded by the ECtHR in article 10 cases, particularly necessity (in a democratic society) and proportionality. The ECtHR has, in fact, been consistently highlighting the importance of freedom of expression in democratic societies, the role of the press as a 'watchdog'[75] and the right of the public to be informed, highlighting that 'prior restraints on the activities of journalists call for the most careful scrutiny on its part and are justified only in exceptional circumstances'.[76] In artistic freedom cases, however, at least until 2010, similar findings have been scarce, with the difference between prior restraints and common restrictions against free expression being seldom highlighted. For instance, in *Alınak* the Court found that the 'most careful scrutiny' standard should be applied because of 'the dangers inherent in prior restraint' and further, that, although this applies primarily to the press and the news, 'this danger extends to the censorship of publications other than periodicals that deal with a topical issue', and that it applies therefore also 'to the publication of books in general or other written texts'.[77] In its more recent case

75 *Sunday Times v the United Kingdom* (no 2) no 13166/87, 24 October 1991, para 50; *Alinak v Turkey* no 40287/98, 29 March 2005, para 67; also *Karademirci and Others v Turkey*, nos. 37096/97 and 37101/97, ECHR 2005, para 40; *Unifaun theatre productions Ltd and Others v Malta*, 37326/13, Judgment (Merits and Just Satisfaction), 15 August 2018, para 80: 'Article 10 of the Convention does not in terms prohibit the imposition of prior restraints on a particular form of communication'.

76 Indicatively only, see *Sunday Times (No. 2) supra* note 75 at para 50; *Observer and Guardian supra* note 15 at para 60. Also, indicatively, *Cumpănă and Mazăre v Romania* no 33348/96, 10 June 2003 (2004), para 118; *Stoll v Switzerland* App no 69698/01, 25 April 2006 at para 153; *Castells v Spain, 23 April* 1992, Series A no 236, para 48. Also *Ahmet Yıldırım v Turkey* App no 3111/10, ECHR 2012, para 57 (blocking of the applicant's website).

77 *Alinak supra* note 75 at paras 37–38 (regarding censorship of a pro-Kurdish theatre play and referring to *Association Ekin v France* no 39288/98, § 57, ECHR 2001-VIII); cf also *Otto-Preminger-Institut v Austria*, 20 September 1994, Series A no 295-A, Joint Dissenting Opinion of Judges Palm, Pekkanen and Makarczyk at para 4 (noting that 'there is a danger that if applied to

law, the Court appears to be more consistent in finding that 'a legal framework is required, ensuring both tight control over the scope of bans and effective judicial review to prevent any abuse of power'.[78] Broad justifications in restricting artworks, plays, films, etc., especially when showing evidence of artistic value, cannot justify restrictions solely because the views advanced are labelled 'offensive' or 'progressive'. On the contrary, the more the evidence of artistic value, the less interference should take place, even in taboo issues – or else, Bollywood movies such as *Udta Punjab*, one of the first films on caste discrimination (although such movies and artworks are increasingly made available),[79] would have been legitimately censored. The meaning of censorship as 'exceptional', therefore, requires from the State to establish exactly how these types of creative expressions affect States' vital interests, and this with sufficient *clarity*.[80] The ECtHR could arguably benefit from the powerful statements of the US Supreme Court on prior restraints, primarily as expounded in *Near v Minnessota* (1931),[81] *Bentham Books* (1963)[82] and arguably also *Pentagon Papers* (1971).[83] The Supreme Court has been much more dynamic in declaring that more prior restraints should be applied only exceptionally, and the government should have the burden of proving why they are necessary, with a heavy presumption playing against constitutional validity.[84] Content regulation, in particular, under the American pro-liberty view should never be a justification for removal or seizure of works, even when these are contrary to national secrets or other necessities related to public order.[85]

protect the perceived interests of a powerful group in society, such prior restraint could be detrimental to that tolerance on which pluralist democracy depends'). cf also dissenting opinion of Judge Lohmus in *Wingrove v UK* App no 17419/90, Merits and Just Satisfaction, 25 November 1996, at 5 and 61, para 1.

78 *Unifaun theatre supra* note 75 at para 80; *Ahmet Yıldırım supra* note 76 at para 64; *Alekhina supra* note 58 at para 260.

79 Arti Singh and Abdul Azeez, 'Caste in Contemporary Bollywood Movies: An Analysis of the Portrayal of Characters' (2021) 49 *Asian Journal of Social Science* 93–100.

80 cf *Ulusoy and Others v Turkey* App no 34797/03, Merits and Just Satisfaction, 3 May 2007, para 53.

81 *Near v Minnesota* 283 US 697 (1931) (US). The Supreme Court first reiterated Justice Holmes' classic view in *Shenck v US* 1919 ('The most stringent protection of free speech would not protect a man in falsely shouting fire in a theatre and causing a panic').

82 *Bantam Books, Inc. v Sullivan* 372 US 58 (1963) (holding that 'any system of prior restraint holds a heavy presumption against its constitutional validity').

83 *New York Times Co. v United States* 403 US 713 (1971) per curiam (US courts in New York had ordered temporary restraint of the *New York Times* that included publication of – vulgarized – versions of classified material on the War in Vietnam on the grounds of national security).

84 ibid at 723 (referring to *Organization for a Better Austin v Keefe*, 402 US 415, 402 US 419).

85 *Board of Education, Island Trees Union Free School District No 26 v Pico* 1983 (regarding the removal of books from school library shelves); see also Chapter 6 of this book (on public art).

3.1.2.2 Challenging Classification for Theatre, Video Art and Cinematography

It may be the case, however, that domestic courts are unwilling or unable to effectively challenge censorship boards' decisions. The role of human rights bodies in those cases is crucial: the ECtHR, for instance, may determine not only whether domestic laws are compatible with the convention, but further, whether these laws include the possibility of judicial review – and whether the associated rights are adequately protected. In the past this was not evident, as the ECtHR would only too often recur to its margin of appreciation doctrine. In *Wingrove*,[86] a widely discussed case from the late 1990s, the British Board of Film Classification (created by the British Cinematography Act in 1909) refused to grant a cinematographic visa to a short (18-minute) video titled *Visions of Ecstasy* because it 'portray[ed] inter alia, a female character [alluding to Santa Theresa] astride the recumbent body of the crucified Christ engaged in an act of an overtly sexual nature',[87] and was therefore considered blasphemous.[88] The author of the video unsuccessfully appealed against the decision to the respective Video Appeals Committee,[89] yet was unable to request judicial review in the United Kingdom because, at the time of the appeal, the British procedural laws did now allow courts to 'look at the merits of any decision made by such a body'.[90] The Court, instead of scrutinizing the legitimacy of the particular restriction ad hoc and in light of the convention, allowed the British authorities substantial discretion.[91]

86 See indicatively, Eleni Polymenopoulou, 'Does One Swallow Make a Spring? Artistic Freedom at the European Court of Human Rights' (2016) 16 *Human Rights Law Review* 511, 523–24; Ilias Trispiotis, 'The Duty to Respect Religious Feelings: Insights from European Human Rights Law' (2013) 19 *Columbia Journal of European Law* 499 at 551; George Letsas, 'Is There a Right Not to Be Offended in One's Religious Beliefs?' in Lorenzo Zucca and Camil Ungureanu (eds), *Law, State and Religion in the New Europe: Debates and Dilemmas* (Cambridge University Press 2012) 239, 239 (advancing 'an understanding of democracy and liberal equality that shows why there is no right to be insulted in one's religious beliefs in public space').

87 *Wingrove supra* note 77 at 5 and 61, para 13 (reiterating the decision of the board). cf *Otto-Preminger-Institute v Austria* App no 13470/87, Judgment, 20 September 1994, para 49 discussed in Chapter 7 of this book.

88 ibid para 13.

89 ibid para 21. The Appeals Committee agreed that 'the formulation of the law of blasphemy, as accepted by the Panel, was an "accurate statement of the present law'.

90 ibid paras 30–31.

91 ibid para 58: 'a wider margin of appreciation is generally available to the Contracting States when regulating freedom of expression'.

Recent practice suggests that the ECtHR is becoming more assertive, at least in artistic freedom cases. In a recent case regarding theatre play classification, the Board of the Maltese Film and Stage Censors classified a theatre play as 'totally banned' in accordance with the Maltese Cinema and Stage Regulations.[92] The applicants complained as the board did not give them a chance to be heard, 'nor were any reasons for the decision ever communicated to them',[93] while the Maltese first instance courts had made substantial remarks with respect to the script.[94] In the particular case, the Maltese Constitutional Court was unable to exercise substantial control, reiterating the judgment of the first instance courts and agreeing that their script contained 'disparaging and insolent remarks towards more than one belief, towards women and towards the suffering of the Jews in the Second World War'.[95] The court specified what effective judicial review means, in that it requires also a 'framework establishing precise and specific rules regarding the application of preventive restrictions on freedom of expression',[96] and that it should be based 'on a weighing-up of the competing interests at stake and designed to strike a balance between them'.[97] It further found a violation of the convention – not because of the classification procedure per se, but because the board classified stage productions on the basis of regulations and guidelines that were not accessible to the public,[98] and on the basis of criteria that 'left room for an unfettered power since the law did not indicate with sufficient clarity the scope of any discretion conferred on the authority and the manner of its exercise'.[99]

In a unique case of censorship, the inverse happened: a classification board gave permission, and subsequently, the domestic courts reversed its decision. The case arose before the Cinematographic Classification Council of Chile during the Pinochet dictatorial regime. It originated in a request to ban Scorsese's film *The Last Temptation of Christ* (based on Kazantzakis's novel).[100]

[92] *Unifaun supra* note 75 at para 57. These regulations provided inter alia rules on 'good behavior in public'.
[93] ibid para 9.
[94] ibid paras 19–37 (this court agreed with the board concluding that 'the play in its entirety was offensive to Maltese society' rejecting the defendants' request to at least perform the play, following testimonies of expert witnesses who had either read the script or watched a rehearsal).
[95] ibid para 47.
[96] ibid para 80; *Ahmet Yıldırım supra* note 76 at paras 64–65; Alekhina *supra* note 58 at para 260.
[97] ibid.
[98] ibid para 84.
[99] ibid.
[100] *Olmedo Bustos et al. v Chile*, OC-73/ 2001, IACtHR Series C 73, 5 February 2001 (*Last Temptation of Christ*).

The board originally refused, yet later granted a visa.[101] This decision however was followed by a motion by seven State attorneys (acting on their own behalf, and also, interestingly 'on behalf of the person of Christ and the Catholic Church'). Shortly after the Supreme Court of Chile sided with the attorneys and found that censorship was justified – with reference to the Chilean Constitution that permitted the banning of movies to protect the Catholic Church.[102] The case was brought before Inter-American Commission by an NGO that represented a number of activists and members of civil society, requesting authorization of the film's cinematographic exhibition – and amendments in the local legislation.[103] Eventually, the case was referred to the IACtHR (as in the meantime Chile ratified the American Convention on Human Rights (1969), which prohibits censorship *stricto sensu*, with the exception of protection of childhood and in the case of public entertainments).[104] The Inter-American Court ultimately found Chile to be in breach of the American Convention and obliged it to change its constitution.[105]

3.1.2.3 Challenging Censorship in Painting and the Visual Arts

The first case that came to the attention of the UN Human Rights Committee in 2004 (over thirty years after the covenant's entry into force) was also a case of seizure, at the request of the Korean *minjung* painter ('people's artist') Shin Hak-Chul, whose work had been consistently censored.[106] The case at hand concerned a large painting on canvas titled *The History of Modern Korea-Rice Planting*, depicting typical rice plantations in a rural setting (inspired in fact by

[101] ibid annex 1 (because of 'new historical, cultural, and social factors of sufficient merit').

[102] Inter-American Commission, Report N° 31/98, Petition no 11.803, received on 3 September 1997, paras 9–13 (referring to Court of Appeal of Santiago, Chile, of 20 January 1997 and Supreme Court of Chile 17 June 1997). The claimants argued that their 'right to honor established in Article 19.4 of the Constitution for the person of Christ, living Christians, the Catholic Church, the appellants themselves, and the right to freedom of conscience [. . .]'.

[103] ibid 8–10, para 45. E.g. the first alleged victim, a human rights lawyer, complained 'because he was prevented from having access to an artistic film with an apparently religious content' and the second, a law student, added also that 'his freedom of conscience was affected by the impossibility of having access to information'.

[104] ACHR, art 13, para 4: 'Notwithstanding the provisions of paragraph 2 above, public entertainments may be subject by law to prior censorship for the sole purpose of regulating access to them for the moral protection of childhood and adolescence'.

[105] ibid para 71.

[106] *Hak-Chul Shin v Republic of Korea* (926/2000), Views, CPR/C/80/D/926/2000 (2004).

the painter's village), with the addition of symbolic objects and persons (such Coca-Cola, Ronald Reagan and ET, the extra-terrestrial character).[107] The painting remained unnoticed by the authorities for two years, until it was distributed and widely publicized as part of a student project.[108] This, however, led to Hak-Chul's arrest and subsequent indictment for breach of Korean national security law.[109] Despite the author's assertion that the painting represented the 'peaceful unification and democratization of his country based on his experience of rural life during childhood',[110] it was ultimately perceived as communist propaganda by the Constitutional Court of Korea, as well as 'class struggle, led by farmers seeking to overthrow the Republic of Korea due to its relationship with the United States and Japan'.[111] The Committee emphasized that the imposed restrictions constituted a breach of the right to freedom of expression under the covenant and most vividly also pointed that the State party must demonstrate in specific fashion the precise nature of the threat to its public interest, and thoroughly justify why seizure of the painting and the author's conviction were necessary.[112] This follows the general stance of the Committee, according to which prior restraints should also be subject to its scrutiny[113] – namely, with reference to the legality, necessity and proportionality test.

[107] Anon, 'Controversial Painting "Rice Planting" Unveiled to Public for First Time since 1989' (Hankyoreh, Korean News, 30 January 2018) <https://english.hani.co.kr/arti/english_edition/e_national/830066.html>; Hyung-Jun Hwang, 'Controversy over Anti-state Propaganda Painting' (Dong-a-Ilbo, 30 December 2017) <www.donga.com/en/article/all/20171230/1175265/1>.

[108] Binna Choi and Seewon Hyun, 'Language of Criticism: What Is an Artist? What Is a Practice? (Interview with Shin Hakchul)' in Sohyon An et al (eds), *Access to Contemporary Korean Art 1980–2010* (Forum 2018).

[109] ibid at 2.4ff (referring to domestic proceedings: Seoul Criminal District Court, 12 November 1992; Seoul District Criminal Court, 16 November 1994 and Supreme Court of Seoul, 13 March 1998). Interestingly, Chul was acquitted at first instance, and the Appeal court also dismissed the prosecutor's appeal against acquittal, yet the Seoul Supreme Court on cassation decided that the author should be retried because 'the expression in question [was] actively and aggressively threatening the security and country or the free and democratic order'. The Supreme Court found a breach of article 7 of the National Security Law, in that the picture constituted an 'enemy-benefiting expression' contrary to article 7 of the National Security Law. See also Karl Schoenberger, 'Artistic Expression Facing a Crackdown' (*LA Times*, 11 October 1989) <www.latimes.com/archives/la-xpm-1989-10-11-mn-204-story.html>.

[110] ibid at 2.2 and 3.1.

[111] ibid at 3.3 (based on an opinion by an expert witness).

[112] ibid at 7.

[113] UN Human Rights Committee, 'General Comment no 34' *supra* note 20 at para 22.

3.2 MINIMAL RESTRICTIONS IN THE EXERCISE OF ARTISTIC FREEDOM

3.2.1 *Subsequent Imposition of Liability*

Contrary to the imposition of prior restraints, common restrictions to artistic freedom refer to the imposition of liability *after* diffusion or publication. Article 19, paragraph 3 ICCPR sets out a number of grounds as acceptable limitations, such as: (a) respect for the rights or reputations of others; (b) protection of national security or of public order (*ordre public*), or of 'public health or morals'. The discussions during the *travaux* also reveal that 'the basic purpose of this article was to protect the individual and this is therefore why it should contain as few restrictions as possible'.[114] At the same time, access to arts, or *freedom of the arts* as a cultural right is subject to no limitations whatsoever – this also stands true for all rights guaranteed under the ICESCR.[115] This means that the rule is freedom, and limitations are only exceptional for both common restrictions to speech *and* prior restraints.[116] In addition, human rights treaty bodies have established detailed tests regarding the values that should be commensurate when restricting freedom of speech. The jurisprudence of all human rights treaty bodies reveals that restrictions to freedom of expression should be construed *narrowly* and in line with the necessity and proportionality tests. The UN Human Rights Committee, for example, highlights in its jurisprudence that 'any restriction on freedom of expression must not be overly broad in nature, that is, it must be the least intrusive among the measures that might achieve the relevant protective function and proportionate to the interest whose protection is sought'.[117]

[114] Bossuyt *supra* note 17 at 398 and A/5000.

[115] Christian Tomuschat, 'Human Rights: Tensions between Negative and Positive Duties of States' (2009) 14 *Austrian Review of International and European Law* 19, 23 ('In the [CESCR Comments] one does not even find a hint that these rights have certain limits drawn by the rights of others or the availability of the goods or services in issue'); and generally, Christian Tomuschat, 'Civil and Political Rights – Economic, Social and Cultural Rights. Complementarity and Opposition' (2007) 35 *Thesaurus Acroasium* 3–48.

[116] This is also read in the text of the article, which provides that '[the right to freedom of expression] may [. . .] be subject to certain restrictions, but these shall *only be such* as are provided by law and are *necessary* [. . .]' (emphasis added).

[117] By way of illustration, see UN Human Rights Committee, *Belyazeka v Belarus* no 1772/2008, 6 June 2012, CCPR/C/104/D/1772/2008; *Laptsevich v Belarus* no 780/1997, 20 March 2000, para 8.1.

3.2.2 *Balancing Conflicting Interests at the ECtHR*

3.2.2.1 Effectively Protecting the Arts

The European Court of Human Rights in numerous judgments flags that 'freedom of expression … is subject to a number of exceptions which, however, must be narrowly interpreted and the necessity for any restrictions must be convincingly established'.[118] In performing its role to interpret and apply the European Convention, the ECtHR has established various guidelines, parameters and tests while increasingly also taking into account the particular context of the infringement. As the Court often says, it 'is intended to guarantee not rights that are theoretical or illusory but rights that are practical and effective'.[119]

The assessment of free speech infringements therefore starts with the so-called three-part test of the Court, which focusses on the necessity and proportionality criteria.[120] An assessment of the infringement at stake follows by determining whether the reasons advanced by the authorities are necessary – or in other words 'relevant and sufficient'[121] and whether the reaction of the authorities (which could range from a small fine or penalty, to severe penalties, seizure of artwork, website removals or even arrest and imprisonment) is proportionate.[122] The same methodology is followed by the UN Human Rights Committee in dealing with violations of the covenant,[123] the difference being that the phrase 'democratic society' is only found in the European Convention. As a result, the scrutiny applied by the Court in terms of the necessity criterion is also one that engages with value-based judgments as to the meaning of democracy.

In addition, the Court typically seeks to find whether the authorities managed to strike a fair balance between the rights, values or public interests at stake under article 10 of the European Convention. Yet, at the same time, it maintains that other interests may take precedence. A good illustration is offered by the *Handyside* case, decided by the ECtHR in 1976, which remains

[118] ECtHR, *Sunday Times (No. 2) supra* note 75 at para 50; *Observer and Guardian supra* note 14 at para 59.
[119] E.g. *Airey v Ireland*, 9 October 1979, Series A no 32, 12–13, para 24.
[120] ibid at 13–17.
[121] E.g. *Cumpănă and Mazăre supra* note 76 at 90.
[122] cf *Chauvy and Others v France* no 64915/01, § 70, ECHR 2004-VI.
[123] See e.g. generally UN Human Rights Council, 'General Comment no 31, Nature of the General Legal Obligation on States Parties to the Covenant', 26 May 2004, UN Doc CCPR/C/21/Rev.1/Add.13, para 6.

the landmark case on freedom of expression. There, the Court found that freedom of expression encompasses opinions that 'offend, shock or disturb the State or any sector of the population' (the so-called 'Handyside' formula),[124] and that general principles such as the need for 'pluralism, tolerance and broad-mindedness' should prevail in democratic societies.[125] It also stipulated that all restrictions to freedom of expression ought to be construed *narrowly* and in accordance with the principle of proportionality. Yet, this Court has equally found the rights-holders have 'an obligation to avoid as far as possible expressions that are gratuitously offensive to others . . . and which therefore do not contribute to any form of public debate capable of furthering progress in human affairs'.[126] This methodology, and especially the doctrine of the 'margin of appreciation', has been widely commented upon[127] and a more detailed account would fall outside the scope of this study. It is also one that is generally followed by other human rights bodies, particularly the Inter-American Court of Human Rights.[128]

The case law of the Court taken as a whole has not evolved in the sense of giving more weight to artistic freedom as compared to other values. Only few judgments rendered after 2005 may, arguably, 'support the suggestion that, in the context of European democratic societies, artists and writers could rely on defences specifically adapted to them'.[129] Yet, such defences are still emerging in the jurisprudence of the Court and include humour; satire; fiction; and symbolism in cases regarding public morality, extreme arts and religious sensibilities, as will be elaborated in more detail in the second part of this book.

What may be mentioned in this section, nonetheless, is that artistic expressions may face such constraints because of their content, but also because of the particular style, place and circumstances of an artistic event or performance. In *Alekhina*, for instance, the issue was not only the content of the song

[124] ECtHR, *Handyside v United Kingdom* no 5493/72, 7 December 1976, para 49. cf *De Haes and Gijsels v Belgium* nos 7/1996/626/809, Reports of Judgments and Decisions 1997-I, 24 February 1997 (with respect to journalistic freedom).

[125] ibid at para 49. cf ECtHR, *Vereinigung Bildender Künstler v Austria* no 68354/01, 25 January 2007, para 26; *Klein v Slovakia* no 72208/01, 31 October 2006, para 35; *İ.A. v Turkey* no 42571/98, ECHR 2005-VIII, para 28; ECtHR, *Kuliś and Różycki v Poland* no 27209/03, Merits and Just Satisfaction, 6 October 2009, para 28.

[126] *Otto-Preminger-Institut v Austria supra* note 77 at para 49; *Wingrove supra* note 77 at 52.

[127] Indicatively, David Harris et al, *Harris, O'Boyle and Warbrick: Law of the European Convention on Human Rights* (4th ed, Oxford University Press 2018) 3–40.

[128] By way of example only, see *Hellera Ulloa v Costa Rica*, Series C, no 107, 2 July 2004; *Canese v Paraguay*, Series C, no 111, 31 August 2004, para 96 (criminal defamation of a former candidate for election to the Paraguay).

[129] See on 'artistic defenses' before the ECHR, analytically, Polymenopoulou *supra* note 86 at 516ff.

(which, according to the Russian courts, was a manifestation of hooliganism, extremism and incited to religious hatred),[130] but also the fact that the group chose to perform it from the altar of one of the oldest cathedrals in Moscow.[131] The Court had to examine a twofold complaint related to artistic freedom, both in relation to the punishment for the particular performance (imposition of liability),[132] and the banning of the relevant video recording on YouTube (censorship) under the Russian Suppression of Extremism Act.[133] The Court took a holistic perspective in examining this case,[134] while the 'performance' in particular was seen as 'a mix of conduct and verbal expression [which] amounts to a form of artistic and political expression covered by Article 10',[135] therefore implying that the particular choice of performance was justified in these particular circumstances.

3.2.2.2 Restrictions or Duties and Responsibilities?

One stumbling block in this elaborate methodology is the fact that, contrary to the other articles of the European Convention, article 10 refers not only to restrictions of expression, but also to 'duties and responsibilities'.[136] Over the last few years, the European Court when dealing with freedom of expression cases (and arguably anxious to guarantee the quality of information in Europe) has insisted on the applicability of the dubious safeguard in various settings. In its well-established jurisprudence on article 10, the Court has kept emphasizing that these duties and responsibilities, whose scope is entirely abstract are, however, 'liable to assume significance' – for example, 'when [. . .] there is question of attacking the reputation of private individuals and undermining the "rights of others"'.[137] In more controversial judgments, the Court has gone as far as considering whether the journalist in question complied with the

[130] *Alekhina supra* note 58 at paras 4–5 and 48ff. The performance was recorded as the group had invited journalists as audience to gain publicity, while 'words such as "holy shit", "congregation" and "in heaven" were audible', while the dissident nature of the song was also confirmed by the expert opinions,

[131] ibid para 13.

[132] ibid para 174ff.

[133] ibid paras 231ff and 242.

[134] ibid paras 214–16 (considering that the group did not really disrupt any religious services, nor did they cause any injures to people inside the cathedral). See also discussion on religious sensibilities in Chapter 7.

[135] ibid at 206.

[136] cf Article 19 of the ICCPR reads: 'this article carries with it special duties and responsibilities. It may therefore be subject to certain restrictions'.

[137] *Bladet Tromsø and Stensaas v Norway* [GC] no 21980/93, ECHR 1999-III, para 65.

ethical requirements of their profession in order to assess whether he or she acted in accordance with his or her 'duties and responsibilities'.[138] As a result, several commentators have expressed concern about a possible 'chilling effect' of the case law of the Court on freedom of expression in Europe, particularly in relation to the press. This criticism is justified, since 'duties and responsibilities' are not areas that should be controlled by the law, but rather left to self-regulation.[139] Duties and responsibilities play an elementary role in relation to the role of the arts and artists in contemporary societies, especially in respect of well-known artists who are often in the media,[140] or those whose work touches upon particularly sensitive areas. This however should be arguably addressed as part of ethical responsibility and artistic professionalism, and included in guidelines of artist-run companies and self-regulating bodies, rather than courts.

3.2.3 *Preventing Private Actors from Interfering?*

3.2.3.1 Private Exhibitions and Events

In the context of exhibitions and events that are State-sponsored, censorship is more likely to be dismissed as illegitimate. This happened in the cancellation by the Berlin Deutsche Opera of *Idomeneas*, scheduled to take place in 2006, out of fear of extremist attacks, or Salakhova's *Waiting Bride*, a marble sculpture representing a fully veiled woman that was removed from the Venice biennale at its own pavilion.[141] Similar censorship however may occur in respect of privately organized events and exhibitions – for instance, those organized by galleries or cultural centres run by banks and other financial institutions. From the perspective of the artists and performers, whether the organizer is a public or private entity is generally of little significance. Examples of works and events that have been censored or cancelled out of fear of protests or vandalism and subsequently acquired publicity include the

[138] As an indication only, see *Prager and Oberschlick v Austria*, 26 April 1995, Series A, no 313; *Stoll v Switzerland* App no 69698/01, 10 December 2007, paras 145–61; *Flux v Moldova* (no 6) App no 22824/04, 29 July 2008.

[139] cf Dirk Voorhoof, 'Freedom of Expression, Journalists' Rights and Duties and the Impact of Ethics and Self-Regulation in the Light of Article 10 ECHR', paper prepared for IRCM Seminar on Freedom of Expression, Strasbourg, 2008 <www-ircm.u-strasbg.fr/seminaire_oct2008/docs/Report_by_Dirk_Voorhoof_Session_II.pdf>.

[140] cf *The Camden Principles supra* note 28, 'Principle 9: Media Responsibilities' (on the responsibilities of 'all media').

[141] Aaron Rosen, *Art and Religion in the 21st Century* (Thames and Hudson 2015) 216.

removal of a sculpture by Eric Fischl, *Tumbling Woman*, from the exhibition space of the Rockefeller Center in New York (depicting a naked woman with her legs and arms above her head, to commemorate those who jumped from the building of the World Trade Center),[142] and the suspension of Gurpreet Kaur Bhatti's *Behzti* in Birmingham (United Kingdom), scheduled to be performed at the Birmingham Repertory Theatre, for fear of Sikh protests.[143]

Private, non-state actors are not *in principle* encumbered with human rights obligations. Their conduct, however, may give rise to State responsibility, particularly where such conduct prevents the exercise of rights otherwise incumbent on the State to protect and fulfil.[144] States cannot escape their human rights obligations by insisting that non-state entities possess a parallel obligation to safeguard human rights.[145] As a result, it would be inaccurate to suggest that the obligation of States to refrain from censoring artistic freedom can go as far as encompassing a similar obligation on non-state actors. This is especially true in the case of events involving the likelihood of protests or vandalism, as clearly no one can compel private actors to face the potential danger of seeing their properties and assets vandalized. In order to find whether a positive obligation exists to protect artistic freedom in this scenario, individual rights would need to be balanced against community interests, including therefore against private actors' right to property, among others.[146] This, however, implies the existence of a second problem, namely, legitimate censorship by private actors (so-called Inter- American Court of Human Rights 'collateral censorship'), eventually culminating to a culture of 'events cancellation',[147] and subsequently, self-censorship.

According to the current interpretation of the covenant by the UN Human Rights Committee, 'there may be circumstances in which a failure to ensure covenant rights as required by article 2 would give rise to violations by States Parties of those rights, as a result of States Parties' permitting or failing to take appropriate measures or to exercise due diligence to prevent, punish,

[142] The Associated Press, 'After Complaints, Rockefeller Center Drapes Sept. 11 Statue', (*NY Times*, 19 September 2002) <www.nytimes.com/2002/09/19/nyregion/after-complaints-rockefeller-center-drapes-sept-11-statue.html>.

[143] Emily Butchelar, 'Behzti Is No Longer Taboo', 5 May 2010, <www.indexoncensorship.org/2010/05/behzti-religion-offence-sik/>.

[144] Andrew Clapham, 'Non-State Actors' in *Moeckli, International Human Rights Law* (Oxford University Press 2014) 560–61. Also generally, Ilias Bantekas and Lutz Oette, *International Human Rights Law and Practice* (3rd ed, Cambridge University Press 2020) 832ff.

[145] ICCPR, art 2, para 1.

[146] cf *Appleby v United Kingdom* App no 44306/98, 6 May 2003, para 39.

[147] See Laurence Cuny, *Relocating Artists at Risk in Latin America* (ifa Edition Culture and Foreign Policy, 2021).

investigate or redress the harm caused by such acts by private persons or entities'.[148] In extreme cases, therefore, States may be held accountable for permitting events and performances that inflict harm on private individuals. This is true in respect of exhibitions promoting or concealing criminal activities (the exhibition *Bodies*, for instance, in which cadavers of suspicious origin were exposed potentially concealing human trafficking, which will be discussed in detail in Chapter 6). Clearly, however, this should not constitute an excuse by which to justify censoring avant-garde and non-mainstream art, as in the case of the exhibition *Queermuseum* – the largest ever Queer Art exhibition, organized in Santander Cultural Centre in Rio – subsequently cancelled following a petition by an extreme right-wing group (although currently exhibited at Rio Museum).[149]

An interesting typology concerns situations where States are obliged to criminalize private conduct deemed to be discriminatory on racial or ethnic grounds. Contrary to the ICCPR, the ICERD refers explicitly to the private sphere, and condemns *all propaganda* and *all organizations* that promote hatred.[150] In addition, the CERD has been regularly addressing State obligations with respect to the regulation of hate speech in the private sphere. Consequently, States are arguably competent to regulate private actors in 'violation' of the ICERD – for example, by taking appropriate measures against exhibitions, performances or private spectacles that promote racial hatred and intolerance against communities, peoples and ethnic groups. A similar trend is manifested with respect to religious intolerance. Both the CERD and UN experts serving on mandates related to religious freedom and the elimination of intolerance, for instance, have emphasized that 'acts of religious intolerance or other acts that may violate the right to freedom of religion or belief can be committed by States but also by non-State entities or actors' and that 'States have an obligation to address acts that are perpetrated by non-State actors' as part of their obligations under article 18 of the

[148] UN Human Rights Committee, 'General Comment no 31, The Nature of the General Legal Obligation Imposed on States Parties to the Covenant", (adopted on 29 March 2004), CCPR/C/21/Rev.1/Add. 1326 May 2004, at para 8.

[149] See Ernesto Londoño, 'In Brazil, "Queer Museum" Is Censored, Debated, Then Celebrated' (NY *Times*, 26 August 2018) <www.nytimes.com/2018/08/26/world/americas/queer-museum-rio-de-janeiro-brazil.html>.

[150] ICERD at 2, 4 and 5; OHCHR, 'Mapping State Obligations for Corporate Acts: An Examination of the UN Human Rights Treaty System', Report no 1, 18 December 2006. cf Patrick Thornberry, 'Confronting Racial Discrimination: A CERD Perspective' (2005) 5 *Human Rights Law Review* 239, 252.

ICCPR.[151] Artworks are no exception to this, and, as pointed out in the relevant 2020 UN action plan launched to respond to the growth of xenophobia and intolerance, 'hate speech can be conveyed through any form of expression, including images, cartoons, memes, art objects, gestures and symbols'.[152]

3.2.3.2 Digital Art and Social Media

Censorship of the digital arts, digital music, video art, films and audiovisual productions promoted on social media and internet platforms is an acute problem for artists and musicians. Most artists, especially those in the process of establishing themselves, increasingly rely on social media and digital platforms to network, promote and diffuse their work, which makes digital challenges (and more broadly media law) an important part of artistic and creative freedom. The legal challenges that arise are especially topical given that intermediaries such as Facebook, YouTube and Instagram exercise control over content dissemination.[153] At the same time, extreme forms of expression, online pornography and paedophilia, copyright infringement through illicit downloading, defamation and hate speech have only increased platform vigilance, as discussed earlier with respect to terrorist networking and recruitment.

The topic has not yet been considered extensively by human rights bodies, nor UNESCO, save for general remarks and recommendations on the 'digital environment'.[154] Unfortunately, also, to date, there has been no relevant comment by the CESCR (save for a brief section in General Comment no 25, issued in 2020).[155] On the contrary, there has been substantial research from the standpoint of internet regulation and intermediary liability.[156] In rare cases, some platforms have been held liable for online content. In *Delphi*, for example, the ECtHR found the largest Estonian news portal liable for

[151] A/HRC/2/3 *supra* note 47 at para 35. See also Chapter 7 with respect specifically to cartoons controversies.

[152] United Nations Strategy and Plan of Action, September 2020, at 10.

[153] cf Land *supra* note 18 at 443 (arguing likewise that 'States compound this problem by outsourcing regulation of online content to these intermediaries').

[154] 'Human rights in the digital age', Keynote speech by Michelle Bachelet, UN High Commissioner for Human Rights, Japan Society, New York, 17 October 2019; the UNESCO 2015 Recommendation concerning the Preservation of, and Access to, Documentary Heritage Including in Digital Form.

[155] UN CESCR, 'General Comment no 25, Science and Economic, Social and Cultural Rights' (article 15 (1) (b), (2), (3) and (4) of the International Covenant on Economic, Social and Cultural Rights), 30 April 2020, E/C.12/GC/25, paras 72–76.

[156] Land *supra* note 18 at 443–44 (noting that 'intermediary liability refers to the practice of holding intermediaries such as internet service providers "liable for the content disseminated or created by their users'); also *Fields supra* note 62; McKeown *supra* note 62.

comments posted online by individual end-users, having posted defamatory allegations and hateful comments against a shipping company,[157] and this, despite the fact that the particular platform used a notice-and-take-down system. This approach, albeit exceptional, has been criticized as overprotective, imposing a chilling effect on online speech, and may be equally dangerous for social media platforms that focus on arts and culture. In fact, in the absence of regulation, States largely outsource their commitments to service providers, which may culminate in the prosecution of art platform owners and news portals. As noted by the Special Rapporteur on Freedom of Expression, David Kaye, 'States regularly require companies to restrict manifestly illegal content such as representations of child sexual abuse, direct and credible threats of harm and incitement to violence, presuming they also meet the conditions of legality and necessity', including by setting liability regimes and notice-and-take-down measures.[158] Yet, in some cases, States may demand removing content or links extraterritorially on the grounds that such content violates local laws.[159] This may include specific artists or artworks active on social media, including keywords, shortcuts and links in relation to their work.[160]

CONCLUDING REMARKS

This chapter examined the problem of censorship in the arts and the art worlds. It focused on censorship in its strict sense (*prior censorship*), distinguishing it from the broad notion of censorship (which is not a legal term and encompasses virtually all situations where the free flow of information is unduly inhibited). Censorship *stricto sensu* refers to the suppression of information, art, music and other creative expressions before its actual diffusion to the public and at the local level it may take the form of a prior restraint (emanating from any legislative, judiciary or administrative body).

The question that arises under international law, therefore, is whether such local laws are compatible with free speech standards. We observed that,

[157] ECtHR, *Delphi AS v Estonia* App no 64569/09, 10 October 2013.

[158] UNGA, 'Report of the Special Rapporteur on the Promotion and Protection of the Right to Freedom of Opinion and Expression', David Kaye, 6 April 2018, A/HRC/38/35.

[159] ibid para 18 (referring to 'global removals'); PEN America, OHCHR, Mapping State Obligations for Corporate Acts: An Examination of the UN Human Rights Treaty System, Forbidden Feeds: Government Controls on Social Media in China', 13 March 2018 at 36–37 (referring to some States' demands to remove content extraterritorially) and 43ff (on the impact of censorship on art and music).

[160] cf PEN *supra* note 159 (on Chinese artists).

although the term is not explicit in international law instruments, a general prohibition of censorship is deduced by freedom of expression provisions. The exact scope of the prohibition, however, remains somewhat ambiguous, given that for some types of content (such as obscenity and the protection of minors,[161] but also, hate speech, revisionism and incitement to terror), prior restraints are generally considered acceptable. The relevant treaty provisions in human rights treaties however are relatively ambiguous, and the exact line between acceptable prior restraints and illegitimate censorship is never sufficiently clear. For example, penalization of advocacy of racial hatred[162] and Holocaust denial[163] is generally considered compatible with international human rights (arguably entailing the permissibility of prior restraints), yet, the penalization of expression of opinions about historical facts is not (given that the ICCPR 'does not permit general prohibition of expressions of an erroneous opinion or an incorrect interpretation of past events').[164] This entails an additional problem, namely the fact that content providers, media producers, museum, galleries and other non-state actors will most likely seek to be on the safe side rather than risking liability, therefore imposing restrictions that go way beyond these international standards (or even local laws). This produces in turn a complex phenomenon, the legitimacy of the so-called 'collateral censorship' in the sphere of visual arts that are created or advertised online – and the 'event cancellation' culture in the sphere of performance. To avoid such restrictive interpretations of free speech and creativity, therefore, and provided that there is no intent to abuse one's right, it only seems parsimonious to apply the most lenient standards – and the *in dubio pro artis* criterion – in the case of creative works, especially those highly symbolic works, which are evidence of human creativity and genius.

[161] ACHR, art 13 *supra* note 104.

[162] Article 20 of the ICCPR and article 4 of the ICERD.

[163] Faurisson *supra* note 68.

[164] UN Human Rights Committee *supra* note 19 at para 49.

4

Positive Obligations in Relation to Artistic Freedom

This chapter examines positive obligations in relation to artistic freedom, especially in light of the International Covenant on Economic, Social and Cultural Rights (ICESCR). At its face, this may sound like an oxymoron. First, article 15, paragraph 3 is the only provision that refers to a *freedom* rather than a right. The way this article is framed denotes in addition an obligation to merely 'respect' this right. This is generally understood as implying a negative obligation rather than a positive one – a 'minimalist undertaking' as Alston and Quinn note.[1] Second, obligations related to '*freedoms*' generally have been generally understood in contemporary political philosophy as negative ones, in the sense of abstaining from setting 'obstacles, barriers or constraints'.[2] This point is exemplified also in Isaiah Berlin's thoughts about liberty: Berlin cherished liberty in the sense of 'ability to do as one wishes',[3] yet also found that 'the inability of humans to fly is generally not thought of as lack of freedom'.[4] The classic concept of State obligations is based on the hypothesis that positive and negative obligations are entirely distinct categories, and that positive obligations are more challenging than negative ones because they involve State action. Subsequently, a rigid distinction has been made: first generation rights such as those guaranteed in the International Covenant on

[1] Philip Alston and Gerald Quinn, 'Nature and Scope of States Parties' Obligations under the International Covenant on Economic, Social and Cultural Rights' (1987) 9(2) *Human Rights Quarterly* 156, 184.

[2] Stanford Encyclopedia of Philosophy, 'Positive and Negative Liberty' (revised 2 August 2016) <https://plato.stanford.edu/entries/liberty-positive-negative/#PosLibConNeu>.

[3] Joseph Hamburger, *John Stuart Mill on Liberty and Control* (Princeton University Press 2001) 4.

[4] See e.g. David Currie, 'Positive and Negative Constitutional Rights' (1984) 53 *University of Chicago Law Review* 864, 868.

Civil and Political Rights (ICCPR) entail negative obligations, while second generation rights such as those in the ICESCR entail positive ones.

This last hypothesis is largely contested today.[5] First, all types of rights have at least some normative force: they 'permit their holders to act in certain ways, or give reasons to treat their holders in certain ways or permit their holders to act in certain ways, even if some social aim would be served by doing otherwise'.[6] This applies regardless of typologies and whether rights belong to one category or the other. As the Vienna Declaration proclaimed in 1993, 'all human rights are universal, indivisible, interdependent and interrelated. The international community must treat human rights globally in a fair and equal manner, on the same footing, and with the same emphasis'.[7] Second, negative and positive obligations are not entirely distinct from each other,[8] and do not correspond to 'strictly negative' or 'strictly positive' duties. 'Positive duties' have been increasingly recognized by human rights bodies and courts around the world. They are now well established in international instruments that guarantee primarily civil rights such as the European Convention[9] and the ICCPR.[10] Third, cultural rights entail mixed obligations – both positive and negative. Their exact scope, however, remains imprecise.[11] This is especially true since cultural rights have evolved from being under-developed[12] to

5 Christian Tomuschat, 'Human Rights: Tensions between Negative and Positive Duties of States' (2009) 14 *Austrian Review of International and European Law* 19, 19; Alston and Quinn *supra* note 1 at 184.

6 Stanford Encyclopedia of Philosophy, 'Rights' (revised 24 February 2020) at 4, <https://plato.stanford.edu/entries/rights/>.

7 Vienna Declaration and Programme of Action, A/CONF.157/23 12 July 1993, at 1.

8 See e.g. Brice Dickson, 'Positive Obligations and the European Court of Human Rights' (2010) 3 *Northern Ireland Legal Quarterly* 203, 203 (arguing that all rights have correlative obligations).

9 cf David Harris et al, *Harris, O'Boyle and Warbrick: Law of the European Convention on Human Rights* (4th ed, Oxford University Press 2014) 22.

10 UN Human Rights Committee, General Comment no 31, 'Nature of the General Legal Obligation on States Parties to the Covenant', 26 May 2004, UN Doc CCPR/C/21/Rev.1/Add.13.

11 Patrice Meyer-Bisch, 'Les droits culturels: forment ils une categories specifique des droits de l'Homme ?' in Patrice Meyer-Bisch (ed), *Les droits culturels: une catégorie sous-developpée de droits de l'homme ?* (1993) at 18–19 [in French] ('les droits culturels sont actuellement dans le flou'); Elissavet Stamatopoulou, *Cultural Rights in International Law: Article 27 of the Universal Declaration of Human Rights and Beyond* (Martinus Nijhoff 2007).

12 Indicatively, Meyer-Bisch *supra* note 11 at 11 (calling these rights 'forgotten rights'); generally, Stamatopoulou *supra* note 11. cf Yvonne Donders, 'The Legal Framework of the Right to Take Part in Cultural Life' in Yvonne Donders and Vladimir Volodin (eds), *Education, Science, and Culture: Legal Developments* (Ashgate and UNESCO 2007) 231, 232 (calling these rights 'the Cinderella of Human rights').

having a spill-over effect on all other rights,[13] and arguably also expanding in other areas of law (and through concepts such as cultural diversity).[14] In addition, new cultural rights keep emerging (such as a right to 'cultural mixing'),[15] arguably taking the focus away from those cultural rights that unfortunately remain under-developed.

The aim of this chapter is not to engage in a cultural rights critique, nor to provide an exhaustive description of positive obligations under all human rights instruments that refer to artistic freedom (some of them were mentioned earlier in Chapter 2). Rather the chapter focusses on classic positive obligations (such as an obligation to provide effective remedies), as well as on the linkages between artistic freedom and obligations stemming from the right to participate in cultural life under article 15, paragraph 1 of the ICESCR. It also discusses positive obligations in the exercise of artistic freedom (i.e. artistic practice), including non-discrimination and equality obligations.

4.1 PROVIDING EFFECTIVE JUDICIAL REMEDIES

4.1.1 *Effective Remedies against Censorship in Performance Art, and Music*

In case of artistic freedom violations, States must ensure that appropriate mechanisms are in place for individuals to be able to form legal claims. These claims are not necessarily constitutional – or human rights – claims. They may also be based on moral rights and remedies arising from intellectual property law, aiming at protecting authors against censorship of artistic freedom – including against seizure, removal or destruction of works.

The right to effective judicial remedies is an independent right under article 2, paragraph 3 of the ICCPR. It is also reiterated in the Human Rights Committee's General Comments (on States' obligations and freedom

13 E.g. Fribourg Declaration on Cultural Rights, 7 May 2007, preamble, paras 6 and 9 (d) (highlighting that all human rights have a cultural dimension).

14 Laura Pineschi, 'Cultural Diversity as a Human Right? General Comment no 21 of the Committee on Economic, Social and Cultural Rights', in Silvia Borelli and Federico Lenzerini (eds), *Cultural Heritage, Cultural Rights, Cultural Diversity* (Brill 2012); Eleni Polymenopoulou, '"Cultural Diversity" from the Perspective of Human Rights, Media and Trade Law: Cross-fertilization or Conflict?' (2021) 2(7) *Santander Art and Culture Law Review* 123–48.

15 UN Human Rights Council, 'Report of the Special Rapporteur in the Field of Cultural Rights, Karima Bennoune' A/76/178, 19 July 2021 (on the 'human rights-respecting cultural mixing').

of expression, respectively),[16] as well as in the Committee on Economic, Social and Cultural Rights (CESCR)'s General Comment released in 2017 on States' obligations.[17] It further appears in focus-specific *soft law* instruments related to freedom of expression and the prohibition of incitement, such as the Camden Principles on Freedom of Expression and Equality,[18] and the Rabat Declaration.[19] The last one, as Parmar notes, 'guarantees the right to fair trial and the right to an effective remedy as well as legal assistance for members of minorities and vulnerable groups'.[20]

Artists who are discriminated against should have easy access to legal remedies in order to seek redress for any infringement equality and non-discrimination under article 3 of the ICCPR. Remedies need to be available, as well as effective. Judicial review in particular is key in relation to censorship decisions, especially those regarding classification of films and audiovisual material. States that have ratified the ICCPR, in addition, should 'provide the Committee, in accordance with reports submitted pursuant to article 40 [of the ICCPR], with the relevant domestic legal rules, administrative practices and judicial decisions' and send to the committee information about available remedies available in the event of alleged infringement.[21]

The importance of effective judicial remedies has been highlighted by human rights bodies. The approach to effective remedies is generally similar to free speech and media freedom cases.[22] In *Alekhina*, for example, concerning Pussy Riot's performance on 'Punk Prayer' discussed earlier in Chapter 3, the applicants complained before the European Court among other things also for lack of effective remedies. The Court subsequently found that 'the ban on access to them did not meet a "pressing social need" and was disproportionate to

[16] UN CESCR, 'General Comment no 17 (2005), The Right of Everyone to Benefit from the Protection of the Moral and Material Interests Resulting from Any Scientific, Literary or Artistic Production of Which He or She Is the Author' (article 15, paragraph 1 (c), of the covenant), 12 January 2006, E/C.12/GC/17 at para 18 (extensively discussing access to judicial and other appropriate remedies).

[17] UN CESCR, 'General Comment no 24 (2017), State Obligations under the International Covenant on Economic, Social and Cultural Rights in the Context of Business Activities', 12 September 2011, E/C.12/GC/24, at para 8.

[18] ARTICLE 19, *The Camden Principles on Freedom of Expression and Equality* (London, 2009), Principle 4.

[19] See Chapter 3 on hate speech.

[20] Sejal Parmar, 'The Rabat Plan of Action: A Global Blueprint for Combating "Hate Speech"' (2014) *European Human Rights Law Review* 21, 31.

[21] UN Human Rights Committee, 'General Comment no 34, The Right to Freedoms of Opinion and Expression' (Article 19), 12 September 2011, UN Doc CCPR/C/GC/34, para 8.

[22] E.g. *Manole and Others v Moldova* (just satisfaction) no 13936/02, 13 July 2010 at para 107; *Informationsverein Lentia and Others v Austria*, 24 November 1993, Series A, no 276 at para 39.

the legitimate aim invoked' and that therefore 'the interference was thus not "necessary in a democratic society"'.[23]

4.1.2 *Reparations for Demolition of Art Installations*

Those whose rights have been violated are entitled to prompt and adequate reparation. Reparations are measures 'necessary to make the effects of violations disappear' – their nature and amount depend on the harm caused at both 'material and moral levels'.[24] Reparations for violations of artistic freedom may consist of restitution, compensation, satisfaction or guarantees of non-repetition, as it is the case with any other right.

In its second case on artistic freedom decided in 2017, the UN Human Rights Committee elaborated more on the form that these reparations could take when artistic freedom is violated. The case concerned a large installation titled *Bridges of Memory* placed on nine bridges over the Mapocho River in Santiago, Chile, on the occasion of the anniversary of the 1973 military coup. The work, which consisted of seventeen banners painted by Chilean artists 'on the subject of the defence of human rights in a democracy', was taken down by a number of Chilean squads (*Carabineros*) for public order considerations. After finding the seizure illegitimate, the committee recommended that Chile provide full reparation to the artists, including the return of the works seized and a public acknowledgement of the violation of their rights under article 19 of the ICCPR.[25]

4.2 POSITIVE OBLIGATIONS UNDER THE ICESCR

4.2.1 *Obligations Relevant to Participation in Cultural Life*

Obligations related to artistic freedom under article 15, paragraph 3 should be read in conjunction with the obligations under article 15, paragraph 1 (on the right to participate in cultural life) as well as those recognized in article 19 of the ICCPR (on the right to freedom of expression). These should also be

[23] See *Alekhina and Others* App no 38004/12, 11 September 2018 at para 268.

[24] *Miguel Castro Castro Prison v Peru*, Merits, Reparations, and Costs, Interpretation of the Judgment, Inter-Am. Ct. H.R. (Ser. C) no 181 (2 August 2008) at para 416.

[25] *Claudia Andrea Marchant Reyes et al. v Chile*, 7 November 2017, UN Doc CCPR/C/121/D/2627/2015, paras 9–10 (regarding the Santiago Court of Appeal Case, 16 September 2013). See also Chandra Morrison, 'Public Art Replacement on the Mapocho River: Erasure, Renewal, and a Conflict of Cultural Value in Santiago de Chile' (2018) 23 *Space and Culture* 149; Sarah Joseph, 'Art and Human Rights Law' in Jani McCutcheon and Fiona McGaughey (eds), *Research Handbook on Art and Law* (Edward Elgar 2020) 389, 401.

considered in light of articles 2–5 of the ICESCR that outline 'cross-cutting state obligations of a general nature applicable to all individual rights, such as issues of non-discrimination and equality'.[26]

4.2.1.1 Artistic Freedom and Participation in Cultural Life

Freedom is a constitutive element of the right to access culture, in the sense of *contributing* to cultural life. As noted by O Keefe, 'although the drafters omitted the word "freely" [. . .] when framing the text of Article 15, they clearly intended that the right to take part in cultural life should comprehend creative freedom'.[27] This is also evident in UNESCO's early work on cultural development. For instance, according to the UNESCO statement of 1970, 'the right to culture includes the possibility for each man to obtain the means of developing his personality through his direct participation in the creation of human values, and of becoming, in this way, responsible for his situation, whether local or on a world scale'.[28] Symonides, too, in 1993, classified the 'right to creativity' under the premise of cultural rights, arguing that 'the concept of creativity is very close to that of "participation" and may be seen as part of the right of participation [in culture]'.[29]

Surely artistic freedom is not as broad as 'access to culture'. It would be equally wrong to consider all cultural expressions as 'artistic'. Yet, both art and creativity fall within the broad concept of 'culture'.[30] As Shaver and Scanga argue, 'article 15 does not suggest that cultural life should evolve in any certain direction, but rather emphasizes the need for encouragement, freedom and popular participation [. . .] In this way, rights-bearers themselves act both

[26] Eibe Riedel, Gilles Giacca, and Christophe Golay, 'The Development of Economic, Social, and Cultural Rights in International Law' in Eibe Riedel, Gilles Giacca, and Christophe Golay (eds), *Economic, Social, and Cultural Rights in International Law: Contemporary Issues and Challenges* (Oxford University Press 2014) 3, 9.

[27] Roger O'Keefe, 'The "Right to Take Part in Cultural Life" under Article 15 of the ICESCR' (1998) 47(4) *International and Comparative Law Quarterly* 904, 910.

[28] UNESCO, 'Statement on Cultural Rights as Human Rights' in UNESCO, *Studies and Documents on Cultural Policies* (1970) 105, 107, para 11.

[29] See Janusz Symonides, 'Cultural Rights: A Neglected Category of Human Rights' (1998) 158 *International Social Science Journal* 55, 59; Meyer-Bisch *supra* note 11 at 36 ('*droit à la participation culturelle*'); Donders *supra* note 12 at 235. Also, e.g., Julie Ringelheim, 'Cultural Rights' in Daniel Moeckli, Sangeeta Shah, and Sandesh Sivakumaran (eds), *International Human Rights Law* (Oxford University Press 2014) 283.

[30] On the polysemous meaning of culture, see indicatively, O'Keefe *supra* note 27 at 905ff ; Donders *supra* note 12 at 235; Ringelheim *supra* note 29; also Pok Yin Chow, *Cultural Rights* (Brill-Nijhoff 2018) 35–37; and Chapter 2 (on terminology issues).

individually and collectively to shape the evolution of cultural life, as co-creators of culture'.[31]

A parallel could also be drawn here with the blending of the concepts of 'artist' and 'audience' in those artistic movements that have mainstreamed the public's participation in the creative process – and which are now also an undisputable part of States' intangible cultural heritage.[32] Examples range from participatory children's theatre to installation art, environmental art and performance arts that have emerged as features of festivals, biennales and trade fairs.[33] Happenings in particular, as evidenced in Alain Kaprow's work,[34] were one of the first movements to invite the public to the 'scene'. A good illustration of this is his work *Reinventions of Yard* (1991):

> Yard was originally made in the sculpture garden of the Martha Jackson Gallery in New York. It consisted of hundreds of used tires covering the ground in no particular order. Five tarpaper mounds emerged from the tires [. . .] Visitors were encouraged to walk on the tires, and to throw them around as they pleased [. . .] The conventional spectators became the participants who executed the changes. Here, also, the traditional notion of the uniquely talented artist (the genius) was suspended in favor of a tentative collectivity (the social group as artist). Art was like the weather.[35]

Marina Abramović, too, one of the most influential contemporary performance artists, describes the evolution of the arts in the involvement of the public in this way:

> . . . my relationship to the public is changing. It used to be very simple: the public was sitting in the audience and I was performing in front of them. [. . .] In Sydney, for 'Marina Abramović: In Residence', I will be like a conductor in the exhibition space, but it will be the public who will take the physical and emotional journey.[36]

Other, primarily American, artists have also been interacting with the public as a means to create provocative art – such as when 'Annie Sprinkle,

31 Lea Shaver and Catarina Scanga, 'The Right to Take Part in Cultural Life' (2010) 27(4) *Wisconsin International Law Journal* 637, 645.

32 UNESCO, Convention on the Safeguarding of the Intangible Cultural Heritage 2003, article 2, paragraph 1 (a) enunciates that ICH is manifested inter alia in performing arts.

33 See e.g. Mark Shuster, 'Culture in the City' in UNESCO, *Courier: Culture and Development. A Life Worth Living* (September 1996) 32.

34 On these movements, see e.g. Barbara Ferriani and Marina Pugliese (eds), *Ephemeral Monuments: History and Conservation of Installation Art* (2013); Martha Buskirk, *International Texts in Critical Media Aesthetics (Book 3)*, 26 April 2012.

35 <www.allankaprow.com/about_reinvetion.html>.

36 <https://kaldorartprojects.org.au/projects/project-30-marina-abramovic/>.

formerly a career actress in pornographic films, appeared onstage in New York to perform [. . .]' and ' during the show, legs spread, invited audience members onstage to view her cervix by means of a speculum'.[37]

4.2.1.2 Shaping Collective Cultural Representations

Art, especially the power of image, contributes to shaping a community's culture, and more broadly also social and cultural representations. Any individual who is exercising their expression in a 'creative' or 'artistic way' and in any public form (for instance, by displaying works, performing, participating in concerts, making films, etc.) is 'participating' in one way or another in cultural life. Farah and Tremolada make an interesting distinction between two classes of culture in which 'participation' is perceived. The first class describes 'the cultural practices that a social group acquired from the past through intergenerational passage', while the second, alludes to popular culture and 'cultural performances, often commercialized, through which a subgroup of a society manifests its unique identity'.[38] Elements of both classes of culture form ultimately 'the origin of all intangible cultural elements [. . .] which is found in the intrinsic capacity of human beings' 'to create original meanings and imaginaries that build social practices and representations'.[39] If this is so, then any individual involved in the cultural industry has some sort of 'special power' to shape a community's representations and imagery. Artists, musicians, film directors, photographers and popular culture actors are such agents *par excellence* – they should have therefore precisely this agency to create, embody and transform cultural representations.

The impact of this process on the formation of a collective culture is evident. Let us take the example of a well-known image in cinematography exported around the world and an idol in American twentieth century's pop culture – Marilyn Monroe. The image of Monroe is not necessarily an objective one, neither physical. Rather, it consists of an image perceived through the senses, and persists in time by virtue of an artistic lens of creativity and imagination. It is the two-dimensional and fictitious Monroe that has

[37] Anne Salzman Kurzweg, 'Live Art and the Audience: Toward a Speaker-Focused Freedom of Expression' (1999) 34 *Harvard Civil Rights-Civil Liberties Law Review* 437, 437.

[38] Paolo Farah and Riccardo Tremolada, 'Conflict between Intellectual Property Rights and Human Rights: A Case Study on Intangible Cultural Heritage' (2016) 94 *Oregon Law Review* 125, 135–36.

[39] ibid, citing Lourdes Arizpe, *Intangible Cultural Heritage, Diversity and Coherence* (Museum International 2004) 130, 131; see also Lourdes Azirpe, 'Back to the Drawing Board' in UNESCO *supra* note 33 at 14–15.

been carved in people's collective memory, perhaps even more than the roles she has undertaken. What people remember of Monroe is not the actual physical person – it is rather, Monroe in *that* movie, or Monroe in *that* photograph, Monroe in *that* Andy Warhol's poster – or in *that* Banksy's stencil and so on.

This may not be as straightforward as it seems, and definitely not for artists who do not enjoy Warhol's, or Banksy's reputation.[40] The debate on 'high' and 'poor' arts is still ongoing, especially with respect to funding of the arts and controversial artistic manifestations. Such divide, however, does not exist under the ICESCR or any other human rights instrument, and rightly so. Contrary to, say, funding obligations of State institutions (especially in relation to extreme, obscene or otherwise 'transgressive' art),[41] free speech guarantees apply to all human beings indistinctly. Whether or not the 'value' of art is a defining characteristic of what constitutes 'art' is beside the point.

4.2.2 *Positive Obligations Relevant to Artistic Freedom and Practice*

4.2.2.1 Take Steps . . . by All Appropriate Means

From the CESCR perspective, progressive realization entails primarily 'asking States to give details of legislation protecting the freedom of artistic creation and performance'.[42] After ratifying the Covenant, States should undertake a review of their relevant legislation, in order to make it compatible with international legal obligations related to both freedom of speech and access to arts and culture.[43] Under article 2, paragraph 1 of the ICESCR, in particular, States need to 'take steps . . . with a view to achieving progressively the full realization of the rights recognized in the present Covenant by all appropriate means'.

It is generally accepted that the term 'steps' in this case does not prevent obligations from being immediate. Some State obligations relating to article 15 are, in fact, of immediate applicability, as the committee has found. For example, both freedom from censorship and the right to non-discrimination raise immediate obligations – including also gender discrimination.[44] In other

40 cf Chapter 3 (on the exhibition *Ode to the Sea* and representations shaping the 9/11 narrative).

41 cf Chapter 6 (on morality and funding of the arts).

42 Alston and Quinn *supra* note 1 at 179–80; O'Keefe *supra* note 27 at 910.

43 cf also UNESCO, *Re|Shaping Cultural Policies* (UNESCO 2018) at Recommendation no 4 (hereafter: UNESCO Report 2018).

44 ibid para 5. The CESCR finds that '15 (3) would seem to be capable of immediate application by judicial and other organs in many national legal systems'. See also UN CESCR General Comment no 3, 'The Nature of States Parties' Obligations' ('art. 2, para. 1, of the covenant), E/1991/23 at para 1; UN CESCR, 'General Comment no 16, The Equal Right of Men and

words, States should make sure that once they ratify the ICESCR, they eliminate policies and practices encouraging prior restraints in arts and science – including in the sphere of regulation. At the same time, they should strive to make national laws fully compatible with international legal obligations, as well as 'take steps' to ensure that artistic freedom, as an element of participation in cultural life, is fully realized. They should therefore take 'positive and continuing'[45] measures to preserve or develop policies with respect to content restrictions, such as reviewing hate speech legislation, legislation related to defamation or obscenity laws and making sure that artists are safe from unlawful prosecutions. Practices that encourage discrimination in artistic practice, both direct and indirect, as it will be explained in the next section, are also immediate.

With respect to 'appropriate measures', the Committee has noted in its General Comment on State obligations that each State must decide what is the 'most appropriate way under its own particular circumstances'.[46] As Alston and Quinn note, if the Committee is silent on the precise steps to be taken, then desirable performance of legal obligations should match a State's objective capabilities.[47] For the right to artistic freedom to be effective, therefore, such appropriateness may include additional entitlements, such as the adoption of legislation and relevant judicial or other effective remedies.[48] Further, States may adopt cultural policies that ensure artists have a maximum exposure to different types of art. At the same time, however, cultural policies affecting a particular segment of the population, such as artists with disabilities, should also make sure there is direct consultation with representatives of that group.[49]

4.2.2.2 To the Maximum of Its Available Resources

States should promote 'artistic freedom', within their overarching obligation of freedom to access culture, to the maximum extent of their available resources.

Women to the Enjoyment of All Economic, Social and Cultural Rights', UN Doc E/C.12/2005/4, 11 August 2005. Generally, Christine Chinkin, 'Gender and Economic, Social, and Cultural Rights' in Riedel et al. *supra* note 26.

45 Alston and Quinn *supra* note 1 at 184–85; O'Keefe *supra* note 27 at 906.

46 UN CESCR, General Comment no 3 *supra* note 44 at paras 4–5.

47 Alston and Quinn *supra* note 1 at 185; also, generally, Maria-Magdalena Sepúlveda, *The Nature of the Obligations under the International Covenant on Economic, Social and Cultural Right* (Intersentia 2003) 195ff.

48 UN CESCR, General Comment no 3 *supra* note 44 at 5.

49 cf UN CESCR, 'General Comment no 5, Persons with Disabilities Re|Shaping Cultural Policies, 9 December 1994, E/1995/22, para 14: '[P]olicy-making and programme implementation in this area should be undertaken on the basis of close consultation with, and involvement of, representative groups of the persons concerned'.

This part of article 2 therefore requires efficient management of budgetary constraints and available fiscal space, which may not necessarily require additional resources. By way of illustration, artistic freedom may just as well be served by decreasing certain taxes for artists (e.g. income tax, sales tax on artworks of struggling artists), or art-related materials and equipment, such as paper, colours, etc. Moreover, art may become an optional course in schools and so in addition to making art more accessible, artists are provided with a basic income that allows them to create art. The State may, in pursuit of this purpose, relax the formal requirements for hiring art teachers at schools.

As the CESCR has highlighted, the obligation to strive to ensure the widest possible enjoyment of rights remains even if available resources are demonstrably inadequate.[50] In relation to cultural life, generally, this means that all States should at least engage part of their budget to promote artists' free participation in cultural life.[51] In relation to artistic freedom specifically, however, this might entail, for example, 'ensuring the multiplicity of bodies called upon to assess works of art and the regular renewal of their membership ... so as to safeguard the freedom of creative artists'.[52]

Along these lines, several States have created cultural institutions to empower their cultural industry, or made commitments to grant a percentage of their funding to support arts and culture. France has been a pioneer in this respect, having committed to support contemporary arts (*arts plastiques*) in the public space with the so-called 'law of artistic 1 per cent' (related to obligations to decorate public buildings such as universities and activity zones)[53] and the creation of regional centres to support the arts, including also street art and public art (although, typically, artistic projects will need to be inscribed in the ministry's cultural strategy and priorities to be eligible for funding).[54] In other cases, a particular kind of art, or music, or dance leads to the growth of 'cultural

50 UN CESCR, 'General Comment no 1, Reporting by States Parties', 27 July 1981, E/1989/22 and Right of everyone to take part in cultural life (art. 15, para 1 (a), of the International Covenant on Economic, Social and Cultural Rights) 21 December 2009, E/C.12/GC/21 at para 16 (b) on accessibility.

51 O'Keefe *supra* note 27 at 907ff and footnote 17, noting that 'from time to time the Committee has enquired bluntly into the percentage of the national budget allocated to culture' citing also E/1988/14, para 266; E/1992/23, paras 214, 247, E/1993/22, paras 62, 97, 1.

52 ibid 915, citing the 1980 UNESCO, Recommendation on the Status of the Artist (Paris 1980) at 10(g).

53 Degree n°2002-677 of 29 April 2002 (amended). See Jean-Marie Rentier, 'Le « 1 % culturel : L'obligation de décoration des constructions publiques' in *L'art et le droit : Ecrits en hommage à Pierre-Laurent Frier* (Maryse Deguergue ed, Éditions de la Sorbonne 2010) 301–27 [in French].

54 Order of 5 May 2017 on the funding of 'Centre national des arts de la rue et de l'espace public' [in French].

tourism' and more broadly development of urban cultural economies.[55] A good example is Argentinian tango. Tango tourism has been 'at the core of Buenos Aires' growth as a global city', and amounted in 2010 to an estimated gain of about '450 million per year for the industry'.[56]

> [Buenos Aires] has seen the growth of myriad private and public ventures turning the city into [. . .] a Disney World of Tango [. . .] from those developed more informally by tango teachers to more standardized packages offered by specialized travel agencies, and tango-themed hostels and hotels [. . .]. These developments have been accompanied by a proliferation of tango magazines and guides listing all the available milongas, practice sessions, and classes, with detailed hours and directions. In sum, this sector is directly involved in maintaining Buenos Aires as the tango capital of the world and is most implicated in transformations of the city's tango economy.[57]

Obligations to provide a minimum funding for culture would apply at all times, including also during crises, such as the Covid-19 pandemic. In fact 'even in times of severe economic contraction and the undertaking of measures of structural adjustment within a State, vulnerable members of society can and indeed must be protected by the adoption of relatively low-cost targeted programmes'.[58] Artists as a whole cannot be considered a 'vulnerable' group requiring increased protection, as is the case, for instance, with 'Roma, people with mental disabilities, people living with HIV, and asylum seekers',[59] or other groups that are socially excluded.[60] It is nonetheless true that the exclusion of nomads and travellers in some States[61] has a severe impact on

[55] On the development of 'art centres' worldwide and emerging markers, see John Zarobell, *Art and the Global Economy* (University of California Press 2017).

[56] For an excellent overview and analysis, see Arlene Dávila, 'Political Economy of Space' in *Culture Works, Book Subtitle: Space, Value, and Mobility across the Neoliberal Americas* (NYU Press 2012) 135, 139ff.

[57] ibid 144–45.

[58] UN CESCR, 'General Comment no 21, Right of Everyone to Take Part in Cultural Life' (art 15, para 1 (a), of the International Covenant on Economic, Social and Cultural Rights) 21 December 2009, E/C.12/GC/21 at 12, para 23.

[59] Lourdes Peroni and Alexandra Timmer, 'Vulnerable Groups: The Promise of an Emerging Concept in European Human Rights Convention Law' (2013) 4 *International Journal of Constitutional Law* 1056.

[60] Audrey Chapman and Benjamin Carbonetti, 'Human Rights Protections for Vulnerable and Disadvantaged Groups: The Contributions of the UN Committee on Economic, Social and Cultural Rights' (2011) 33 *Human Rights Quarterly* 682, 685 (referring to a study of the Icelandic Human Rights Centre that identifies thirteen groups as vulnerable).

[61] See e.g. 'Concluding Observations on the Fourth Periodic Report of Switzerland', 18 November 2019, E/C.12/CHE/CO/4 at paras 56–57 (with respect to Yenish, Sinti/Manouche and Roma cultural rights).

those groups' artistic and musical expression, especially when disasters and pandemics strike. Musical identities are a defining element of lifestyle of nomad communities, such as Roma and Sinti populations.[62] For example, gypsy music is a vital element for the preservation of rites, especially 'rites of passage such as weddings, circumcisions, baptisms and funerals',[63] which are cultural practices in need of protection and safeguarding.

4.2.2.3 Achieving Progressively

The concept of progressive realization in the context of article 2 is a central element of the covenant,[64] adding an important layer to the full realization of cultural rights as a whole. In brief, this means that States' actions and efforts should be directed towards progress – rather than retrogression. States should be held accountable in case of retrogressive measures – an obligation which should be monitored on the basis of State reporting procedures before the CESCR. Small steps should be taken in this regard. For example, some States commit to support at a minimum artists and musicians who live and work under precarious conditions. As soon as this is achieved, States should progress to additional measures, such as, for instance, social aid schemes and artist residences. France is a good example of this: a State providing special subsidies for artists, writers and musicians who are able to produce evidence of professional occupation, as well as actual artistic practice, including emergency aid schemes (for instance, during Covid-19).[65]

4.2.3 *The Application of the 4-A Scheme in Artistic Freedom*

The CESCR has elaborated criteria in relation to the implementation of State obligations under article 2, paragraph 1 of the ICESCR and article 15. They largely follow the '4-A scheme of structuring governmental human rights obligations', as developed by the first UN Special Rapporteur on the Right to Education, Katarina Tomasevksy, in 2002[66] – or simply, 4A scheme, as it has

62 Irén Kertész Wilkinson 'Gypsy' [Roma-Sinti-Traveller] *Grove Music Online*, at 6 and 10 (referring e.g. to Jazz manush by German Sinit); Svanibor Pettan, 'Encounter with "The Others from Within": The Case of Gypsy Musicians in Former Yugoslavia' (2001) 43 *The World of Music* 119, 133 (on various 'musicianships' of Gypsies in central Europe).

63 ibid at 8.

64 Alston and Quinn *supra* note 1 at 172.

65 <www.mesures-covid19.urssaf.fr/autres-publics-marins-artistes-auteurs/#artiste-auteurs>.

66 Katarina Tomasevksy, 'Annual Report of the Special Rapporteur on the Right to Education, submitted to the Commission on Human Rights', E/CN.4/2002/60 7 January 2002.

come to be known in economic, social and cultural rights (ESCR) theory. These criteria are clearly not well suited to describe obligations in relation to the concept of 'freedom'. They can, however, provide guidance in understanding the rights enunciated in article 15 of the covenant, taken as a whole. For example, availability in accessing arts is typically understood as making actual artworks and cultural products (such as plays, films, books, musical pieces) available within a State through cultural policies and all other appropriate means.[67] In light of artistic freedom, therefore, art should be actually *freely* created and diffused, and not the fruit of State propaganda, or self-censorship. Authors of works of art should not be obliged to be members of particular associations in order to be considered artists, nor should there be any formal criteria by which artists are denied such an identity.[68] This is because the right to access the arts, participate in the art sphere, as well as to benefit from intellectual property are intrinsic to human beings and enhance their well-being.[69] The 1980 UNESCO Recommendation on the Status of the Artist, which sets broad criteria on defining 'artists' is also indicative in this respect.[70]

Likewise, accessibility involves the public as much as the artist; it is crucial that the public has full access to *all* artistic concepts and ideas, without censorship or discrimination.[71] This includes at least three elements: first, enhancing the physical ability of the public to access the arts; second, financial accessibility, in the sense of providing access to art and culture at an affordable price and; third, non-discrimination and equal opportunities among individuals or groups desirous of access to the arts.[72] This obligation in turn also entails that States need to ensure that art is not confined within elitist spaces, thus allowing art to be immersed in daily life, and that States should ensure that dissemination of artworks is possible in the public space and in the context of domestic cultural policies. The elaboration of further State obligations could also benefit from the input of art history, and the fact

[67] cf UN CESCR, General Comment no 21, *supra* note 58 at 12, para 16. Also O'Keefe *supra* note 27 at 906 (noting that 'article 15 is also a question of the substantive ability to enjoy and create cultural works').

[68] cf IACtHR, *Compulsory Membership in an Association Prescribed by Law for the Practice of Journalism*, Consultative Opinion 5/85, Series A, 13 November 1985 (IACtHR) 30.

[69] UN CESCR, General Comment no 17 (2005) *supra* note 16 at para 2.

[70] UNESCO, Recommendation on the Status of The Artist (Paris 1980) at 5 (III) (a) [guiding principles].

[71] See IACtHR, *Compulsory Membership supra* note 68 at 30.

[72] cf UN CESCR, General Comment no 21 *supra* note 67 at 4, para 16, b: that 'everyone should have the right to [*freely*] seek, receive and share information on all manifestations of culture in the language of the person's choice, and the [*free*] access of communities to means of expressions and dissemination'.

several movements in the late nineteenth and the beginning of the twentieth century focused on the concept of accessible and participatory arts, in particular Bauhaus,[73] which aimed at blurring the lines between elitist and popular art.

Economic accessibility (*affordability*) of the arts too requires minimum access to art, literature, music, films, etc. by everyone – be it through national music days, festivals or public broadcasting and audiovisual means. The CESCR has also stipulated in this regard that privatization 'should not lead the enjoyment of Covenant rights to be made conditional on the ability to pay, which would create new forms of socioeconomic segregation' and that it should not 'result in excluding certain groups that historically have been marginalized, such as persons with disabilities'.[74] This obligation is also inextricably linked with artistic freedom, and with respect to cultural access, not only with respect to artistic education – which should be affordable and of good quality – but also the increasing emergence of private cultural institutions.[75] From the perspective of the artist, however, this means that regardless their financial situation, States should make sure that artistic creativity is supported.[76] This could mean, for instance, that opportunities exist for artists to be able to develop professionally, or experiment with new materials and techniques, including online digital platforms. A core minimum support should be provided, especially with respect to artistic education (under article 13 of the ICESCR) and affordable materials. Artistic freedom and access to arts in this case would entail, for example, an obligation to provide free artistic materials and instruments to students of fine arts schools and conservatories.

Accessibility also needs to comply with the principle of non-discrimination. Whether a particular artwork or film remains accessible or not through other means should not constitute a justification for non-diffusion through a particular medium. In *Ozkan*, a case decided by the European Commission of Human Rights, the applicant complained that he was not able to watch René Clément's movie *Les yeux interdits* (Forbidden Games, 1952) on Turkish television because the broadcaster (TRT) cancelled the transmission after

73 Hugh Honour and John Fleming, *World History of Art* (7th ed rev, Taschen) 821–22 (noting that Gropius, the founder of Bauhaus advocated the unification of art and design in everyday life).

74 UN CESCR, General Comment no 24 (2017) *supra* note 17 at para 22.

75 ibid.

76 cf UN CESCR, General Comment no 21 *supra* note 67 at 16 (b).

the film had started.[77] The Commission decided that the cancellation did not amount to censorship insofar as the movie remained accessible by other means.[78] The outcome of the case, however, would be much more contentious in relation to cancellation of live events such as concerts, festivals and performances.

'Adaptability' in relation to cultural accessibility under the ICESCR has been interpreted by the CESCR as 'refer[ring] to the flexibility and relevance of strategies, policies, programmes and measures adopted by the State party in any area of cultural life [which must be respectful of the cultural diversity of individuals and communities]'.[79] The last phrase of this paragraph is a particularly important tool in situations of emergency and indeed while many rights under article 4 of the ICCPR are derogable, cultural rights are in principle not.[80] Hence, both 'flexibility' and 'relevance' of strategies are important in this case, as States have the obligation to adapt their cultural policies to respond to the particular circumstances. States' obligations in relation to artistic accessibility, therefore, should provide artists with at least some materials that are vital for artistic creation, as well as access to the Internet to continue diffusing their work. These should continue being 'available, accessible and affordable' at all times during emergencies and pandemics, even if this means additional spending for the State. In the same way that education continues in times of disasters, pandemics should alert States to adapt their cultural policies 'to the maximum of their available resources', primarily by allowing additional funding to cultural institutions that adapt by digitizing collections and access to arts. The International Council of Museums (ICOM) statement is of relevance here, which, amidst the Covid-19 outbreak, 'called on policy and decision-makers to urgently allocate relief funds to salvage museums and their professionals'.[81]

[77] *Noyan Özkan v Turkey*, European Commission of Human Rights App no 23886/94 (decision). According to the Applicant, this 'contravened the internal discipline of TRT and its broadcasting principles'. According to TRT the cancellation of the film was justified, given that 'the film had been duly examined by the board of censorship before it was scheduled', and transmission was stopped only because TRT received 'unforeseeable reactions to the film and in order to prevent undesirable consequences'.

[78] ibid. 'There are sufficient alternative sources available to the public for watching the film, i.e. cinemas, video-tapes and private television channels. Consequently, the applicant is not deprived of access to the film in question'.

[79] cf General Comment no 21 *supra* note 67 at 4, para 16, d.

[80] Amrei Müller, 'Limitations to and Derogations from Economic, Social and Cultural Rights' (2009) *Human Rights Law Review* 557, 558.

[81] International Council of Museums (ICOM), *Statement on the Necessity for Relief Funds for Museums during the COVID-19 Crisis.*

Tomasevsky's criteria of 'adequacy'[82] in relation to the arts require 'appropriateness' or 'acceptability' of artistic expressions, including also 'cultural acceptability'. The 'adequacy' criterion is twofold: first, it refers to decent quality of the artistic expressions available. In relation to access to culture under article 15(1)(a) of the ICESCR, this means that a State's cultural authorities as well as private individuals should be, in principle, at liberty to set criteria of artistic excellence and merit in choosing and promoting specific types of artworks by means of cultural policies. 'Artistic merit' is highly controversial in both art theory and the law, as it will be discussed in Chapter 6. Yet events and the creation of artworks are directly subsidized by the State, whereby the latter can clearly decide on their content, by setting criteria and guidelines. Adequacy however also refers to the preservation of cultural diversity. It may therefore involve limitations to artistic freedom (in the sense that its exercise should be respectful of the culture and cultural rights of minorities and indigenous peoples, as the committee states),[83] but also, positive measures – especially in pluralistic yet divided societies, where there is a vital need to continue living together. For example, in its last concluding observations on Israel, the CESCR showed concern about the lack of measures taken to promote cultural diversity, especially in relation to access to cultural life.[84]

4.3 NON-DISCRIMINATION AND EQUALITY OBLIGATIONS IN THE ART WORLDS

4.3.1 *Towards the Elimination of Discriminatory Practices against Artists and Creatives*

4.3.1.1 Towards Elimination of Direct Discrimination

Direct discrimination consists of treating persons in equal or comparable situations differently. The prohibited discriminatory grounds of the ICCPR or the ICESCR can be 'of any kind, such as race, colour, sex, language, religion, political or other opinion, national or social origin, property, birth or

[82] UN CESCR, General Comment no 21 *supra* note 67 at 4, para 16 (e). 'Adequacy' refers to 'the realization of a specific human right in a way that is pertinent and suitable to a given cultural modality or context'.

[83] ibid at (c) and (e).

[84] 'Concluding Observations on the Fourth Periodic Report of Israel', 12 November 2019, E/C.12/ISR/CO/4, para 68.

other status'. As the last phrase ('other status') implies, the grounds are open-ended,[85] and are indeed gradually interpreted as such. The recognition of race as an 'inherently suspect' discriminatory ground predates the human rights system.[86] Other grounds, however, such as sexual orientation and gender identity are also now routinely addressed in State reporting procedures,[87] the concepts of 'vulnerability' and 'disadvantage' are also increasingly gaining terrain in human rights theory.[88] Yet, not every 'distinction' is discriminatory. Differences in treatment that have 'an objective and reasonable basis' do not constitute discrimination.[89] In other words, decisions that constitute a difference in treatment should be legitimate in accordance with the principle of non-discrimination and thoroughly justified, 'requir[ing] particularly weighty and convincing reasons for justification'.[90]

The CESCR has elaborated on the meaning of 'discrimination' in relation to arts accessibility in its general comment on the right to take part in cultural life.[91] According to the committee, 'no one shall be excluded from access to cultural practices, goods and services'.[92] The fine line between censorship and lawful discrimination is not easily distinguishable. For example, prior to World War II, the performance of samba and capoeira constituted criminal offences in Brazil, despite the fact that both were immensely popular among African descendants. The purpose underlying their criminalization was indirectly discriminatory as it clearly affected black communities and their supporters more than others. It was only after the 1940s when the legal framework evolved that these kinds of cultural manifestations ceased to be considered illegal.[93]

85 Daniel Moeckli, 'Non-discrimination' in Daniel Moeckli, Sangeeta Shah and Sandesh Sivakumaran (eds), *International Human Rights Law* (4th ed, Oxford University Press 2020) 153.

86 *Korematsu v United States* 323 US 214 (1944) (noting that race is inherently suspect, yet ultimately found that discrimination on these grounds was justified).

87 See generally Mindy Jane Roseman and Alice Miller, 'Normalizing Sex and Its Discontents: Establishing Sexual Rights in International Law' (2011) *Harvard Journal of Law and Gender* 313, 344 (fn 127).

88 On the concept of 'vulnerability' under human rights law, see Chapman and Carbonetti *supra* note 60 at 683–84.

89 See e.g., *Abdulaziz, Cabales and Balkandali v the United Kingdom* [1985] ECtHR App nos 9214/80; 9473/81; 9474/81, paras 82 and 83 (violation of article 14 on the grounds of sex).

90 cf also *Marckx v Belgium*, 13 June 1979, Series A, no 31, para 33; *Abdulaziz supra* note 89 at 143; Moeckli *supra* note 85 at 155.

91 UN CESCR, General Comment no 21 *supra* note 67 at para 23.

92 ibid at 26.

93 David Ruebain and Marcelo Paixão, 'Equality in Higher Education: Experts' Perspectives' (2012) 8 *The Equal Rights Review* 143.

At domestic level, such issues are typically addressed as supplementary claims to contractual breaches, chiefly arising out of artistic performances, exhibitions or other types of collaboration. The US Supreme Court, for example, ruled in the late 1990s that 'discrimination might in some cases be justified in order to preserve expressive [artistic] integrity', in order to absolve private parties from liability for discrimination.[94] This is a peculiar and perhaps case-specific argument that allows private parties to fully discriminate as they please. This approach however has been largely adopted by US State courts and used in some cases against artists (most notably in the case of the actress Vanessa Redgrave).[95]

As discriminatory grounds are expanding in human rights law, similar cases may arrive before human rights bodies. This would occur, for instance, if LGBTIQ-related artworks were excluded from an exhibition (or art contest, grant application or fellowship process or artists' residences), even though the work was comparable to that of other participants. In this case, both the right of the artist (to exercise their artistic freedom) and of the public (to access that work) would be violated.

Laws providing that women require permission from their guardian in order to participate in cultural life are directly discriminatory, as they provide different statuses for men and women. Male guardianship laws in Saudi Arabia, for example, although relaxed in some areas,[96] significantly affect women artists' right to receive education in arts or to become professional artists, curators, musicians, actresses, as official approval by the guardian is still formally needed. It is today still difficult for women to enrol in fine arts education,[97] or open a gallery, practice the arts or send their candidature to a film contest if their guardian is not in agreement. This is a breach of ICESCR standards, as

94 *New York State Club Ass'n v City of New York* 487 US 1 (1988); Lois Krieger, 'Miss Saigon and Missed Opportunity: Artistic Freedom, Employment Discrimination, and Casting for Cultural Identity in the Theater' (1992) 43 *Syracuse Law Review* 839, 850.

95 *Redgrave v Boston Symphony Orchestra, Inc.* 855 F.2d 888 (1st Cir.1988) (regarding the lawsuit of Vanessa Redgrave against the Boston Symphony Orchestra (BSO) for cancelling a scheduled performance because of her public support for the Palestinian Liberation Organization). See Krieger *supra* note 92 at 848–49; also Marjorie Heins, 'Vanessa Redgrave v. Boston Symphony Orchestra: Federalism, Forced Speech, and the Emergence of the Redgrave Defense' (1989) 30 *Boston College Law Review* 1283, 1289ff.

96 Eleni Polymenopoulou, 'Human Rights in the Six States of the Gulf Cooperation Council (GCC): From Vision to Reality' (2020) 3 *Cardozo International Comparative, Policy and Ethics Law Review* 929, 964ff.

97 See e.g. '"I am my own guardian": Feminist Saudi street artist Saffaa protests sexist law (*ABC News*, 2017) <www.abc.net.au/news/2017-10-08/feminist-artist-protests-saudi-arabias-male-guardianship-law/9022770>.

according to the UN Committee on ESCR, education is the means to *freely* develop one's personality and dignity. In sharp contrast, secular States requesting fine arts students or exhibition participants to remove religious symbols or uncover their face or hair, or even penalizing any covering of the face for religious reasons, could also be in violation not only of privacy rights,[98] but also of those individuals' right to participate in artistic and cultural life.

4.3.1.2 Towards Elimination of Indirect Discrimination

Discrimination also takes place if a State sets conditions or limitations in the exercise of artistic freedom, which although connected to laws of general application affects disproportionality a particular segment of the population. Cases related to discrimination on the grounds of nationality – or national origin – for example would be harder to resolve. For example, in some Gulf States, certificates of citizenship are needed to prove nationality in order to be able to present artistic work in a gallery or participate in exhibitions.[99] This clearly affects disproportionately the rights of long-term residents in engaging freely in artistic practice. Yet, States are not necessarily compelled to grant privileges to non-nationals, or 'give preferential treatment to their own citizens or nationals from countries with whom they have the closest links'.[100] This, however, would be different if these States requested certificates of ancestry[101] – for nationals wishing to exhibit or present their work – as this would clearly be discriminatory on the basis of national origin.

Non-discrimination obligations, however, even as a form of indirect discrimination, do not capture the entire range of discriminatory practices in artistic and cultural policies, especially where private actors are involved. The exclusion, or misrepresentation of contemporary art or artists in private, non-profit organizations such as museums and galleries, is arguably not caught by the discrimination clauses of the ICCPR and the ICESCR – and arguably the Convention on the Elimination of All Forms of Discrimination against Women (CEDAW). For instance, the International Survey of Painting and Sculpture at the Museum of Modern Art (MoMA) in New York presented in the early 1990s an exhibition that 'claimed to review the world's most

98 See however, *SAS v France* [2014] ECHR 695 (no violation by reason of France's margin of appreciation and the 'living together' theory).

99 Suzi Mirgani, 'Authenticating an Emirati Art World: Claims of Tabula Rasa and Cultural Appropriation in the UAE' in Suzi Mirgani (ed), *Art and Cultural Production in the Gulf Cooperation Council* (Routledge 2018) 12–27 (discussing cases in the UAE).

100 *Abdulaziz* cited *supra* note 89 at para 113.

101 cf Mirgani *supra* note 99.

important contemporary art', yet 'among the 169 artists on show, only 13 women were to be found'.[102] Clearly such a choice could give rise to discrimination claims on the grounds of sex. Yet, for a claim to be successful under the ICESCR (or the ACHR), there needs to be evidence that such selection was unreasonable and unjustified, as discussed above, and moreover, that the State failed to comply with non-discrimination obligations in the particular situation. It is unlikely that the claim would be successful (assuming that the United States would have ratified the ICESCR, which to date, has not happened). The applicable US law in 1983 had not set any conditions inhibiting equal participation between men and women in the arts and MoMA could fairly easily prove that arts had reached a state where men and women were equally represented in the art world.

Things would be different however, were a State or State-sponsored authority to deliberately discriminate, or permanently or purportedly exclude women, or a particular segment of the population from arts and culture, especially if this was sanctioned by law. This could apply *mutatis mutandis* in artistic freedom cases – and the 'cultural dimension' of discrimination. For example, in cases where discrimination leads to permanent exclusion from cultural life, artistic education or employment as a professional artist (curator, musician, film-maker, etc.), States must prove and thoroughly justify[103] compelling reasons for such actions.

This said, discrimination could take place also *within* minorities too. For example, a hip-hop artist living in the United Kingdom explains how being a female and black leads to exclusion from the community: 'Hip-hop is intrinsically black music [. . .] But there's this idea within some non-black Muslim communities that anything that comes from black culture is inherently bad or evil [. . .]'.[104]

4.3.1.3 Eliminating Discrimination in the Digital Art World

Most artists work online, sharing or displaying digital content in one way or another. The preservation therefore of internet neutrality (i.e. an obligation on internet service providers to allow access to content equally) is of a particular

[102] See Anon, 'The Guerrilla Girls' Fight against Discrimination in the Art World' (*Deutsche Welle*, 2017) <www.dw.com/en/the-guerrilla-girls-fight-against-discrimination-in-the-art-world/a-37852529>.

[103] UN CESCR 2009 at para 48; cf UN Human Rights Committee, General Comment no 34 *supra* note 21 at para 39 (in relation to States parties obligation to avoid imposing onerous licensing conditions and fees on the broadcast media).

[104] Aina Khan, 'Britain's Black Muslims: Ignored, Discriminated and Resisting' (*Al Jazeera*, 22 June 2018) <www.aljazeera.com/indepth/features/britain-black-muslims-discriminated-resisting-180322181443300.html>.

interest to visual artists working in digital media and the 'tech art' community;[105] those who rely on the Internet to communicate with the public and promote or sell their work; or those who connect through P2P networks.[106] This is not only due to the typically precarious conditions artists may need to work in,[107] as clearly they will not be able to 'buy' fast lanes to promote their artworks and will need to remain on 'slow' websites.[108] Allowing for wholesale regulation of the Internet could have a disastrous impact on projects that use web-based technologies,[109] or the 'New Art Online' presented under the auspices of the New Museum in Manhattan, New York;[110] Occupy Museum (part of the Whitney Museum of American Art Biennale in 2017);[111] and numerous other artistic initiatives, including also those undertaken after the Covid-19 outbreak.[112]

In the United States the debate has been open at least since 2010 when the so-called Internet Neutrality Act was passed by the Federal Communications Commission (FCC) and under the Obama administration. In 2014 however the US Court of Appeals for the D.C. Circuit[113] struck down the Act, allowing for monopolies to establish their position in the market. In 2015 the FCC voted again with a very narrow margin in favour of internet neutrality,[114] and in June 2018, it changed its position again in favour of 'investment and innovation'.[115]

[105] Anna Louie Sussman, 'The Repeal of Net Neutrality Could Harm Artists – Here's How' (9 January 2018) <www.artsy.net/article/artsy-editorial-repeal-net-neutrality-harm-artists>.

[106] Paddy Johnson, 'How Will the Repeal of Net Neutrality Impact Artists?' (11 June 2018) <https://hyperallergic.com/446564/net-neutrality-repeal-artists/>.

[107] Indicatively, ILO, 'Employment Relationships in the Media and Culture Industries', presented at the Global Dialogue Forum on Employment Relationships in the Media and Culture Sector, 14 and 15 May 2014, GDFMCS/2014 paras 4–6; also J. Vincent, *The Social Situation of Musical Performers in Africa, Asia and Latin America* (Sectoral Activities Programme, Working Paper no 172, ILO 2001), p. iii.

[108] Sussman *supra* note 105.

[109] <www.artsy.net/article/artsy-editorial-repeal-net-neutrality-harm-artists>

[110] <www.artsy.net/newmuseum>

[111] The project 'in 2016 invited financially strapped artists to share their experiences about debt, and apply to have their work displayed as part of a project called DebtFair' at <https://hyperallergic.com/tag/occupy-museums/>.

[112] By way of example, see <www.artsy.net/article/artsy-editorial-museums-finding-new-ways-connect-art-lovers-online-quarantine>.

[113] *Verizon v FCC*, US Court of Appeals for the D.C. Circuit (2014). See on this, Christopher Yoo, 'Common Carriage's Domain' (2018) 35 *Yale Journal on Regulation* 992, 992–93.

[114] See the Open Internet Order (2015), whereby the FCC voted in favour of classifying internet providers as 'common carriers', see Yoo *supra* note 113 at 1003.

[115] Internet Freedom Order (2015) at <www.fcc.gov/restoring-internet-freedom> and Yoo *supra* note 113 at 1004ff.

4.3.2 *Real Equality in the Art World*

4.3.2.1 Is Real Equality Ever Possible?

Discriminatory laws and policies are gradually interpreted – not only those that do not treat equals equally. They are also interpreted as those that do not 'treat persons who are in substantially different positions differently',[116] and also those that do not provide for adequate exceptions in respect of persons in disadvantageous situations.

In areas such as political pluralism and the protection of religious beliefs, for example, both the Human Rights Committee,[117] and *to some extent* also the ECtHR,[118] States may accord a degree of accommodation. This is not because such exceptions are compulsory; in fact they are not. Rather, States may be held responsible for two other reasons: either because they fail to respect their own previous commitments to accommodate diversity,[119] or because they fail to explain, in specific situations, how and why an 'accommodation' in favour of a minority would impact the application of the rule of general rule. The jurisprudence of the Human Rights Committee on article 27 of the ICCPR (in relation to minority rights and the right to participate in their culture) however has been scarce, and generally restricted to a handful of cases that are not directly relevant to artistic practice (especially for indigenous 'persons' belonging to minorities[120] and the use of minority or indigenous languages).[121]

The issues raised in this concept of equality, however, are still debated under international law, especially given the limitations of available case law.

[116] cf *Thlimmenos v Greece* [GC] no 34369/97, ECHR 2000-IV, para 44.

[117] Indicatively, Ana Filipa Vrodjlak, 'Liberty, Equality, Diversity: States, Cultures, and International Law' in Ana Filipa Vrodjlak (ed), *The Cultural Dimension of Human Rights* (Oxford University Press 2013) 26, 29–35, 35–36.

[118] Indicatively, Sophie van Bijsterveld, 'Equal Treatment of Religions? An International and Comparative Perspective' in Titia Loenen and Jenny E Goldschmidt (eds), *Religious Pluralism and Human Rights in Europe* (Intersentia 2007).

[119] For example, in *Manole* (cited *supra* note 22) the Court found Moldavia responsible for not being up to its own commitments.

[120] In addition, until the 1990s, minority claims were generally inadmissible, see e.g. *Peter Drobek v Slovakia*, Communication no 643/1995, 14 July 1997 in *Selected decisions of the Human Rights Committee – Volume 6*, CCPR/C/OP/6 at 14–15.

[121] By way of example, see *Allan Singer v Canada*, Communication no 455/1991, Views adopted on 26 July 1994, at para 11.2 (States cannot restrict use of language in the public space).

To date (2021), the CESCR has adopted only ten communications since the adoption of the Optional Protocol to the ICESCR in 2009 (OP-ICESCR), yet none of them on article 15. Likewise, the CESCR's concluding observations on State party reports do not specifically focus on artistic freedom and typically, not even on access to culture (article 15(1)(a)), but rather cultural rights in general. Typically, observations on State reports focus on discriminatory treatment of minority languages[122] and the need to foster indigenous languages, typically also re-referring to the need to preserve cultural diversity.[123] Occasionally, the committee addresses discrimination in art funding. For example, in the last concluding observations on Canada, the committee addressed the problem of structural discrimination in black arts and specifically the 'inadequate funding for and promotion of African art and culture' and recommended 'that the State party promote and increase the funding to the art and culture of African-Canadians'.[124]

It would be interesting therefore to see how the application of the non-discrimination provisions may unfold in the future also in relation to artists, both in universal standards and States practice. A good parallel could be for example the 'accommodation privileges' accorded under domestic laws in several cases in the domain of sports and athletes with disabilities.[125] Similar conclusions would be forthcoming in the domain of arts and culture, in any artistic contest requiring physical participation – such as examinations for admission to a fine arts school or conservatory.

4.3.2.2 Affirmative Action and Artistic Freedom

'Affirmative action' in favour of disadvantaged group's under human rights law can only be entrenched on special regimes of obligations, such as those established by the International Convention on the Elimination of All Forms of Racial Discrimination (ICERD), the CEDAW and the Convention on the Rights of Persons with Disabilities (CRPD). Positive action has been

122 'Concluding Observations on the Sixth Periodic Report of the United Kingdom of Great Britain, and Northern Ireland', E/C.12/GBR/CO/6, 14 July 2016 (lack of effective measures adopted by the State party to promote the use of the Irish language in Northern Ireland).

123 Indicatively, UN CESCR, 'Concluding Observations on the Sixth Periodic Report of Colombia', 19 October 2017, E/C.12/COL/CO/6, paras 65–66; Concluding Observations on the Seventh Periodic Report of Ukraine', 2 April 2020, E/C.12/UKR/CO/7, paras 47–48. cf also E/C.12/ISR/CO/4 *supra* note 84.

124 'Concluding Observations on the Sixth Periodic Report of Canada', 23 March 2016, E/C.12/CAN/CO/6, para 60.

125 E.g. *PGA Tour Inc. v Martin* (00-24) 532 US 661 (2001) 204 F.3d 994 (*Casey Martin* case).

recognized also by the Human Rights Committee under article 27 of the ICCPR for persons belonging to minorities (who 'shall not be denied the right [. . .] to enjoy their own culture') ('minority regime').[126]

These special regimes not only prohibit discrimination in relation to specific target groups. They also provide for at least some kind of affirmative action, and in fact, 'preferential treatment'. As such, unavoidably they involve at least some amount of confrontation – between interests, individuals, groups and ultimately values. For example, confrontation may arise where a State adopts special measures to enhance participation of black women in the arts, such as by increasing pay scales, appointing women as curators or increasing their quotas in biennale exhibitions. Necessarily one or more white males will be left unhappy, perhaps also white females, or black men. In this, a choice needs to be made, arguably political: either to balance two individual rights to non-discrimination (in the enjoyment of cultural rights, for example), or promote diversity in the public sphere. The first scenario would require the judiciary to balance two a priori equal rights, while the second would require the legislator to decide in advance that one right, individual or collective, weighs more heavily than the other in the pursuit of substantial equality.[127]

The concept of 'affirmative action', generally, is still debated in the United States and other parts of the world.[128] Non-discrimination obligations do not currently extend to allow all underrepresented groups from entering the art market or presenting their work in public spaces on an equal basis. Liberal States are not required to regulate the art market or film industry so tightly as to promote all types of art, films or music equally. In addition, service providers such as Netflix have indeed been making efforts over the last few years to promote equality and diversity.[129] The debate on 'equality' in artistic freedom is clearly also relevant here: in the contemporary world any 'film-maker' or musician's artistic freedom is breached if the chances that his work ever reaches Netflix, YouTube or SoundCloud is zero. Arguing, however, that the said providers should have responsibility under the ICESCR framework

[126] Indicatively, Alexandra Xanthaki, 'Multiculturalism and International Law: Discussing Universal Standards' (2010) 32 *Human Rights Quarterly* 21, 28–30.

[127] cf Olivier de Schutter, 'Three Models of Equality and European Anti-discrimination Law' (2006) 57 *Northern Ireland Legal Quarterly* 1, 2–3.

[128] ibid at 869ff. To date, the ICESCR counts 170 ratifications, the most recent ones being Antigua and Barbuda (2020), Qatar (2018) and Myanmar in (2017).

[129] See e.g. UN Women: 'Netflix and UN Women launch special collection curated by 55 groundbreaking women in entertainment', Press release, 4 March 2020; UN HRC 'General Comment no 28, The Equality of Rights between Men and Women, (article 3), 29 March 2000, para 3: 'The State party must not only adopt measures of protection, but also positive measures in all areas so as to achieve the effective and equal empowerment of women'.

still appears far-fetched. The question of transnational corporations' (TNCs) responsibilities in relation to ESCR has been already on the table, primarily due to the 'almost unparalleled capacity of TNCs to infringe such rights' and the frequent lack of regulation by host State governments.[130] These questions until now have primarily focused on selective ESCR matters (for instance, corporate responsibility and environmental issues or equality in relation to the workforce)[131] and little has been said or done in relation about discrimination and equality obligations concerning access to culture under article 15. In the absence of effective media regulation outside broadcasting, service providers have been generally free to respond to criteria as set by the market, rather than human rights law.

Last, a reference should be made here also to the principle of cultural diversity. The precise scope of obligations stemming from 'cultural diversity' are far-reaching. 'Cultural diversity' as such has been enunciated in various soft law instruments, most noteworthy the 2001 UNESCO Universal Declaration on Cultural Diversity and the 2005 UNESCO Convention on the Protection and Promotion of the Diversity of Cultural Expressions (DCE Convention).[132] This convention however was specifically tailored to promote access of the South to the North's cultural industries in the hope of supporting developing States' cultural industries, especially within the WTO setting.[133] Its scope is also unclear, given that cultural content is defined as 'the symbolic meaning, artistic dimension and cultural values that originate from or express cultural identities'.[134] In addition, it provides overall for relatively complex and vague principles and obligations (such as 'equitable access to cultural expressions' and 'international solidarity'),[135] and is accompanied by only a weak mechanism of supervision, based on cooperation and negotiation.[136] As a

[130] Justine Nolan and Luke Taylor, 'Corporate Responsibility for Economic, Social and Cultural Rights: Rights in Search of a Remedy?' (2009) 87(2) *Journal of Business Ethics* 433, 434.

[131] See e.g. *International Network for Economic, Social and Cultural Rights Corporate Accountability Working Group* (2005).

[132] 20 October 2005, 2440 UNTS 311. As of March 2021, the DCE Convention has 143 members including the EU.

[133] ibid at 636–37; also Tania Voon, 'Culture, Human Rights, and the WTO' in Vrodjlak (ed) *supra* note 117 at 186–202. Also John Morjin, 'The Place of Cultural Rights in the WTO System' in Francesco Francioni and Martin Scheinin (eds), *Cultural Human Rights* (Martinus Nijhoff 2008) 285–316; Polymenopoulou *supra* note 14 at fns 91–93 and accompanying text.

[134] DCE Convention, art 4, para 2.

[135] ibid arts 2 and 5. See Indicatively see Tania Voon, 'UNESCO and the WTO; A Clash of Cultures?' (2006) 55 *Oxford Review of International and Comparative Law Quarterly* 635, 639ff; Polymenopoulou *supra* note 14 at fns 89–90 and accompanying text.

[136] DCE Convention, art 25. See analytically, Voon *supra* note 135 at 645–46.

result, despite the affirmations in its Preamble on the linkages between 'freedom of thought, expression and information', diversity of the media and cultural diversity, this particular convention is unlikely to have an impact on the effective implementation of the right to artistic freedom in States parties.

One principle of interest, eventually, is the obligation of 'openness' that is also mentioned in the convention.[137] With reference to other human rights instruments this obligation could, eventually, be interpreted as an obligation to relax travelling requirements in the case of States that impose them. Freedom of movement is indispensable to allow artists to travel and participate in artistic and cultural manifestations around the world. As the former director of the Contemporary Art Institute Künstlerhaus Bethanien emphasized:

> The postmodern invention and worldwide spreading of residential arts centres are one response to the needs of artists and intellectuals to experience the world and its many environments and cultures [. . .]. The networking of centres across national and cultural barriers is part of the postmodern game, as is the crossing of borders between arts and technologies that many of these centres are able to provide.[138]

States, therefore, should take measures to facilitate travel and ensure cultural mobility for artists, musicians, dancers and other performers presenting and performing their work. This obligation includes consideration of gender-based discrimination (for instance, in the case of women artists who cannot travel due to restrictions related to male guardianship). Due to space limitations, a thorough analysis of obligations triggered under special circumstances such as war, conflict and humanitarian emergencies will not be examined. It could, however, be argued that in the context of conflict and prolonged occupation, these standards should take into account that artists may be also protected as cultural rights defenders.[139] Censorship and raids of cultural centres, for example, are regularly reported both in the Occupied

[137] ibid art 2, Principle 8 ('openness to other cultures of the world').

[138] Michael Haerdter, 'The Age of the Migrant Artist' in UNESCO *supra* note 33 at 16.

[139] cf Shaheed *supra* note 34; also 'Report of the Special Rapporteur on the Stuation of Human Rights Defenders, Margaret Sekaggya', 28 February 2011, A/HRC/16/44/Add.1 (urgent appeal regarding attacks that took place at the Visual Cultural Centre in Kiev, Ukraine); and generally, UN Human Rights Council, A/HRC/43/50 Cultural Rights Defenders, Report of the Special Rapporteur in the Field of Cultural Rights, Karima Bennoune', 20 January 2020, A/HRC/43/50, at 3, para 8 (d).

Palestinian Territories[140] and beyond,[141] while Gaza-based artists, even those with an international reputation, face significant travel restrictions.[142]

CONCLUDING REMARKS

The primary State obligation accompanying artistic freedom is a 'negative' one (in the sense of obligations to abstain from interfering with artistic freedom): the prohibition of censorship. Even this, negative, obligation par excellence however is accompanied by a positive one: an obligation to provide effective remedies (and, eventually, judicial review) in cases of unlawful interference with the right to artistic freedom and creative practice. This includes also an obligation to allow for judicial review of all decisions of classifications committees and censorship boards, especially those related in relation to films and audiovisual material. Moreover, artistic freedom is a full part of article 15 of the ICESCR, and should be rightly read in light of this article in its entirety, in particular the right to participate in cultural life under article 15, paragraph 1 of the ICESCR. The criteria established to describe positive obligations accompanying cultural rights (minimum core, availability, accessibility, adaptability, etc.) are clearly not well suited to describe obligations in relation to the concept of 'freedom'. As this chapter argued, however, obligations related to artistic freedom (and subsequently artistic practice) should be read in light of obligations accompanying the right to participate in cultural life (e.g. the fact that arts should be available, freely created and diffused, and not the product of self-censorship or event cancellation culture). Moreover, they should be interpreted in conjunction with articles 2–5 of the ICESCR that outline general and cross-cutting state obligations, including non-discrimination and equality obligations.

As discussed in this chapter, therefore, emphasizing positive obligations in relation to artistic freedom is crucial in obtaining substantial equality in cultural life. Examples range from those countries that maintain guardianship

[140] More recently, UN News, *Arrests of Palestinian Rights Defenders Part of 'Wider Crackdown'* (11 August 2021) <https://news.un.org/en/story/2021/08/1097602>, and indicatively, <www.frontlinedefenders.org/en/case/raid-yabous-cultural-centre-and-judicial-harassment-its-director-rania-elias>.

[141] For example, Rifat Fareed, 'Kashmir Police Arrest Graffiti Artist over Palestine Mural' (*Al Jazeera News*, 16 May 2021) <www.aljazeera.com/news/2021/5/16/police-crackdown-in-kashmir-over-on-pro-palestine-demonstrations>.

[142] James McAuley, 'Dreaming of van Gogh in Gaza' (*Washington Post*, 21 January 2020) <www.washingtonpost.com/world/middle_east/dreaming-of-van-gogh-in-gaza/2019/09/24/2db02cb1-cbe0-4f29-b46c-40b352c0b574_story.html>.

laws and otherwise restrict women's (artists') freedom of movement; those that do not take adequate and appropriate measures to facilitate access of persons with disabilities to artistic practice; those that place restrictions on persons (or children) of different ethnic and religious background; those that do not grant sufficient representation to members of minorities and indigenous peoples, or LGBTQ communities and members of other vulnerable groups; and those that censor human rights defenders who use creative practice to advocate in favour of reform.

5

Street Art, Graffiti and Art in Public Space

That art of the public space is always beautiful and popular is a myth. It just so happens that many times it is poorly made and highly unpopular. This is clearly unrelated to artistic talent or reputation. In fact, many controversial works in the public space belong to famous artists. When Picasso's monumental sculpture named *Chicago Picasso* was placed in the middle of Daley Plaza to contribute to Chicago's 'cultural rebirth' in 1967, one notable art critic did not hesitate to write in the local newspaper: '... some soaring lines, yes. Interesting design, I'm sure. But the fact is, it has a long stupid face and looks like some giant insect'.[1]

In addition, avant-garde and contested art that does not resonate well with public morality standards, even when cherished by cultural authorities, runs a higher risk of being vandalized. Vandalism in this context is generally associated with graffiti, which is a typically rude, provocative and at times transgressive form of expression – an 'unedited mirror of culture' as Lovata and Olton note.[2] A few years ago, the French public authorities decided to place in the garden of Louis XIV palace in Versailles a giant sculpture with a striking resemblance to a vagina. This was Anish Kapoor's installation *Dirty corner* (dubbed the *Queen's vagina*). The installation was vandalized more than three times, and in 2015 it was tagged with anti-Semitic graffiti, which the artist

1 Mike Royko, 'Picasso and the Cultural Rebirth of Chicago' (16 August 1967) <https://press.uchicago.edu/Misc/Chicago/730719.html>.

2 Troy Lovata and Elizabeth Olton, 'Introduction' in Troy Lovata and Elizabeth Olton (eds), *Understanding Graffiti: Multidisciplinary Studies from Prehistory to the Present* (2nd ed, Routledge 2016) 11, 12. For various definitions, see also Al Roundtree, 'Graffiti Artists "Get Up" in Intellectual Property's Negative Space' (2013) 31 *Cardozo Arts and Entertainment Law Journal* 959, 962–63; analytically, Marta Iljadica, *Copyright Beyond Law: Regulating Creativity in the Graffiti Subculture* (Hart 2016) at 102ff.

refused to remove (as a sign of protest against the 'abominable words').[3] Similar controversy sparked in Austria in 2003, when the municipality of Salzburg considered it a good idea for a young group of Viennese artists to exhibit an *Arc de Triomphe* made of plasticine with a recognizable penis as a fountain – only to find it vandalized later.[4] In more conservative settings, even the mere sight of nudity in the public space can spark immense controversy. For example, Damien Hirst's twelve monumental bronze sculptures representing a foetus growing in the womb that were placed in the premises of Sidra hospital in Doha, Qatar, were covered for five years, before being unveiled in 2018.[5]

Decisions on the placement or relocation of artworks (and, conversely removal of illicit street art) from the public space raise substantial dilemmas in cultural law. By necessity they involve a consideration of questions as thorny as the funding of artworks, the dynamics of public morality, urban planning considerations and the involvement of communities in cultural governance. They also imply financial commitments, especially since the removal cost of graffiti is rising. An editorial ran by the *New York Times* in 1973, for example, reveals that the cost of removing graffiti in New York alone was about 10 million dollars 'without making an appreciable dent in the spread of graffiti',[6] whereas in the entire United States during the 1990s, this cost 'exceeded $4 billion annually'.[7] In London alone, in 2002, the total cost of graffiti was estimated by the City of London at 'over £100 million per annum'.[8]

Hence, while seemingly a narrow topic, art in public spaces evokes an array of complex questions. Politics aside, their resolution requires interpretation and application of rules encompassing at least three inter-linked bodies of law:

3 Henri Neuendorf, 'Anish Kapoor Refuses to Remove Vandals' Anti-Semitic Slogans from Versailles Sculpture' (7 September 2015) <https://news.artnet.com/art-world/kapoor-vandalism-anti-semitic-330664>; also Hili Perlson, 'Anish Kapoor Forced by French Court to Remove Anti-Semitic Vandalism from Versailles Sculpture' (*Art News*, 21 September 2015) <https://news.artnet.com/art-world/anish-kapoor-dirty-corner-antisemitic-vandalism-versailles-334043>.

4 Bert Demarsin et al, *Art and Law* (Hart 2008) 29–31 (on 'Gelitin and Their Arc de Triomphe' 28, and noting however that the sculpture was exhibited in front of the Salzburg Museum of contemporary arts).

5 Naomi Rea, '"We Are Not Expecting Everyone to Like Them": Damien Hirst's Graphic Fetus Monuments Return to View in Doha' (*Art Net*, 19 November 2018) <https://news.artnet.com/art-world/damien-hirst-public-fetus-works-go-back-up-in-doha-1398895>.

6 Murray Schumach, 'At $10-Million, City Calls It a Losing Graffiti Fight' (NY *Times Archives*, 28 March 1973) <www.nytimes.com/1973/03/28/archives/at-10million-city-calls-it-a-losing-graffiti-fight-lindsay-decrying.html>.

7 Amardo Rodriguez, 'On the Origins of Anonymous Texts That Appear on Walls' in Lovata and Olton *supra* note 2 at 21, 22 (citing Brewer and Miller).

8 London Assembly, *Graffiti in London* (Report of the London Assembly Investigative Committee 2002) at 4; also cf Susan Hansen, '"This Is Not a Banksy!": Street Art as Aesthetic Protest' (2015) 29(6) *Journal of Media & Cultural Studies* 1.

intellectual property (IP) law; cultural heritage law; and human rights law. These regimes overlap with each other, but at times also clash. In addition, private interests and the interests of the public are virtually always at stake. This is true for instance with graffiti on private property (i.e. do the owners of a wall on which graffiti was unlawfully created have the right to keep the work or destroy it as they please?) but also, in the case of commissioned, yet unpopular, art as in *Chicago Picasso*. Contractual liability and IP rights too are part of the equation, as will be discussed in this chapter, with respect to the protection of artists' moral rights and the preservation of the integrity of artworks.

Due to the complexity of the topic, the first section of this chapter offers some introductory comments on the nature and evolution of graffiti, highlighting terminology issues related to street art. It further discusses the legal framework of these creative expressions in the public space, including State obligations emanating from human rights treaties, and linkages with cultural rights and cultural heritage law. In the second section the chapter examines questions related to urban planning and vandalism, focusing on the practice of human rights bodies and their interpretation of artists' 'freedom' to perform, display and exhibit their work in festivals, public events and more generally the public space – including also graffiti artists who work illegally. The chapter includes a discussion on the IP rights perspective, and protection of authors' moral rights (and their right to oppose destruction or relocation of their artworks, sculptures and installations) insofar as they relate to artistic freedom. It discusses, in particular, protections of artists and sculptors' artistic freedom in the context of moral rights in the United States, comparing this framework to the artistic freedom approach of human rights law. A detailed comparative approach to street art however (and particularly issues related to copyright in street art),[9] albeit fascinating, is an area of law that falls outside the scope of this study.

5.1 THE HUMAN RIGHTS LAW PERSPECTIVE ON GRAFFITI AND STREET ART

5.1.1 *Definitions of Graffiti and Street Art*

5.1.1.1 Terminology Issues

The term 'graffiti', is defined in principle as 'the practice of tagging and use of materials such as sprays, posters and stencils on surfaces located in public

9 For an overview in comparative law, see Enrico Bonadio, *The Cambridge Handbook of Copyright in Street Art and Graffiti* (Cambridge University Press 2019).

places'.[10] Generally, however it is used interchangeably with both 'graffiti art' and 'street art'. The former denotes graffiti with materials other than pure spray paint, such as, (e.g. stencils, stickers and posters), and is in fact more often than not political or satirical. 'Street art' in turn is a much broader term and encompasses graffiti art, but also, more complex works and installations in the public space (e.g. large murals and installations creating optical illusions).[11] Furthermore, contrary to the common presumption that considers them 'outlaws', graffiti artists are in fact more often than not trained in fine arts, design, animation, etc.[12] Finally, in order to understand the fluidity of the concept of 'street art', it is worth noting that the French equivalent of *street art* (*arts de la rue*) denotes an activity that is generally lawful and commissioned – especially since the French regional Centres for Street Art (CNAREP) have been subsumed under the auspices of the French Ministry of Culture.[13] *Arts de la rue* in this sense is typically commissioned, referring not only to visual artworks but also any kind of artistic expression in the public space, including performance, music and theatre – as well as children's theatre and events (arguably equivalent to *arts in the public space*). 'Urban art' cannot be used as a full substitute for 'street art'. Although born in urban settings (freight trains, abandoned yards and industrial areas mostly), graffiti art is not only found there, or at least not anymore. Much of it also exists in small towns and rural settings, as well as other 'unexpected locations'.[14]

5.1.1.2 Transgressive or Mainstream?

Graffiti has been historically an inherently illegal activity (the Oxford Dictionary, for example, includes the element of illegality in its definition of graffiti).[15] It is hardly of any recent vintage. Tagging on the Parthenon was

10 Rafael Schacter and John Fekner, *The World Atlas of Street Art and Graffiti* (Yale University Press 2017); Garry Hunter, *Street Art from Around the World* (Arcturus 2012).

11 Darcy Schild, 'Some Artists : An Artist Uses Spray Paint to "Carve" through Walls, and the See-Through Murals Make for Wild Optical Illusions' (17 September 2019) <www.insider.com/spray-paint-optical-illusions-2019-9>.

12 ibid (explaining that 'street art is frequently confused with graffiti, but street artists often use formal art techniques – printmaking, silk-screening, even sculpting – in contrast to the immediate, almost painterly methods of spray-can-wielding graffiti artists').

13 <www.culture.gouv.fr/Sites-thematiques/Theatre-spectacles/Organismes/Structures-de-creation-et-de-diffusion/Centres-nationaux-des-arts-de-la-rue-et-de-l-espace-public-CNAREP>.

14 Pitchaya Sudbanthad, 'Roundtable: Street Art' (*The Morning News*, 23 March 2005) <https://themorningnews.org/article/roundtable-street-art> (transcript of interview with Wooster Collective).

15 <https://en.oxforddictionaries.com/definition/graffiti> ('writing or drawings scribbled, scratched, or sprayed illicitly on a wall or other surface in a public place'). See also Lovata and

apparently one of the favourite pastimes of Phidias' workmen,[16] and the renovators of the Colosseum too;[17] it was equally discovered in the Pompeii ruins.[18] In the 1920s, graffiti became popular among gangs,[19] and in the second half of the twentieth century it resurfaced in the streets of New York as a creative offshoot of May 1968 – the apex of feminism, pacifism, rock music and the hippie movement. At the same time, graffiti *art* entered the sphere of institutions and exhibition spaces and is found incorporated in paintings – as in the case of Jean-Michel Basquiat, for example, who started his career as a graffiti artist. Graffiti artists have been inspired by the Beat Generation literature (William Burroughs, Jack Kerouac), as well as 'official' modern art – particularly abstract expressionism (Jackson Pollock) and pop art (Warhol, Lichtenstein). The interplay between arts and social change also started around the 1980s – a poignant illustration is offered by Keith Haring whose work was deeply influenced by the AIDS/HIV epidemic – and continues to date (with the variety of street artworks inspired by the Covid-19 pandemic).[20] By the 1990s graffiti had reached its fame as an unlawful, subversive, yet meaningful form of expression.[21] Baudrillard finds that it constitutes a 'symbolic destruction of social relations'.[22] Today, it is relatively common for top street artists to shift from street work to museums and galleries – even though

Olton *supra* note 2 at 14; cf also Paula Westenberger, 'Copyright Protection of Illegal Street and Graffiti Artworks' in Bonadio *supra* note 9 at 55, 58 (distinguishing between types of 'illegality'); generally also see Danwill Schwender, 'Promotion of the Arts: An Argument for Limited Copyright Protection of Illegal Graffiti' (2008) 55 *Journal of Copyright Society of the USA* 257, 260ff.

16 Andrew Szegedy-Maszak, 'Well Recorded Worth: Photographs of the Parthenon' in Jenifer Neils (ed), *The Parthenon: From Antiquity to the Present* (Cambridge University Press 2010) 331, 351–52.

17 J. A. Baird and Claire Taylor, 'Ancient Graffiti' in also A. R. Williams, 'What Does First-Century Roman Graffiti Say? Work at Rome's Colosseum Turns up 2,000-Year-Old Scrawling' (*National Geographic*, 13 January 2013) <www.nationalgeographic.com/news/2013/1/130129-roman-italy-graffiti-colosseum-archeology-photo>.

18 See Cathay Smith, 'Street Art: An Analysis under US Intellectual Property Law and Intellectual Property's "*Negative Space*" Theory' (2014) 24(6) DePaul Journal of Art, Technology & IP Law 259, 260; Schwender *supra* note 15 at 260 (at fn 21) (citing Walmesley and *Beautiful Losers: Contemporary Art And Street Culture*: 'The ancient city of Pompeii proudly displays its graffiti, with guidebooks providing as much information on the scrawls of the common man as they do sanctioned fresco works').

19 Susan Philips, 'Deconstructing Gang Graffiti' in Jeffrey Ian Ross (ed), *Routledge Handbook of Graffiti and Street Art* (Routledge 2016) 48, 48.

20 Tyson Mitman, 'Coronavirus Murals: Inside the World of Pandemic-Inspired Street Art' (*The Conversation*, 18 May 2020) <https://theconversation.com/coronavirus-murals-inside-the-world-of-pandemic-inspired-street-art-138487>.

21 Lovata and Olton *supra* note 2 at 12.

22 ibid (citing Baudrillard 1993, 77).

the sentiment of freedom is not comparable. Magazines and art galleries,[23] as well as roundtables and scientific reviews (such as the *Street Art and Urban Creativity* journal) are specifically dedicated to street art. From the perspective of a lawyer, graffiti is intriguing. No other movement has, as Gastman and Neelon emphasized, 'so thoroughly confounded the deeply held concepts of private and public property'.[24]

A trend to consider graffiti more favourably is clearly visible in academia, both in relation to its copyrightability,[25] and to some extent also, decriminalization.[26] This is equally reflected in judicial attitudes in several jurisdictions.[27] In *Pictures on the Berlin Wall*, for example, a case about graffiti on the Berlin Wall, the local German court accepted that graffiti is copyrightable even if 'the way in which the work was produced is evidently unlawful, by virtue of an act of damage to property subject to civil and criminal sanctions'.[28] US courts, too, in more recent decisions, demonstrate a tendency whereby 'protection through copyright management information' may overcome the 'unclean hands' doctrine.[29]

Regardless of the validity of these arguments, there is also the business case in favour of graffiti, as many of these works have positively contributed to cultural tourism, regardless if commissioned or not. Street-art tourism has

[23] Sudbanthad *supra* note 14.

[24] Roger Gastman and Caleb Neelon, *The History of American Graffiti* (Harper Design 2011) 23; Luma Zayad, 'Tagged: Graffiti's Advancements in Mainstream Culture through Expanded Copyright Protection in *Williams v. Cavalli*' (2019) 26 *DePaul Journal of Art, Technology & Intellectual Property Law* 161, 161.

[25] See, indicatively, Zayad *supra* note 24 at 71; Roundtree *supra* note 2 at 962 (fn 16); Sara Cloon, 'Incentivizing Graffiti: Extending Copyright Protection to a Prominent Artistic Movement' (2017) 92 *Notre Dame Law Review* 54, 55–56; Enrico Bonadio, 'Graffiti, Street Art and Copyright' (2018) 4(1) *Street Art and Urban Creativity Journal* 75, 76; also Celia Lerman, 'Protecting Artistic Vandalism: Graffiti and Copyright Law' (2013) 2 *New York University Journal of Intellectual Property and Entertainment Law* 295, 312–13; Westenberger *supra* note 15 at 56ff; generally, Iljadica *supra* note 2.

[26] Indicatively, Ian Edwards, 'Banksy's Graffiti: A Not-So-Simple Case of Criminal Damage?' (2009) 73 *Journal of Criminal Law* 345, 345 (arguing that 'the work of artists such as Banksy forces a reappraisal of the precision and applicability of criminal damage'); Gabry Vanderveen and Gwen van Eijk, 'Criminal but Beautiful: A Study on Graffiti and the Role of Value Judgments and Context in Perceiving Disorder' (2016) 22 *European Journal on Criminal Policy and Research* 107, 125 (suggesting that 'a more lenient policy may signify awareness to different views on what public space should look like').

[27] Westenberger *supra* note 15 at 56ff and generally the contributions in Bonadio *supra* note 9 (and insights, e.g. from France, Germany, Italy, Greece).

[28] *Re Pictures* on the *Berlin Wall* (Case I ZR 68/93) [1997] ECC 553, see, indicatively, Iljadica *supra* note 2 at 107–08; Marc Mimler, 'Street Art, Graffiti and Copyright: A German Perspective' in Bonadio *supra* note 9 at 188–206; also Westenberger *supra* note 15 at 60.

[29] Zayad *supra* note 24 at 169–72; Enrico Bonadio, 'Street Art, Graffiti and Copyright: A US Perspective' in Bonadio *supra* note 9 at 105–22.

been booming and world street art festivals are opening up to highly profitable markets of alternative collectors and the profitable 'snowboard, surf and skate' culture.[30] States are increasingly interested in strategies to attract tourists by enhancing their profile as open and culturally diverse. These strategies are based on the city's urban profile, and do not distinguish between illicit and commissioned street art. The official 'Visit London' website, for example, proudly announces that 'London has one of the biggest and best collections of un-commissioned street art in the world' that visitors can easily discover, by booking one of the many local graffiti and street art tours.[31] These tours are typically complemented by workshops where one will be able to meet 'real street artists' – as in the case of the top TripAdvisor 'Street Art Paris graffiti mural workshop taught by real, yes, real, Parisian graffiti artists'.[32] In Berlin and New York, workshops are also available for children and school tours.[33] In Beijing, graffiti has not only started popping up in various neighbourhoods, but also, a particular section of the Great Wall has been dedicated to graffiti creations.[34] Even in the Gulf, street art and urban lifestyle are increasingly relatively popular, and to some extent fashionable. The municipality of Riyadh, in the Kingdom of Saudi Arabia, for example, launched in April 2019 a series of 'Beautifying Riyadh's Murals' events by inviting the best Saudi graffiti artists to beautify public places as part of the Kingdom's Vision 2030.[35] This, in turn, means that it is highly unlikely for local authorities to take down artworks from which they benefit. Visual street art is in fact already largely institutionalized, being part of festivals and exhibitions and museums that contribute to reshaping the counter cultural narrative in the context of museum institutions.[36] This is due to the immense success of the urban-style

30 <https://hkwalls.org/>.

31 <www.visitlondon.com/tickets-and-offers?ref=nav>.

32 <http://streetartparis.fr/graffiti-mural-workshop/>

33 <https://grafftours.com/graffiti-workshops-nyc/group-graffiti-lesson/>; <https://urban-nation.com/plan-your-visit/>.

34 'Features: The Great Wall of China: Tangible, Intangible and Destructible' <www.chinaheritagequarterly.org/features.php?searchterm=001_greatwall.inc&issue=001>, based on a well-publicized study of the Australian National University (ANU) (revealing that graffiti art on the Great Wall was popular already in the sixteenth century 'when soldiers' wives decorated parts of the wall with images of clouds, lotus blossoms and fluffy balls'). See also Carolyne Look, 'Graffiti on the Great Wall: The Hidden Street Art Culture of Beijing Street' <www.gsdmagazine.org/graffiti-on-the-great-wall-the-hidden-street-art-culture-of-beijing/>.

35 Anon, 'Saudis Bid to Beautify Their Cities with Street Art' (*Arab News*, 15 April 2019) <www.arabnews.com/node/1482066/saudi-arabia>. Generally, Sabrina de Turk, *Street Art in the Middle East* (IB Tauris 2019).

36 E.g. Andrew Wasserman, 'Sites of Counter-Culture: The Move of the New Museum to the Bowery' in Cher Krause Knight and Harriet Senie (eds), *Museums and Public Art?* (Cambridge

street art fashion, which is now a defining element of urban lifestyle, and products, including clothing, accessories and sports equipment. Ultimately, street art has become a significant commodity in the agenda of the tourism industry and in urban development – and an 'unavoidable element of cities around the world'.[37]

5.1.2 *Graffiti as a Grey Area in Law*

5.1.2.1 Legal Treatment in Domestic Laws

Both graffiti and street art are punishable under domestic criminal laws – most typically by laws concerning damage or defacement of property (criminal damage).[38] Street art, in addition, may be caught under other types of legislation, particularly criminal laws relating to vandalism and public morality (or 'social behaviour'),[39] as well as administrative laws. The latter could include, urban planning regulations; protection of cultural heritage and historic buildings; and laws on clean environment and 'neighbourhoods'.[40] In addition, street art may be encompassed under anti-graffiti-specific legislation. New York City, for example, has passed by-laws on the 'defacement of property by means of aerosol spray' as early as the 1970s. Originally misdemeanours, these offences have been reclassified in New York as 'crimes' under the city's *zero tolerance* approach to graffiti, initiated by former New York mayor, Rudolph Giuliani. In addition, criminal liability emerges regardless of the actual content of the work (e.g. in case that the actual representation is deemed to be obscene, blasphemous, hateful, etc.), which in turn may also give rise to a second criminal offence. An example is the case of the widespread graffiti slogan 'Putin is a d*head' that was scrawled virtually in every wall in Ukraine

Scholar 2018) 181, 185ff (discussing the relocation of the *New Museum* in New York to a 'former skid-row' and the exhibition *Counter-culture*).

37 Alexandra Duncan, 'From the Street to a Gallery' in Lovata and Olton *supra* note 2 at 126, 129; cf also Smith *supra* note 18 at 262 ('Street art today has become a hot commodity').

38 cf UK Criminal Damage Act 1971, which contains provisions on 'Destroying or damaging property' and punishes damages with imprisonment and penalties; French Criminal Code, Chapter V (penalties ranging from 1,500 to 30,000 euros). Indicatively, Edwards *supra* note 26 at 345, 348ff.

39 By way of example, see the UK Anti-social Behaviour, Crime and Policing Act 2014 (Publication of Public Spaces Protection Orders) Regulations 2014.

40 For example, the UK Clean Neighbourhoods and Environment Act 2005. See indicatively, Enrico Bonadio, 'Street Art, Graffiti and Copyright: A UK Perspective' in Bonadio *supra* note 9 at 159–74; also cf Andrew Millie, 'Crimes of the Senses: Yarn Bombing and Aesthetic Criminology' (2019) 59 (6) *The British Journal of Criminology* 1269, 1269.

following the Russian annexation of Crimea (and shortly after a Ukrainian diplomat had used the vulgar word for Putin 'delighting protesters and angering Moscow').[41] In this case the author of the graffiti could be prosecuted not only for damage and vandalism but also insult of public officials and state symbols.[42] The public's reactions to such street art simply makes freedom of expression debates more visible and more intense.

5.1.2.2 State Obligations under Human Rights Law

The protection of graffiti artists and other artists who work in the public space is not expressly found in any human rights instrument. Protections, however, applicable to artistic freedom and more broadly cultural rights (including also the protection that should be afforded to cultural rights defenders) apply in all types of creative expression.[43] Additional State obligations in relation to authorizations and the use of the public space may also be relevant. As discussed in Chapter 4, positive obligations accompanying participation in cultural life and making arts accessible under article 15 of the International Covenant on Economic, Social and Cultural Rights (ICESCR) should be read in light of artistic freedom and article 27 of the Universal Declaration of Human Rights (UDHR). Positive obligations therefore may imply opportunities for artists to present their work in the public space, such as parks and public gardens, especially on the occasion of open-air festivals and summer events. This was also highlighted in the report of UN Special Rapporteur on Cultural Rights Karima Bennoune in 2019 in relation to culture and the public space, which underlines the linkages between cultural rights and 'vibrant and accessible public spaces',[44] highlighting that 'public authorities should promote the presence of arts in public spaces as part of the right to have access to a wide variety of artistic expression'.[45]

The same findings apply to vulnerable groups considered beneficiaries of street art. Children are eventually the first such category, given the importance of the arts for the development of the child. This point is specifically raised in the reports of the UN Committee on the Rights of the Child in its elaboration

[41] Adam Taylor, '"Khuilo": The Offensive Term That Has Attached Itself to Putin' (*Washington Post*, 17 June 2014).

[42] The Criminal Code of the Russian Federation No 63-Fz of 13 June 1996, art 319: Insult of a Representative of Power.

[43] See Chapter 2 of this book.

[44] Karima Bennoune, 'The Importance of Public Spaces for the Exercise of Cultural Rights, Report of the UN Special Rapporteur on Cultural Rights', 30 July 2019, A/74/255, paras 58–60.

[45] ibid at para 63.

of article 31(1) of the Convention on the Rights of the Child, which provides that 'States Parties recognize the right of the child to rest and leisure, to engage in play and recreational activities appropriate to the age of the child and to participate freely in cultural life and the arts'.[46] According to the committee, street art contributes to generating a 'culture of childhood',[47] and is a particularly important element for children's development – physical, emotional, cultural and sentimental.[48] With respect to visual street arts, in particular, positive obligations would include the commissioning of at least a minimum number of meaningful and culturally relevant street art works, to the extent of a State's available resources – as well as minimizing vandalism and arguably also random graffiti tags (i.e. those without aesthetic value) in order to maintain a clean environment.

In addition, artists should have the opportunity to assemble for the purpose of performances and public display of their works (for instance, in festivals) *freely*, without cumbersome formalities and excessive pre-authorizations. In other words, States have obligations not to interfere in cultural gatherings, which are, additionally, protected under the freedom of peaceful assembly. In its General Comment no 37, for example, the Human Rights Committee has highlighted that freedom of association (article 21 of the ICCPR) is applicable in assemblies that serve cultural objectives or entertainment.[49] Accordingly, States have a negative obligation not to interfere, and not to set prior authorizations,[50] especially cumbersome and bureaucratic ones. As the committee notes, '[f]reedom of peaceful assembly is a right and not a privilege and as such its exercise should not be subject to prior authorization by the authorities'. According to its General Comment no 37, the Human Rights Committee emphasized that a primary negative duty of States applicable in peaceful assemblies is the obligation not to interfere, as well as to arrange for notification requirements (rather than prior authorizations). As the Committee states, a prohibition of peaceful assembly should only be a measure of 'last resort', and States must impose only the 'least intrusive' measures to restrict it.[51] Furthermore, it could be argued that cultural activism by means of artistic

46 Convention on the Rights of the Child, art 31, para 1.

47 Committee on the Rights of the Child, 'General Comment no 17 (2013), The Right of the Child to Rest, Leisure, Play, Recreational Activities, Cultural Life and the Arts' (art 31), 17 April 2013, CRC/C/GC/17, paras 11–12.

48 ibid at para 15.

49 UN Human Rights Committee, General Comment no 37, The Right of Peaceful Assembly', (art 21) CCPR/C/GC/37, 17 September 2020, para 12.

50 ibid paras 70–74.

51 ibid paras 37–38.

performances or concerts in the public space are also protected through freedom of assembly provisions, especially when amounting to human rights activism.[52] The same standard, however, cannot arguably be applied to milder types of activism that amount to vandalism, as is the case with street artists, who deploy a range of tactics 'to critique, subvert, and otherwise "jam" the workings of consumer culture'.[53] This type of 'jamming' will be typically undertaken against advertisements and arguably falls outside the protective scope of cultural rights. An example is the work of 'Zevs', a French graffiti artist who acquired his fame[54] by doing what he called 'logo liquidations' (*liquidation de marque*),[55] that is, tagging advertisement posters in Parisian bus stops.

5.1.2.3 Arguments against Removal from the Public Space

The punishment for graffiti or graffiti art by criminal sanctions is rarely contested in court. Such a 'rare occasion' was the case of a well-known Swiss graffiti artist named Naegeli, who was held criminally liable for damages under Swiss law for damaging 'by means of an aerosol spray' another person's wall. In addition to the action in tort, a criminal prosecution also took place (for the prevention of public disorder).[56] When the case arrived in Strasbourg, the now defunct European Commission of Human Rights ruled against graffiti art.[57] One of Naegeli's arguments was that the law on the protection of private property against damage did not apply in his case, since the buildings he had bomb-sprayed had not been damaged but, on the contrary, augmented in value.[58] The commissioners, although considering the question of a potentially different treatment of the arts as 'open-ended', did not go as far as to endorse Naegeli's claim.

Does this mean, therefore, that at some point the question could have attracted a different solution, whereby a human rights court would recognize the value of graffiti as street art and as an exercise of artistic freedom? Theoretically, under the

52 On this argument, see also Eleni Polymenopoulou, 'Expressing Dissent: "Gag Laws", Human Rights Activism and the Right to Protest' (2021) 32 *Florida Journal of International Law* 1.

53 Marilyn DeLaure and Moritz Fink (eds), *Culture Jamming: Activism and the Art of Cultural Resistance* (NYU Press 2017).

54 <www.debuckgallery.com/artists/zevs/>, noting that Zevs has 'risen to become one of the most prominent figures on the contemporary street art scene'.

55 Duncan *supra* note 37 at 129.

56 ibid *in fine*. Before the Court, Switzerland claimed that the prevention of public disorder was also at stake.

57 See *N. v Switzerland* App no 9870/82, Commission Decision, 13 October 1983. 'Painting, by means of an aerosol spray, on walls belonging to another person, against the wishes of the owners'.

58 ibid.

present framework of human rights law this perspective cannot be excluded. This is because State obligations to respect, protect and fulfil individual rights do not extend necessarily to removing graffiti or street art from the public space – and not even to giving private interests a carte blanche privilege. Human rights law contains rules of a constitutional nature, applicable to all human beings – with no exceptions or distinctions. As stipulated in article 27 of the UDHR and article 15(1)(a) of the ICESCR, everyone has the right to participate in the cultural life of the community *freely*.[59] In principle, therefore, it does not depend on any conditions or qualifications – such as the originality of creations for example, or the ability to express the author's personality based on creative choices, as would be the case with IP law.[60] At the same time, recognition of economic rights under human rights instruments is also a solid part of the UDHR[61] and article 15 of the ICESCR.[62] In addition, the exercise of artistic freedom as a human right is not subject to any value-based standards or quality considerations. Artistic freedom can be subject to restrictions and limitations only exceptionally – on specific grounds, narrowly construed and strictly in accordance with necessity and proportionality tests,[63] taking into account the particular circumstances of the artwork's creation. Hence, limitations would 'by default' weigh more heavily in case of conflict between the individual artist's rights and the preservation of public safety. The question may often come up as a matter of cultural policy, especially with respect to large interactive or accessible artworks and installations. This is a usual problem in artworks associated with safety considerations (e.g. an urban sculpture named the *Traffic Light Tree* originally placed at a roundabout in East London was blamed for causing traffic confusion) and even deadly incidents (e.g. a large installation named *Dreamspace* by Maurice Agis in 2008 fell while displayed, killing two people).[64]

On the other hand, arguments against removal of artworks can be reinforced by the rights of the public to access art. Removal of works from the public space, therefore, is a form of interference with the rights of the public to access a particular artwork – which is interesting, as the public

59 See Chapter 2 of this book (on the *travaux* of the UDHR and the ICESCR).

60 Indicatively, CJEU, C-145/10 *Eva-Maria Painer v Standard Verlags GmbH* 1 (on the 'free and creative choices of the author'); US Supreme Court, *Feist Publications, Inc., v Rural Telephone Service Co.* 499 US 340 (1991) (on the requirement of a 'minimum creative spark' for the work to be considered original).

61 Article 29, paragraph 2 of the UDHR proclaims protection of one's moral and material interests and 'resulting from any scientific, literary or artistic production of which he is the author'.

62 Economic rights of authors protected under 15(1) (c) of the ICESCR.

63 See Chapters 2 and 3 of this book.

64 Louise Jury, 'The End of a Dream: Dreamspace Turns into a Nightmare' (*BBC News*, 25 July 2006) <http://news.bbc.co.uk/2/hi/uk_news/england/7856121.stm>.

generally does not distinguish between lawful and unlawful artworks. As the Committee on Economic, Social and Cultural Rights (CESCR) has stipulated in its General Comment on author's rights, in its examination of article 15(1)(b) ICESCR, the rights of authors cannot be 'isolated' from other ICESCR rights – such as the right of the public to 'access art'.[65] This is equally true in respect of the general standards stipulated by the UN Human Rights Committee, the European Court of Human Rights (ECtHR) and other human rights bodies in assessing the legitimacy of restrictions on rights – chiefly, the necessity and proportionality tests. The CESCR, too, has noted in respect of limitations against authors' rights that these 'must be proportionate' and 'compatible with the very nature of the rights protected in article 15(1)(c), which lies in the protection of the personal link between the author and his/her creation'.[66] In other words, the rights of the public are not affected by the actual circumstances of an artwork as commissioned or not. Even supposing that the author himself cannot claim the right to artistic freedom due to its illegal placement, the public still maintains the right to view the work. This could happen, for example, in cases where citizens themselves bring a relevant complaint under mechanisms protecting their access to cultural and artistic works. This would arguably not go as far as giving rise to an obligation not to remove simple graffiti tags (for which authors run the risk of illegality) – or to safeguard illicit art, protecting it from damage. Such issues have not yet been addressed in States' reports before the CESCR (which only briefly touches upon cultural rights),[67] neither a fortiori in individual communications – nor in fact before domestic courts. There is no visible perspective that this will happen anytime soon – as the authorities will most likely be keen on maintaining works in respect of which the public has an interest. For example, Banksy's *Well Hung Lover* painted illicitly on the walls of a public family planning clinic in Bristol is still there today as the local residents voted not to remove it and the borough granted its retrospective permission.[68]

[65] ibid at 35.

[66] UN CESCR, General Comment no 17 (2005), 'The Right of Everyone to Benefit from the Protection of the Moral and Material Interests Resulting from Any Scientific, Literary or Artistic Production of Which He or She Is the Author' (art 15, para 1 (c), of the covenant), 12 January 2006, E/C.12/GC/17 at para 23. See, indicatively, Tzen Wong, Mollie Torsen and Claudia Fernandini, 'Cultural Diversity and the Arts: Contemporary Challenges for Copyright Law' in Tzen Wong and Graham Dutfie (eds), *Intellectual Property and Human Development: Current Trends and Future Scenarios* (Cambridge University Press 2009) 279–328.

[67] See Chapter 4 on States' obligations.

[68] Debra Mancoff, 'Banksy: British Graffiti Artist' in *Encyclopedia Britannica* <www.britannica.com/biography/Banksy>.

This, however, does not mean that all works will be considered immune from removal or destruction. Some degree of qualitative evaluation will need to take place, that is, arguments in favour of preferential treatment regarding artistic freedom under specific circumstances and only examined on a case-by-case basis. At present, such claims of preferential treatment in the form of 'defences' for the arts have been occasionally accepted by the ECtHR in relation to artistic and literary works.[69] Similar defences could also eventually be applied to graffiti and street art, taking into account the site-specificity of the works; the public's preferences; and necessarily also the aesthetic value of these works (as clearly, the public will be unlikely to vote in favour of preserving, say, ugly or bad art). This would also entail that some works will necessarily fall outside the protective scope of human rights law. For example, tags would have minimal chances of surviving the 'balancing exercise' against street art of significant political content or major aesthetic value. In other words, street artist 'Tox' who is considered the 'King of taggers' in London (convicted of criminal damage on multiple counts by a London court in 2011)[70] would arguably not stand the same chance as Banksy's, say, *Spy Booth* in avoiding criminal punishment. In the case of *Spy Booth*, the local council of Cheltenham (United Kingdom) legitimized it retrospectively because it attracted tourists, even though part of the work was actually painted *on* a classified monument.[71]

5.1.3 *Street Art for Future Generations?*

5.1.3.1 Murals and the Preservation of Cultural Identities

The last question to examine is whether the exercise of artistic freedom in the case of street art could, eventually, give rise to a positive obligation by States to preserve and safeguard it. An example of a great street art project in need of restoration is the *Great Wall of Los Angeles* in California – a mural painted on the wall adjacent to a Flood Control Channel in the City of Los Angeles, stretching over half a mile. The *Great Wall* represents the history of ethnic

69 See on this, Eleni Polymenopoulou, 'Does One Swallow Make a Spring? Artistic and Literary Freedom at the European Court of Human Rights' (2016) 3 *Human Rights Law Review* 511, 531ff (noting that established and emerging defences encompass the political nature of the works; their eventual contribution to the public debate; as well as humour and satire).

70 Caroline Davies, "Tox" Graffiti Artist Convicted of Criminal Damage' (*Reuters*, 7 June 2011) <www.theguardian.com/artanddesign/2011/jun/07/tox-graffiti-artist-criminal-damage>.

71 Peter Levy, 'Who Owns Street Art? Missing Banksy Mural Sparks Debate' <https://worldcrunch.com/culture-society/who-owns-street-art-missing-banksy-mural-sparks-debate>

peoples of California. It was created between 1974 and 1984 by teams of young people. It was the first art project of the Social and Public Art Resource Center in Los Angeles (SPARC-LA),[72] and employed 'over 400 youth and their families from diverse social and economic backgrounds working with artists'.[73] It is irrelevant whether this project therefore started as illicit or not. The *Great Wall* is currently considered 'one of Los Angeles' true cultural landmarks and one of the country's most respected and largest monuments to inter-racial harmony'[74] and is even part of the US 'Register of Historic Places'. Similar projects would be, for example, *Calle Regina 56* – a street art project in downtown Mexico City, which commenced in 2009,[75] or the *Community Mural Project*, a series of collaborative murals painted in the 1990s in Durban, South Africa, depicting the South African struggles of independence and the fight against apartheid.[76] Such projects are not only successful in 'beautifying' the towns they have been created in. With the passage of time, they become integral parts of the cities' urban and cultural identities – apart from their great aesthetic value, they also visually express the idea of solidarity among citizens.[77] The question that comes to mind naturally, therefore, is whether any protective mechanisms exist to safeguard and maintain such heritage. UNESCO itself was set up precisely with the aim of establishing the 'intellectual and moral solidarity of mankind'.[78]

An argument in favour of the preservation of such murals could be entrenched on the right to participate in cultural life. Surely, neither individual nor group identities are expressly protected under international human rights law. A right to preserve one's cultural identity, however, is generally deduced from three elements: first, the right to participation in cultural life

72 <https://sparcinla.org/programs/the-great-wall-mural-los-angeles/>.

73 <www.nps.gov/places/great-wall-of-los-angeles.htm>; <https://sparcinla.org/programs/the-great-wall-mural-los-angeles/>.

74 ibid.

75 Pamela Scheinman, 'A Wall in Mexico's City Historic Centre: Calle Regina 56' in Lovata and Olton *supra* note 2 at 219–32.

76 Sabine Marschall, 'A Postcolonial Reading of Mural Art in South Africa' (2000) 14 (2) *Critical Arts: A South-North Journal of Cultural & Media Studies* 96, 101 (noting that while writing on these projects a journalist coined the term 'official graffiti' to denote – and 'urban art tolerated by officials').

77 cf Maliha Ikram, 'Long-Term Preservation of Public Art: From Cultural Heritage to the Confederacy' (2018) 14(1) *Northwestern Journal of Law and Social Policy* 37, 69 (arguing further that the government should maintain such property under the American 'public trust' doctrine). Marschall *supra* note 76 at 68.

78 UNESCO Charter, art 1.

(as noted also by the CESCR);[79] second, the nature of legal obligations imposed on States by the ICESCR and the collective dimension of cultural rights, especially in relation to minority and indigenous peoples' rights.[80] Third, identities are also recognized by the UNESCO as elements of cultural pluralism. Article 2 of the 2001 UNESCO Declaration on Cultural Diversity, for example, provides,

> in our increasingly diverse societies, it is essential to ensure harmonious interaction among people and groups with plural, varied and dynamic cultural identities as well as their willingness to live together. Policies for the inclusion and participation of all citizens are guarantees of social cohesion, the vitality of civil society and peace [. . .].

An obligation to safeguard murals reflective of broad community participation, therefore, particularly in rural and deprived urban areas,[81] could also be deduced from the protection of cultural heritage. The definition of the latter includes artistic expression that 'provides [both "communities and groups"] with a sense of identity and continuity, thus promoting respect for cultural diversity and human creativity'.[82] As a whole, the protection of cultural heritage is increasingly associated with the cultural rights of communities to access that heritage.[83] In addition, graffiti art is associated with strong communal bonds enhancing the sense of identity (including hip-hop and breakdance culture and skating),[84] as graffiti artists generally work in teams (or *crews*) from

79 Indicatively, UN CESCR,'General Comment no 21, Right of Everyone to Take Part in Cultural Life' (art 15, para 1 (a), of the International Covenant on Economic, Social and Cultural Rights), 21 December 2009, E/C.12/GC/21 at 4, para 15 (a).

80 Indicatively, Yvonne Donders, 'Towards a Right to Cultural Identity?' (2002) 15 *School of Human Rights Research Series*; Laura Pineschi, 'Cultural Diversity as a Human Right? General Comment No. 21 of the Committee on Economic, Social and Cultural Rights' in Silvia Borelli and Federico Lenzerini (eds), *Cultural Heritage, Cultural Rights, Cultural Diversity* (Martinus Nijhoff 2012) 28–53; also Eleni Polymenopoulou, 'Cultural Rights in the Case-Law of the International Court of Justice' (2014) 27(2) *Leiden Journal of International Law* 447, 451ff.

81 ibid at 53.

82 UNESCO Convention of Intangible Heritage, art 2 (definition of intangible heritage).

83 On the intersections between cultural heritage and cultural rights, see also UN Human Rights Council, 'Report of the Special Rapporteur in the Field of Cultural Rights, Karima Bennoune', UN 3 February 2016, UN Doc A/HRC/31/59; also UN Human Rights Council, 'Report of the Independent Expert in the Field of Cultural Rights, Farida Shaheed', 21 March 2011, UN Doc A/HRC/17/38.

84 See *Style Wars* (documentary), 1983 <www.imdb.com/title/tt0177262/> (documentary exposing the rich growing subculture of hip-hop of New York City in the late 1970s and early 1980s).

the same neighbourhood.[85] Particular ways of working on street art projects therefore (especially murals) would be likely to fall under the protective scope of intangible heritage. This is especially true for certain types of street art involving craftsmanship,[86] such as *yarn bombing*/knitted graffiti and *crochet art* on trees (commonly perceived as 'markedly feminine' – or the 'softer side' of street art).[87]

5.1.3.2 Murals as Urban Cultural Heritage

What follows, therefore, is whether murals and street art projects such as the *Great Wall* or *Calle Regina* could equally be considered for potential nomination and inclusion in the UNESCO list created under the World Heritage Convention. In theory, this is only possible insofar as it can be proved that a certain artwork is of such outstanding quality that reflects 'the world heritage of mankind as a whole', meeting at least one of the UNESCO list of formal criteria.[88] The World Heritage Convention specifically encompasses monuments and sites in its definition, including also 'works of monumental sculpture and painting',[89] and provides for a State duty to preserve such works in view of transmission to 'future generations'.[90] In practice, however, this is unlikely for States to happen anytime soon, given the scarcity of monumental works of street art and the intense competition for these nominations. A more palatable perspective therefore would be to start including street art of exceptional value in national inventories, enhancing national inscriptions. This

85 Philips *supra* note 19 at 68 (Philips, herself a graffiti artist, explains how crews are different from gangs. Their bond with the urban space and sense of urban belonging is also exemplified by the fact that nicknames are often devised with reference to cities and streets one is working in – for instance, 'Taki 183' with reference to street number 183). cf also Mitman *supra* note 20 at 197; also Schwender *supra* note 15 at 261.

86 cf Francesco Francioni, 'Article 2(1): Defining Intangible Cultural Heritage' in Janet Blake and Lucas Lixinski (eds), *The 2003 UNESCO Intangible Heritage Convention: A Commentary* (Cambridge University Press 2020).

87 Minna Haveri, 'Yarn Bombing – The Softer Side of Street Art' in Ross *supra* note 19 at 48–60. See also Millie *supra* note 40 at 1272–73. See however, Jessica Pabón, 'Ways of Being Seen: Gender and the Writing on the Wall' in Ross *supra* note 19 at 78–91.

88 Operational Guidelines on the World Heritage Convention, WHC.19/01 10 July 2019 ('suggestions of attributes' which 'might be considered as conveying or expressing Outstanding Universal Value').

89 UNESCO 1972 Convention, art 1.

90 ibid art 4: 'each State Party to this Convention recognizes that the duty of ensuring the identification, protection, conservation, presentation and transmission to future generations of the cultural and natural heritage [. . .]'.

would also allow for better allocation of funds for the safeguarding of street art – especially for those murals in need of restoration.

A better approach could find support in human rights law and the right to participate in cultural life. Community murals constitute genuine realizations of the obligations stipulated in article 15 of the ICESCR concerning everyone's right to 'participate in the arts of the community'. The ICESCR, in addition, specifies that 'the steps to be taken by the States Parties to the present Covenant to achieve the full realization of this right shall include those necessary for the conservation, the development and the diffusion of science and culture'.[91] As the South African White Paper on Arts Culture and Heritage (1996) stipulated in relation to the Durban murals, 'access to, participation in and enjoyment of the arts, cultural expressions and the preservation of one's heritage are basic human rights; they are not luxuries nor are they privileges as we have been led to believe'.[92]

In addition, a right to 'access cultural heritage' is deduced by the ICESCR, article 15, paragraph 1 (a) and positive obligations accompanying the right to participate in cultural life.[93] It is also made explicit in other instruments – for example, the Council of Europe's Framework Convention on the Value of Cultural Heritage for Society (2005).[94] The new question, therefore, is whether States should have an obligation to facilitate the public's access to street art as a form of cultural heritage. In certain contexts, this is not solely for the purpose of entertainment. For example, in Mexico, community practices are commonly advertised on murals – the so-called Bardas de Baille[95] – to which the authorities typically turn a blind eye.

Even so, the exact rationale underpinning the protection of illegal street art remains to a large extent contested. This is precisely because of the deep-rooted nature of graffiti as subversive, as explained above. This, in turn, resurfaces the distinctions between 'poor art' and 'high art' for which the debate continues to rage – in the same way it was mooted back in 1945, when UNESCO was created to 'assure the conservation and protection of the

91 ICESCR para 2.

92 Marschall *supra* note 76 at 99.

93 See Chapter 4.

94 This framework convention provides that 'the Parties to this Convention agree to: (a) recognise that rights relating to cultural heritage are inherent in the right to participate in cultural life [. . .]'.

95 Patricia Cué, *Mexican Wall Painting: Bardas De Baile* (Ghost & Co. 2013); Steven Heller, 'The Writing on Mexican Walls Isn't Graffiti – It's "Vernacular Branding"' (*The Atlantic*, 1 August 2013) <www.theatlantic.com/entertainment/archive/2013/08/the-writing-on-mexican-walls-isnt-graffiti-its-vernacular-branding/278116>.

world's inheritance of books, works of art and monuments of history and science [...]'.[96] Should States strive to safeguard graffiti and art murals as they do for Venus de Milo, Roman baths and other antiquities? And if this is so, then should creative graffiti artists be protected on an equal footing with Renoir and Rebrand? States will be necessarily better placed to decide on their cultural (and urban) policies, following a thorough assessment of conflicting priorities and domestic cultural politics, which typically fall outside the sphere of international law.

5.2 ARTISTIC FREEDOM, CULTURAL HERITAGE AND URBAN PLANNING

5.2.1 *Is Contemporary Street Art Cultural Heritage?*

5.2.1.1 *La Demeure du Chaos (Abode of Chaos)*

There could be a valid reason to believe that forty years after *Naegeli*[97] the views of the ECtHR would be at least slightly different today. Yet, even supposing that the Court has now started paying more attention to artistic creation, its case law has not developed in a way that justifies graffiti artists' immunities against criminal liability. In fact, the Court's jurisprudence is complemented by the strict margin of appreciation afforded to national authorities in determining cultural policies and urban planning and maintaining the lawfulness of pre-authorization for graffiti art. Astonishingly, this entails that graffiti art may be illegal even if created on one's *own* walls.

An interesting case is that concerning the property of an artist in Saint-Romain-au-Mont-d'Or, a small city in the French countryside, close to Lyon. The property is known as '*La Demeure du Chaos*' *(Abode of Chaos)*, which started as Mr Ehrmann's personal project in 1999, through which he endeavoured to transform his property, a seventeenth century listed building, into 'a kind of monument to his eclectic religious beliefs, which range from Roman Catholicism to alchemy'.[98] The *Demeure* was used by various artists as a residence,[99] as well as an exhibition space for collective street-art style projects, addressing 'aspects of life like war and destruction and hatred and terrorism'.[100]

96 UNESCO Charter, art 1 ('Purposes and Functions of the UNESCO').
97 See Chapter 1 of this book (on the definition of the art in law).
98 John Tagliabue, 'It's His House. But, Village Traditionalists Ask, Is It Art?' (*NY Times*, 19 July 2006) <www.nytimes.com/2006/07/19/world/europe/19france.html>.
99 *Ehrmann and SCI VHI v France* App no 2777/10, Admissibility, 7 June 2011, at 2 (inadmissible).
100 Tagliabue *supra* note 98.

It was also characterized by the local artistic community as a 'contemporary art museum', with more than 3,000 paintings and construction works forming part of it, including inscriptions; drawings of skulls and salamanders; as well as blocks of black stone on the wall representing meteorites. In 2006, the *Demeure* had achieved 'ERP status' under French law (i.e. establishment receiving the general public), receiving about 120,000 visitors per year and 'reported widely in the press, art reviews, films and documentaries'.[101]

Following a largely mediatized controversy, the French courts found the artist criminally liable for breaching the provisions of the French Planning Code, the *Code de l'urbanisme*. That Code, in fact, contained an exception for statues, monuments and 'works of art' from planning permission.[102] The French courts, however, did not find the exception applicable. At the first round of domestic proceedings, the Lyon Criminal Court found the applicant guilty 'on the charge of failing to comply with the land-use plan' (Planning Code) and for placing on the outer walls of the property without planning permission 'paintings, inscriptions and drawings in red or black, together with blocks of black stone, resulting in the alteration of their external appearance'.[103] It also found a breach of the French cultural heritage law (Heritage Code), which required prior authorization for alterations in respect of any property in a position of joint visibility with edifices in the French secondary list of historical buildings – a church and a manor house.[104] Without examining the eventual contribution of the *La Demeure du Chaos* to the artistic and cultural life of the wider community, it ordered the applicant, owner of the *Demeure*, to pay an extraordinary criminal fine amounting to 200,000 euros, 'in light of the requirements of public safety, construction safety and compliance with the basic rules governing environmental protection'. The fine was maintained by the Court of Appeals of Lyon, which did, however, set aside the restitution order – recognizing the *Demeure* as an artistic creation of 'certain

101 ibid.

102 Article R 421-1 of the *code de l'Urbanisme*, invoked by Lyons Court of Appeal judgment, 13 September 2006, cited in the decision. The code subjected any operations capable of altering the appearance of the property to prior authorization – which *La Demeure* had not applied for.

103 *Ehrmann supra* note 99 (citing the *Tribunal de Grande Instance* of Lyon, 29 November and 4 December 2004).

104 ibid at 3 (referring to the judgment of the Lyons Court of Appeal, 4 December 2004 and Article L. 621-31 of the French Heritage Code). The *Demeure* was also in breach of the local land-use plan that stipulated that 'constructions . . . must blend into the surrounding landscape'.

physical volume'.[105] That decision was quashed by the French Court of Cassation, and, in accordance with French criminal procedure, was referred back to a lower court for a second time – this time the Grenoble Court of Appeal. This court, in turn, found the applicant liable to pay a fine of 30,000 euros for urban planning offences (Planning Code), and also revived the original restoration order.[106] With respect to the artistic nature of the project and freedom of arts claim, it indicated in passing that the question whether the *Demeure* should be characterized as a work of art 'was not for the criminal court to decide'.[107]

In an unusually long admissibility decision, the European Court agreed with the French courts and found the applicant's article 10 claim inadmissible. The restoration order and associated fine for failure to receive prior authorization were both found to constitute measures that were necessary in a democratic society for the prevention of disorder, while the general interest, according to the Court, was 'constituted by the protection of heritage' and 'requir[ing] that the applicants comply with certain planning regulations'.[108]

In spite of the noteworthy justification, it is difficult to overlook the antiquated approach to street art in the contemporary urban space. By finding itself incompetent to pronounce on the nature of the artworks at stake, it implicitly validated the French classification system – which privileges by default one type of 'heritage' (historic monuments) over another (contemporary street art). Furthermore, the Court found that 'the particular case concerned a limitation on the exercise of freedom of expression, which was confined to the boundary wall and outer wall [...] and did not affect the work as a whole'.[109] This is also an odd rationale – in essence a way to avoid discussing further the nature of the artworks at stake, as the point of artistic freedom is to maintain precisely the integrity of an entire artwork against removal or destruction, rather than only part of it.

[105] *Ehrmann supra* note 99 at para 4 (noting that the Court of Appeals of Lyon in fact did recognize that the *Demeure du Chaos* was 'indisputably a work of art', which 'imposes that it is not destroyed, nor modified' (as the original judgment states) [in French, our trnsl.].

[106] ibid at 5.

[107] ibid at 12 (citing the Grenoble Court of Appeal, judgment of 16 December 2008, which also indicated that 'a finding on the artistic nature of a work would mean referring to an aesthetic order [...]. Such an assessment is not within the remit of the judge responsible for enforcing the law').

[108] ibid at 11–12, citing also *Beyeler v Italy* [GC] no 33202/96, ECHR 2000-I) at para 112.

[109] See Chapter 3 (on balancing interests before the ECtHR).

5.2.1.2 The Legacy of 5Pointz

American courts follow an entirely different rationale in considering the nature of street art and outdoor installations. This is especially evident in cases involving IP rights, including both copyright and moral rights.

In order to understand the US perspective, it seems apposite to briefly introduce the reader who is not familiar with IP law to artists' moral rights – and the 'special' way they are protected in the United States. Moral rights were guaranteed in the United States later than anywhere else in the world.[110] Following accession to the Berne Convention, however, the United States adopted the Visual Artists Rights Act (VARA), which is now incorporated in US copyright law.[111] VARA protections are not granted to all works. The relevant provisions apply to *visual arts* only – as per the definition of the US Copyright Act (e.g. under US copyright law a painting or sculpture in a 'single copy or limited edition in 200 copies or fewer' and 'bear[ing] the signature or other identifying mark of the author' is a 'work of visual art').[112] In addition, the VARA makes an important distinction between *all* works of visual art and *some* works of visual art – the ones that are considered of 'recognized stature'. The authors of the former are protected against distortion, deformation, mutilation or other modification of their work.[113] The authors of the latter, however, are granted an additional right, namely, the right to 'prevent any destruction of a work of recognized stature, and by extension any intentional or grossly negligent destruction of that work is a violation of that right'.[114] In other words, in order for the VARA to be triggered, authors need to prove that their work fulfils both general requirements of US copyright law (for instance, that their creation is original), *and* that their work is indeed a 'work of visual art', as defined in the US Copyright Act. If, in addition, the authors manage to prove that their work is of 'recognized stature', then they may also be expressly granted the right to prevent its destruction under the modalities of the VARA.[115]

110 For an overview, Cyrill Rigamonti, 'Deconstructing Moral Rights' (2006) 47(2) *Harvard International Law Journal* 353, 355; Justin Hughes, 'The Line between Work and Framework, Text and Context' (2001) 19 *Cardozo Arts & Entertainment Law Journal* 19; also Bonadio *supra* note 29 at 105–12.

111 US 2001 Copyright Act, Section 106a Rights of certain authors to attribution and integrity.

112 Section 101 of the US Copyright Act (on 'definitions').

113 ibid 106a(3) (A).

114 ibid 106a(3) (B).

115 Section 113, which refers to 'destruction, distortion, mutilation, or other modification, by reason of [artworks'] removal' (noting, for example, that artists must be given a ninety-day notice to remove their work, or else pay for its removal).

VARA protections have two important exceptions. The first is explicit: VARA rights do not apply to works affixed to a surface, that is, which cannot be relocated.[116] This is an important feature of the VARA that makes it less likely to be applicable in large and heavy artistic installations. The second exception is implicit and is deduced by the jurisprudence of US courts, which have accepted – until now – that VARA rights do not apply to works illegally placed on the property of others, against their will or without their consent. In a case decided by the South District Court of New York, for example, a group of artists had made various artworks, both murals and sculptures, in a community garden on the 11th street of New York – which they referred to as 'the Mural Gardens'. When the New York City sold the site for development, the artists attempted to oppose the relocation of their works by invoking US copyright law and brought an action against NYC's housing development fund. When the case arrived before the court the illegal use of the communal garden was a decisive factor for the court's pragmatic assessment of the works' preservation, as '[o]therwise parties could effectively freeze development of vacant lots by placing artwork there without permission'.[117]

It appears, however, that more recently, the value of street art and graffiti is better weighed. The most famous illustration of street art removal and subsequent application of the VARA is arguably 5Pointz Aerosol Art Center, Inc.,[118] which is hailed as momentum for street art. In 2013, a graffiti-covered warehouse in Queens, New York, named '5Pointz', beautiful enough to be listed in travel guides as a 'New York must-see', was taken down by its new owners (a real estate company) without notifying the artists.[119] Cohen and other contributing artists initiated VARA-based litigation, in which they asserted that their work was one of 'recognized stature'.[120] The New York district court found VARA protections applicable and awarded the plaintiffs over 6 million dollars'

[116] US Copyright Act, Section 113, and 113 (d) (1) (A).

[117] *English v BFC&R East 11th Street LLC* 97 *Civ* No7446 (HB) (SDNY 1997) (*Mural Gardens*). See Smith *supra* note 18 at 267–68; Lerman *supra* note 25 at 331; Hughes *supra* note 110 at 27–28.

[118] *Cohen v G & M Realty* (*Aerosol Art Center Inc.*) L.P. 988 F. Supp. 2d 212 ('*5Pointz*'). See also Ikram *supra* note 77 at 69; Lerman *supra* note 25 at 304–05; Perot Bissell, 'Monuments to the Confederacy and the Right to Destroy in Cultural-Property Law' (2019) 128 *Yale Law Journal* 1130, 1152–53.

[119] ibid at 212. See e.g. Lerman *supra* note 25 at 304–05; Bissell *supra* note 118 at 1152–53. Also Ikram *supra* note 77 at 69.

[120] ibid at 215.

worth of damages for the irreparable harm they suffered.[121] This judgment was upheld by the Circuit Court, as well as the Appeals Court in 2020.[122]

This is not to say that VARA-based litigation for street art is a panacea in the United States. In reality, artists can easily 'trade off' their moral rights, abandoning or modifying them by contract.[123] Moreover, after such litigation actually takes place, real estate developers will be clearly more cautious in collaborating with artists, creating a certain 'chilling effect' in the street art world.[124] It remains to be seen whether this chilling effect could be sanctioned by the First Amendment – as in fact certain authors have argued already that 'there is no principled reason why the artist's expression through creation should be granted any higher constitutional protection than the art owner's expression through destruction'.[125]

5Pointz, albeit in an entirely different context involving IP law (rather than human rights law) is still a far leap from *Ehrmann* and other similar cases, both in terms of rationale and final outcome. The Court did not raise the question of the nature and artistic value of the particular work – neither did it engage in questioning whether the work is a single piece, as the author claimed,[126] or a combination of works. In fact, only time and money have managed to overturn the ECtHR judgment: to date, *La Demeure* receives close to 200,000 visitors per year free of charge and is branded by the French media as 'the museum for the future',[127] giving a boost to local markets and the French national railways through which *La Demeure* is more easily accessible, especially for its young visitors – Saint-Romain-au-Mont-d'Or stop.[128]

[121] ibid at 216. See also Alan Fauer, 'Brooklyn Lawsuit Asks If Illegal Graffiti Is Protected by Copyright Law' (*The New York Times*, 15 March 2018). More than 6 million dollars for statutory damages based on the estimated value of the work and attorney faces.

[122] Eileen Kinsella, 'A Stunning Legal Decision Just Upheld a $6.75 Million Victory for the Street Artists Whose Works Were Destroyed at the 5Pointz Graffiti Mecca' (*Art News*, 20 February 2020).

[123] US Copyright Act, Section 113(d)(1) (B); see also Hughes *supra* note 110 at 26; also Richard Serra, 'The Tilted Arc Controversy' (2001) Cardozo Arts and Entertainment 39, 49.

[124] cf Kinsella *supra* note 122.

[125] Bissell *supra* note 118 at 1152–53.

[126] *Ehrmann supra* note 99 at 2. According to the applicant, the *Demeure* was 'a work of art that is made up of 3,123 separate works to which about thirty plastic artists had contributed'.

[127] Julien Bouisset, 'Chaos, prototype du musée de demain' [in French] (*Nouvel Observateur*, 22 October 2019) <www.nouvelobs.com/2049/20191022.OBS20117/la-demeure-du-chaos-prototype-du-musee-de-demain.html>.

[128] <www.renfe-sncf.com/rw-en/blog/destinations/lyon/abode-of-chaos> (advertisement on the French railways site).

5.2.2 *Unpopular Art and the Urban Space*

5.2.2.1 A Human Rights Law Perspective to Richard Serra's *Tilted Arc*

One of the best known art controversies in the United States was Richard Serra's *Tilted Arc*, a sculpture commissioned by the General Services Administration (GSA) of the US Federal Government 'to be installed on the plaza adjacent to the federal office complex'.[129] The artwork followed 'Serra's formalist, minimalist aesthetic'[130] and from the moment of its installation sparked furious debate.[131] A *New York Times* art critic called it 'an awkward, bullying piece that may conceivably be the ugliest work of outdoor art in the city'.[132] In fact, a large segment of the public agreed with the art critic. Close to 1,300 signatures by federal employees were collected, requesting its removal.[133] The public debate on the merits and demerits of the *Tilted Arc* continued for almost four years.[134] Supporters rejected public censorship, deeming it to constitute forward-looking art and site-specific, whereas detractors advanced arguments against its perceived ugliness[135] and the disruption to pedestrian traffic and security.[136] The debate only intensified with time. In the words of the Court of Appeal:

> The pigeons had barely begun to roost on *Tilted Arc* before the sculpture became the object of intense public criticism. GSA received hundreds of letters from community residents and federal employees complaining about the sculpture's appearance and its obstruction of Federal Plaza's previously open space. Initially, GSA took the position that critics should give the work time to gain public acceptance. However, when hostility to the work had not abated after several years, GSA agreed to hold a hearing on the possible relocation of the sculpture.[137]

[129] *Serra v United States General Services Administration*, Court of Appeals, Second Circuit 93 A.L.R.Fed. 897 (1988); 664 F.Supp. 798 (S.D.N.Y.1987).

[130] Eric Brook, '"Tilted" Justice: Site-Specific Art and Moral Rights after U.S. Adherence to the Berne Convention' (1989) *California Law Review* 1431, 1431; see also *Serra supra* note 129 at 5.

[131] US GSA, 'Richard Serra's Tilted Arc' <www.gsa.gov/real-estate/design-construction/art-in-architecture-fine-arts/fine-arts/fine-arts-collection-faq/richard-serras-tilted-arc>.

[132] 'An Outdoor-Sculpture Safari around New' (*New York Times*, 7 August 1981) Section C, p. 1 (digitized version) <www.nytimes.com/1981/08/07/arts/an-outdoor-sculpture-safari-around-new.html>; also Brook *supra* note 130 at 1432.

[133] Serra *supra* note 123 at 39 (in which the artist argues that 'prejudice, even if shared by a majority, ought not be a reason to decide the fate of a work of art').

[134] US GSA *supra* note 133.

[135] ibid: 'an ugly object foisted upon the public by insensitive Government bureaucrats'.

[136] ibid: 'a security hazard that blocked views of the street and could be used as a shield for terrorist attacks against the nearby government office'.

[137] *Serra supra* note 129 at 6.

Following these events, a hearing did indeed take place in March 1985 before a panel presided by the GSA regional administrator, which voted (by a margin of four to one) that the *Tilted Arc* be relocated.[138] The author opposed the sculpture's relocation,[139] and in 1986 filed a lawsuit against the GSA invoking among others, his constitutional freedom of expression and due process rights (First and Fifth Amendment, respectively).[140] The lawsuit was unsuccessful and as a result the *Tilted Arc* was dismantled by the GSA and removed from Federal Plaza.

At its face, the legal issue under US law would be simply to determine the extent of preservation of an artist's moral rights. At the time of the *Tilted Arc* controversy, however, the VARA did not exist. Had it been, the discussion would have been substantially different. More importantly, however, the fact remains that the artwork was commissioned by the government – and as such, constituted in fact governmental property. As the district court found, '*Tilted Arc* was entirely owned by the Government and displayed on Government property. Serra relinquished his own speech rights in the sculpture when he voluntarily sold it to GSA [. . .] the Government's action in this case is limited to an exercise of discretion with respect to the display of its own property'.[141]

This point cannot be overlooked. Artists commissioned to create a particular artwork do so in the context of a contract with the entity ordering the artwork. Any challenges that arise therefore should be primarily addressed in the context of that contract. Commissioned art in the public space runs the risk of being overtaken by circumstances extraneous to the underlying contract – in the same way that illicit art in the public space runs the risk of being removed, damaged, worn out by taggers or 'gradually work[ed] away by weather'.[142] Censorship on the other hand concerns primarily *freedom* in the creative process[143] – and State abstention from interference and decisions on how art should look like, entailing obligations to examine removal decisions with 'utmost scrutiny'.[144]

[138] *Serra supra* note 129 at 7.
[139] ibid; also Serra *supra* note 123 at 42 (arguing on the site-specificity of the work).
[140] *Serra* cited *supra* note 131 at 11; *Serra supra* note 129 at 39; Robert O'Neil, 'Artistic Freedom and Academic Freedom' (1990) 53 *Law and Contemporary Problems* 177, 180.
[141] *Board of Education v Pico* 457 US 853 (1982) (the Court found that content regulation is not a valid restriction). See also Chapter 2 (on US courts' practice).
[142] Benedikt Feiten, 'Answering Back: Banksy's Street Art and the Power Relations with the Public Space' in DeLaure and Fink *supra* note 53 at 221.
[143] cf *Mephisto* 1 BvR 435/68 (24 February 1971) BVerfGE 30, 173 (1971), discussed in Chapter 3.
[144] See Chapter 2, censorship.

Human rights law, however, does not go as far as encompassing the fate of artworks agreed in the context of a private contract, even if the artwork or performance is to be delivered in the public space. In fact, US constitutional protection on this particular point is far stronger, as it sets clearly defined limits even against governmental discretion. The First Amendment grants a unique protection of freedom of speech, and only *content-neutral* restrictions are constitutional (as opposed to content-based).[145] In the *Island Trees* case (*Pico*), for example, concerning the removal of books from public school libraries in West Virginia, State discretion was 'exercised in a narrowly partisan or political manner'.[146] This means, in brief, that cultural authorities within a State are not free to engage in cherry picking in cultural materials provided to the public, according to their own religious and political beliefs, especially if such choices are the product of conservatism. This is because, in the words of Justice Brennan in *Pico*, the government 'is not to strangle the free mind at its source'.[147] In addition, this protection in the United States also applies in the public space via the *public forum* principle, which prohibits municipalities from imposing content-based restrictions on speech.[148] In *Boos v Barry*, decided about the same time as *Serra*, the Supreme Court struck down as unconstitutional a regulation that prohibited protests within 500 feet from a foreign embassy and 'displaying any sign that tends to bring the foreign government into public odium or public disrepute'.[149] The Court found that this was a content-based restriction to freedom of speech – incompatible with the 'adequate breathing space' that the First Amendment should enjoy, and the assertion that 'in public debate, [American] citizens must tolerate insulting, and even outrageous, speech'.[150]

The result of the case at issue, therefore, would have been substantially different if the work was removed because it was expressing a particular idea, which some people found offensive – this would have been a content-based restriction as in *Pico*. In the case at hand no *Pico* issue existed.[151] It would have

[145] This applies to conduct too, see e.g. *Cohen v California* 403 US 15 (1971) (wearing a jacket bearing the words '*F the Draft*'). See infra Chapter 7 of this book (on performances and public morality).

[146] *Board of Education supra* note 141 at 870.

[147] ibid at 865.

[148] See analytically 'Public Forum Principle' <www.law.cornell.edu/constitution-conan/amendment-1/the-public-forum#fn1456amd1>.

[149] *Boos v Barry* 485 US 312 (1988).

[150] ibid at 322 (noting that this judgment struck down as unconditional Columbia's Code), citing *Hustler Magazine, Inc. v Falwell* 485 US 56; *New York Times Co. v Sullivan* 376 US at 376 US 270 On these cases, see also Chapter 3 of this book (on prior restraints).

[151] *Serra supra* note 129 at 20 (noting however that no assertion of facts indicated that GSA officials understood the sculpture to be expressing any particular idea that they disapproved).

also been different if the work expressed ideas that were not culturally adequate – as in the case of a municipality that would order, say, a racist sculpture. In this context, obligations under 'access to arts' would also come into play[152] – and arguably in that case the State would be violating human rights standards by failing to provide culturally adequate and appropriate arts to the public.

5.2.2.2 Debates on Racist and Sexist Art in the Public Space

Expressions of contemporary art in public spaces that may be perceived as racist, hateful, sexist, misogynous, homophobic and generally intolerant are problematic under human rights law. This is because limitations to free speech, discussed analytically in earlier chapters, apply against cultural and artistic expressions. This should also be the case a fortiori when in the public space. In fact, the UN Human Rights Committee has clarified that 'on the basis of maintenance of public order (*ordre public*) it may, for instance, be permissible in certain circumstances to regulate speech-making in a particular public place'.[153] This is especially true of street art, artworks and performances reaching the threshold of unacceptable incitement to hatred, or discrimination – for example, in her reports as UN Special Rapporteur on Religious Freedom, human rights activist Asma Jahangir has pointed to threatening use of local-style street art (chalk writing on walls) to spread hatred and intimidate religious minorities in Pakistan.[154] States typically also undertake obligations compelling them to raise awareness and eliminate stereotyping, such as those found in the Convention on the Elimination of All Forms of Discrimination against Women (CEDAW)[155] and the Convention on the Rights of Persons with Disabilities (CRPD).[156]

Such an approach, arguably, could not go as far as prohibiting private actors from using their space as they please.[157] An exception could be made in respect of expressions existing in a private space, but which are nonetheless in public view or freely accessible by the public (e.g. private actors' exhibitions

152 See Chapter 4 of this book (on the 4-A scheme).

153 ibid para 31; UN Human Rights Committee, *Coleman v Australia*, Communication no 1157/2003.

154 UN Human Rights Council, 'Report of the Special Rapporteur on Freedom of Religion or Belief, Asma Jahangir', 28 February 2008, UN Doc Addendum A/HRC/7/10/Add.1, paras 204–06 (discussing incidents of wall-chalking against Christians).

155 CEDAW, art 5(on the elimination of prejudice and stereotyped roles of men and women).

156 CRPD, art 8 (on raising awareness and combating stereotypes, prejudices and harmful practices).

157 See Chapter 3 of this book (on private actors).

or performances in open-air private property that is adjacent to public spaces). An illustration is the controversy over the sculpture *Fearless Girl*, representing a grown up woman in child dimension placed opposite the New York Stock Exchange and facing the giant Charging *Bull* (or, *Bull of Wall Street*). Originally part of the State Street Global Advisors (SSGA) campaign to promote gender equality, the sculpture has been increasingly perceived by human rights groups as *anti*-feminist (in fact, promoting fake 'corporate feminism').[158]

Similar controversies exist in relation to publicly exhibited sculptures and monuments that are now perceived as racist, colonial, undemocratic, totalitarian, misogynous, and generally, anti-human rights. Various authors have taken the view that museums should not exhibit artefacts collected during the colonial era demonstrating 'cultural racism and appropriation'.[159] In Europe, colonial era statues and racist monuments are being increasingly vandalized. In the United States too, local governors have been under pressure over the last few years to take down monuments glorifying racism and reminding humanity of its colonial past. Responses from the legal perspective, however, vary: Bissell, for example, argues that a 'right to destroy' should be possible under cultural-property law,[160] while Lixinski argues that the framework for transitional justice law provides the best outcomes.[161]

Such debates, however, are for now confined to the theoretical sphere, as in most cases monuments have been taken down or relocated de facto in the context of protests and increased pressure on the authorities.[162] Assuming a legal dispute, however, arises, the jurisprudence of the UN Committee on the Elimination of Racial Discrimination could be helpful. Keane, for example, has thoroughly explained that the ICERD is increasingly interpreted as a living instrument,[163] with reference in particular to *Hagan v Australia*.[164] In *Hagan*, the ICERD Committee considered the use of the racial epithet 'N*' on a sports stand in Australia (named in the 1960s after a sports personality whose nickname was a racial epithet – N*'Brown') which the petitioner found

[158] Ikram *supra* note 77 at 52–58; Sheelah Kolhatkar, 'The Ongoing Saga of the "Fearless Girl" Statue' (New Yorker, 7 January 2022) <https://www.newyorker.com/business/currency/the-ongoing-saga-of-the-fearless-girl-statue>.

[159] Carol Tator, Frances Henry, and Winston Mattis (eds), *Challenging Racism in the Arts: Case Studies of Controversy and Conflict* (Toronto Press 1998) 36ff, at 37.

[160] Bissell *supra* note 118 at 1132ff. cf Ikram *supra* note 77 at 71–72.

[161] Lucas Lixinski, 'Confederate Monuments and International Law' (2018) 35 *Wisconsin International Law Journal* 549, 553.

[162] Polymenopoulou *supra* note 52 at 26.

[163] David Keane and Annapurna Waughray (eds), *50 Years of the International Convention on the Elimination of Racial Discrimination: A Living Instrument* (Manchester University Press 2017).

[164] *Stephen Hagan v Australia* (2003), CERD Communication no 26/2002, UN Doc CERD/C/62/D/26/2002.

'extremely offensive, especially to the Aboriginal people'.[165] The committee found a violation of the treaty, even though the use of the term was not necessarily regarded as offensive in the past. This is because, according to the ICERD Committee, 'the Convention is a "living instrument"', which 'must be interpreted and applied taking into the circumstances of contemporary society'.[166] By the same token, an argument could be made therefore that such monuments, taken by hate speech standards as forms of 'expressions', should be no longer accepted.

CONCLUDING REMARKS

This chapter addressed the complex legal regime covering street art and graffiti, focusing on obligations of preservation and safeguarding in light of artistic freedom, as well as relevant limitations. It started by observing that unauthorized graffiti is still largely considered to be an illicit activity – as well as associated with a variety of misdemeanours (trespassing of property, etc.). The distinction between 'illicit' and 'commissioned' street art and graffiti (which is relatively blurred, if not inexistent in the art worlds) remains generally pertinent in domestic laws. Unauthorized street art therefore remains an offence punishable by a variety of criminal laws and by-laws (on vandalism, protection of public order, urban planning, the protection of the environment, anti-graffiti specific legislation, etc.), and is also a tort when involving private property. This is the case despite the fact that street art is becoming increasingly popular in urban capitals around the world, attracting cultural tourism and income for cities (which subsequently makes demolition of artworks of great aesthetic quality highly unlikely as the 'Banksy phenomenon' has demonstrated). Arguments against criminalization of graffiti were not directly addressed in this chapter. In examining the approach of the ECtHR in the few relevant cases (primarily *La Demeure du Chaos*), the chapter found that the case law has not developed in a way that justifies graffiti artists' immunities against criminal liability. This is even more true given the ECtHR's methodology in addressing human rights violations and particularly the margin of appreciation doctrine, which is afforded to States parties to the European Convention with respect to urban planning provisions. Arguments against removal (i.e. negative State obligations not to interfere with artistic freedom) could be eventually drawn from the IP law regime, and specifically the protection of artists' moral rights. In this respect, this

165 ibid at 3.1.
166 ibid.

chapter compared the approach of the ECtHR with that of American courts in cases related to street art and installations, and suggesting that VARA-based litigation could provide some insight into the European setting too.

Furthermore, the chapter addressed positive State obligations under human rights. It found that (commissioned or authorized) street art and other arts of the public space are jointly covered by the protective regime of free speech in the public space under the ICCPR, and obligations relevant to the participation in cultural life under the ICESCR (especially those related to facilitating 'access to arts'). Limitations to creativity (including also the necessity and proportionality tests) apply therefore equally to the public space. This also implies that the taking down of hateful, racist, homophobic and misogynous expressions is in line with the current interpretation of human rights standards on free speech. This arguably equally means that the monuments of the confederacy, colonial statues and other works that are celebratory of slavery and humanity's racist past may no longer be acceptable in the public space, as many authors have already argued.

The chapter subsequently emphasized the linkages between positive obligations to promote cultural rights, and the creation of opportunities for artists to present their work. These are valuable for novice artists, creative practitioners, performers and musicians whose work addresses the public or interacts with them. Safeguards for political expression should also be applicable to street art, especially when it amounts to human rights activism or when free speech safeguards are not adequate. Last, the chapter suggested that obligations of safeguarding those murals are reflective of broad community participation (and those that provide communities and groups with a sense of identity). They should be therefore deduced from the protective regime of cultural heritage and the principle of cultural diversity, including provisions related to cultural rights of communities to access their heritage and preserve their identities.

6

Public Morality, Obscenity and the Arts

"Limits" is a relative term.

Like beauty, it is often in the eye of the beholder.

—Chris Burden

Three decades ago, between 1989 and 1991, Jeff Koons created a series of human-scale billboard paintings and sculptures named *Made in Heaven*. The works depicted him and his then wife Illona Staller (known as *La Ciciollina*, porn star and member of the Italian parliament) in sexually explicit poses. Originally displayed at an outdoor exhibition of the Whitney Museum, aimed at exploring the role of art in the media,[1] they sparked immediate controversy (even after Koons' divorce and subsequent custody battle which led to their destruction). Was *Made in Heaven* pornographic? Or was there some 'aesthetic legitimacy' in what Koons was doing? And would that legitimacy imply also absolving him from liability for any breaches of public morality offences?[2]

Assuming that the answer to these questions is positive, one could argue that the works were indeed artworks; that part of the works has been already displayed and offered for sale at the Tate Gallery and Sotheby's, respectively (and therefore legitimized by art circles);[3] or simply that this is somehow different from sexually explicit content that is deprived of any aesthetic merit. If this is so, consider now a different scenario, whereby an artist who has served

1 <https://whitney.org/media/1058>.

2 See the comments in the interview of the artist with Pharrell Williams, available at <www.youtube.com/watch?v=aOf_pMWpoPM> (noting that according to the artist, the series was made in a spirit of 'transcendence', alluding among other things to acceptance of the human body).

3 See indicatively, <www.tate.org.uk/art/artists/jeff-koons-2368/jeff-koons-banality-decadence-and-easyfun>; <www.sothebys.com/en/auctions/ecatalogue/2009/contemporary-art-evening-auction-n08592/lot.38.html>.

jail time for paedophilia invites children to his studio, requesting them to undress and pose as nude models (a quite typical process in artistic training and practice). Let us now assume that the children do as requested and that the artist, just like Koons, creates a series of human-scale billboard paintings and sculptures named *Made in Heaven*. The works are not pornographic per se, and not primarily aiming at sexual stimulation, yet represent children as *nudes*. Would the answer be equally positive? Arguably not. The quality and characterization of the artist as a paedophile and the absolute abhorrence of the fictitious crime make the mere thought of such artworks so repulsive, to the point of arguing against any type of merit, aesthetic or other. Video clips such as 'Lemon Incest' performed by Serge Gainsbourg and his then thirteen-year old daughter (showing them performing the song while lying on a bed together) were banned from music channels for years, and are still not fully acceptable as public opinion shows.[4]

In the context of works under contract, exhibitions and performances, morality concerns may amount to artwork adjustments and event cancellations, and even criminal prosecution and punishment, as in the case of the fictitious artist above. Civil law mechanisms, however, may also be available to individuals harmed by a particular behaviour for less serious morality offences that do not involve obscenity or indecency. An action in tort rather than a criminal suit is typically the only legal remedy in respect of less serious offences. For example, an artist appropriating another person's work as their own commits an unprofessional, unethical and arguably also 'immoral' act. This artist, therefore, may be liable for damages in tort, depending on the particular legal system wherein the offence took place and the extent to which it guarantees rights to authorship (also guaranteed under article 15, paragraph 1 (a) (c) of the International Covenant on Economic, Social and Cultural Rights [ICESCR]).

This chapter is spread over two sections. The first section attempts to disentangle the conflation between the concepts of 'indecency', 'obscenity' and 'pornography', and between (indecent) artworks and (immoral) artists. Drawing from domestic court practice it explores controversies related to the representation of nudity and sexuality in visual arts, focusing on the defence of artistic value and whether it can be invoked before international bodies (before the European Court, for example). The second section explores hard cases, such as bodily harm, 'cadaver' art and child pornography in Japanese manga.

4 <www.imdb.com/title/tt6863100/>.

6.1 EVIL, WORTHLESS AND IMMORAL ARTS

6.1.1 *The Contextuality of Morality Considerations*

6.1.1.1 Is There a Universal Standard of Morality?

Morality is defined as a set of 'principles concerning the distinction between right and wrong, or good and bad behaviour'.[5] It is a broad concept that is not defined in the law – rather, it is sometimes *conflated* with law. Yet, the role of a legal system is not necessarily to provide ethical guidance, neither to identify morally unacceptable behaviour. Immorality therefore is illegal only insofar as the law considers it wrong enough to be outlawed, and only insofar as it affects the public interest. The choice to criminalize morally unacceptable behaviour is taken by considering not only individual liberty but also its impact on the public good – what Robert George calls a 'healthy moral ecology'.[6] Subsequently, a legislative choice needs to be made on the type of legal response to morally unacceptable behaviour. This choice is generally understood by courts around the world as the *average person's* morality. The additional parameters that are often taken into account in considering criminalization are principles derived from legal philosophy, and may be as broad as 'harm' (as developed by John Stuart Mill and H. L. A. Hart)[7] and 'offence' (as developed by Feinberg).[8]

Morality-based offences encompassed in the broad term *public morality*, therefore, come in theoretical varieties and with subtleties that are difficult to grasp. Pornography, on the one hand, is generally related to sexual arousal. *The Stanford Encyclopedia of Philosophy* defines it as 'sexually explicit material (verbal or pictorial) that is *primarily* designed to produce sexual arousal in viewers'.[9]

5 <www.lexico.com/definition/morality>.

6 Robert George, 'The Concept of Public Morality' (2000) 45 *American Journal of Jurisprudence* 17, 19 and 24 (arguing that 'The common good of public morality, that is, the good of a healthy moral ecology, generates obligations in justice for all of us, just as do the common goods of public health and safety'); also Christopher Mooney, 'Morality and the Law' (1983) 1(1) *Journal of Law and Religion* 45, 46.

7 John Stuart Mill, *On Liberty* (Cambridge University Press 1989, first ed, 1859); H. L. A. Hart, *Law, Liberty and Morality* (Stanford University Press 1963). See also, generally, David van Mill, 'Freedom of Speech' in *The Stanford Encyclopedia of Philosophy* (2002) <https://plato.stanford.edu/entries/freedom-speech/#JoeFeiOffPri>.

8 Joel Feinberg, *Offense to Others: The Moral Limits of the Criminal Law* (Oxford University Press 1985).

9 Caroline West, 'Pornography and Censorship' in *The Stanford Encyclopedia of Philosophy* (2001) <https://plato.stanford.edu/entries/pornography-censorship/>. Generally also Catharine MacKinnon, *Feminism Unmodified: Discourses on Life and Law* (Harvard University Press

The term *primarily* is crucial, and, as West notes, 'the *Last Tango in Paris* arguably aims to arouse audiences, but this is not its primary aim'.[10] Writers, however, have given significantly more inspired definitions. For example, D. H. Laurence defined genuine pornography 'as that which insults sex and the human spirit'[11] and Havelock Ellis found that pornography is 'the vulgar, disgusting, and stupid form of obscenity'.[12]

Obscenity on the other hand, while often coinciding with representations of sex, is not identical with pornography. It is rather defined as offensive, disgusting and generally repugnant content.[13] In 'obscenity as an aesthetic category', Kaplan makes the difference between various types of obscenity, where sex still maintains a crucial role (although for him, obscenity and arts can coincide).[14] Regardless of such distinctions, obscenity appears to be a tool that maintains standards of conformity. In other words, rejecting something as obscene implies believing in the rightness of one's *own* standards. In turn this also implies the belief in the existence of an *objective* standard that makes it possible to identify an inherent sense of shame or disgust that is (or should be) applicable to all members of a defined community.

Lockhart and McLure highlight this ambiguity:

> No one seems to know what obscenity is. Many writers have discussed the obscene, but few can agree upon even its essential nature. Some find the key to it in the sense of shame; whatever violates the community's sense of shame is obscene.[15]

'Obscene arts', therefore, are not identical to 'pornographic arts'. For example, transgressive artistic manifestations aiming specifically at provocation, protest and disgust such as those involving representations of the human body and animal suffering are surely not pornographic; yet, arguably fall within the scope of obscenity. For example, an installation that consists of

1987); also Catherine Izin (ed), *Pornography: Women, Violence and Civil Liberties* (Oxford University Press 1992).

10 ibid.

11 William Lockhart and Robert McLure, 'Literature, the Law of Obscenity, and the Constitution' (1954) 38 *Minnesota Law Review* 295, 321–22.

12 ibid at 322.

13 According to the current version of the Oxford Dictionary 'obscene' means specifically something that is 'offensive or disgusting by accepted standards of morality and decency', as well as 'repugnant' and 'offending against moral principles' available at <www.lexico.com/definition/obscene>.

14 Abraham Kaplan, 'Obscenity as an Aesthetic Category' (1955) 20 *Law and Contemporary Problems* 544, 546–47 (e.g. one type 'attacks established sexual patterns and practices' and another 'celebrates sex').

15 Lockhart and McLure *supra* note 11 at 320–21.

leaving a sick dog to starve to death (as protest against animal cruelty)[16] can be prosecuted under public morality laws and obscenity, even in the absence of animal protection laws. The same applies to cannibalistic 'art', as in the case of the Norwegian artist who ate a part of his own body as part of a performance (in order to show that he can 'take control of himself'),[17] and the Chinese artist who consumed human foetuses.[18] These works, however, despite the motivation of their authors to provoke and create scandal, pass generally unnoticed by the wider public and are rarely the object of actual prosecutions – causing disdain even among art critics. In contrast, obscene content that reaches a larger audience is generally regulated, especially when blamed for increasing violence in the real world (while violence itself could also be caught by public morality laws, as Saunders argues).[19] The cinematographic release of Kubrick's *Clockwork Orange* (1972), for example, apart from immoral and obscene, was also blamed as a cause of real assaults perpetrated in the United Kingdom.[20] This resulted in refusals of screening by local authorities, despite the granting of a visa classification by the British Board.[21]

6.1.1.2 Obscenity Treaties and Lack of Agreement

Two treaties negotiated under the League of Nations and amended in the early 1950s deal specifically with obscene publications. Both agreements aimed at intensifying the collaboration between signatory Member States, with a view to tracing and suppressing offences connected with obscene publications (and largely legitimizing the various censorship bodies mandated to regulate arts and entertainment pre-World War II).[22] The first is a

16 Kency Cornejo, 'No Text without Context: Habacuc Guillermo Vargas' Exposition #1' (2014) *Art and Documentation* 54, 54.

17 Benjamin Sutton, 'Norwegian Performance Artist Eats His Own Hip' (*Artnet*, 27 May 2014) <https://news.artnet.com/exhibitions/norwegian-performance-artist-eats-his-own-hip-27201>.

18 Meiling Cheng, 'Violent Capital: Zhu Yu on Fire' (2005) 49 *Drama Review* 58 (discussing the works of the experimentalist Zhu Yu).

19 Kevin Saunders, *Violence as Obscenity: Limiting the Media's First Amendment Protection* (Duke University Press 1996).

20 See however, Carolyn Strange, 'Stanley Kubrick's A Clockwork Orange as Art against Torture' (2011) 6(3) *Crime, Media, Culture: An International Journal* 267.

21 Bernard Williams (ed), *Obscenity and Film Censorship: An Abridgement of the Williams Report* 87–88 (Cambridge University Press 1981) (obscenity and film censorship, noting also the concerns about the harmful effect of pornography, e.g. in the cases of the Moors murderers where pornographic material was found in possession of the perpetrators (at 85)).

22 1910 Agreement, Preamble.

1910 international agreement on the 'Suppression of obscene publications'.[23] It compelled Member States to establish authorities charged with the duty to facilitate the tracing and suppression of acts related to obscenity as long as they are of 'international character',[24] as well as to expedite seizure of publications.[25] The second is the 1923 Convention on 'the prohibition of their diffusion and publications'.[26] It compelled Member States to discover, prosecute and punish any person who makes or possesses 'obscene writings, drawings, prints, paintings, etc'.[27] None of these treaties provides a generally accepted definition of obscenity, nor of public morality and for this reason, and given the low number of ratifications,[28] their significance is still marginal. As noted by Lockhart and McLure, the delegates of the Geneva Conference where the 1923 convention was negotiated soon discovered that no acceptable definitions existed.[29]

The lack of agreement in these anti-obscenity conventions reflects the inherent limitations of the discourse on free speech: there is no such thing as 'universal morality'. The actual perceptions of the audience about morality are decisive for the fate of virtually any legal dispute. Obscene and pornographic content generally legitimizes both prior restraints and regulation. Human rights law in this respect largely grants discretion to States, given that under both article 19 of the International Covenant on Civil and Political Rights (ICCPR) and article 10 of the European Convention on Human Rights (ECHR) artistic freedom can be legitimately restricted by States pursuing the legitimate aim of 'public morality protection' and in accordance with the necessity and proportionality tests.[30]

23 Agreement for the Repression of Obscene Publications, signed in Paris, 4 May 1910, amended by the Protocol signed in New York, 4 May 1949.

24 1910 Agreement, art 1 (1).

25 ibid art 2. The full list of parties to the 1910 Agreement is at <https://treaties.un.org/Pages/ViewDetails.aspx?src=TREATY&mtdsg_no=VIII-1&chapter=8&clang=_en>. This treaty was originally ratified by most Western European countries, as well as Russia, Brazil and the United States.

26 Convention for the Suppression of the Circulation of, and Traffic in, Obscene Publications, concluded at Geneva on 12 September 1923 and amended by the Protocol signed in New York, 12 November 1947.

27 1923 convention, art 1(I).

28 The 1923 convention counts only a handful of ratification, with States as varied as Salmon Island, Fiji and Zimbabwe, see <https://treaties.un.org/Pages/ViewDetails.aspx?src=TREATY&mtdsg_no=VIII-3&chapter=8&clang=_en>.

29 Lockhart and McLure *supra* note 11 at 320–21 (citing Aldous Huxley, *Vulgarity in Literature* (1930): after 'triumphantly assert[ing] that they did not know what they were talking about, the members of the Congress settled down to their discussion').

30 See Chapter 2 of this book.

6.1.2 *The Applicable Legal Framework*

6.1.2.1 UNESCO, Plato and Human Rights Law

UNESCO, in its 1980 Recommendation on the Status of the Artist, while affirming artistic freedom points to States' duties to promote 'moral arts' that aim at peace, justice, humanity and spiritual enrichment:

> Member States, recognizing the essential role of art in the life and development of the individual and of society [...] Member States should demonstrate and confirm that artistic activities have a part to play in the nations' global development effort to build a just and more humane society and to live together in circumstances of peace and spiritual enrichment.[31]

This UNESCO Recommendation reflects also the public sentiment that arts should serve some higher ideal, arguably also morality. One of the principal reasons may be the conflation between art and morality in the philosophy of the arts. This perception, namely that art is only meaningful when it is beautiful and morally 'good', arguably springs from Plato's ethical criticism of the arts, as discussed in Chapter 1. Contrary to Aristotle, who believed that beauty is a matter of harmony,[32] Plato viewed art as second-hand imitation of reality ('far from reality'), ultimately conferring upon it a secondary status in his *Republic*. He, nonetheless, saw art as having a potentially great impact on the human soul and as being able to corrupt even the most noble of men, and that '[art] stimulates emotions which a good man tries to suppress'.[33] The impact of this view has been pervasive throughout classical philosophy.[34] Influential philosophers of the pre-modern era, especially Kant and Hume, found that 'immoral art cannot be beautiful' and proposed 'to bring the moral evaluation of works of art to bear, in some systematic way, upon their aesthetic evaluation'.[35] Other notorious examples include Tolstoy's *What Is Art* in

31 UNESCO, Recommendation on the Status of the Artist (1980), at 5, Guiding principles III (3).

32 Aristotle, *Poetics*, Book VII, 3–5 ('a beautiful object must not only have an orderly arrangement of parts, but must also be of a certain magnitude; for beauty depends on magnitude and order').

33 See Chapter 1. Also John Herman Randall, 'Plato as the Philosopher of the Artistic Experience' (1968) 37(3) *The American Scholar* 502, 509 (on Plato's Ideal as participatory process).

34 Indicatively, Daniel Jacobson, 'In Praise of Immoral Art' (1997) 25(1) *Philosophical Topics* 155, 156 (noting that 'Rousseau, Tolstoy, and Shaw [...] all advocate some form of Platonic moralism, the central tenet of which is that aesthetic strength is often morally dangerous'); Noël Carroll, 'Art and Ethical Criticism: An Overview of Recent Directions of Research' (2000) 110 *Ethics* 350, 351.

35 ibid at 156 and 158ff (finding that 'Humean moralism is flourishing in contemporary philosophy of art, and the recent literature abounds with similar claims and arguments').

which the writer, engaging with philosophy, finds that 'art [must] communicate a morally good emotion to its audience'.[36] Danto cites a 'not-uncharacteristic passage' from a French philosopher's work published in 1853, titled 'The Birth of the True, the Good, and the Beautiful', whereby

> the artist is before all things an artist; what animates him is the sentiment of beautiful; what he wishes to make pass into the soul of the spectator is the same sentiment that fills his own [...] the artist has done his [work] when he has procured to some noble souls the exquisite sentiment of beauty [...] So art, which is founded on this sentiment, which is inspired by it, which expands it, is in its turn an independent power. It is naturally associated with all that ennobles the soul, with morals and religion; but it springs only from itself.[37]

6.1.2.2 Who Is the Average Person?

Domestic courts around the world occasionally attempt to define pornography, obscenity and other public morality offences, with reference to 'average person' standards. US courts have straggled for a long time to come to some sort of consensus on this matter. In *Roth*, the US Supreme Court defined obscene material as 'material which deals with sex in a manner appealing to prurient interest' with reference to the average person's morality and contemporary community standards,[38] and decided that obscenity generally falls outside the First Amendment's protective purview. Subsequently, however, these 'community standards' were found too stern. In *Miller*,[39] the test was refined, suggesting that one of the 'the basic guidelines for the trier of fact' must be 'whether the work, taken as a whole, lacks serious literary, artistic, political, or scientific value'.[40] Indecency, in turn, appears to set a standard of

[36] Israel Knox, 'Tolstoy's Esthetic Definition of Art' (1930) 27(3) *The Journal of Philosophy* 65–70; Gary Jahn, 'The Aesthetic Theory of Leo Tolstoy's What Is Art?' (1975) 34 *The Journal of Aesthetics and Art Criticism* 59–65. See however, Jacobson *supra* note 34 at 155 (noting that 'the common opinion among philosophers of art is that this later Tolstoy was a crank').

[37] cf Arthur Danto, 'Kalliphobia in Contemporary Art' (2004) 63 *Art Journal* 24, 25.

[38] *Roth v United States* (1957) 354 US 476 ('whether to the average person, applying contemporary standards, the dominant theme of the material taken as a whole appeals to prurient interest') and 487 ('i.e. material having a tendency to excite lustful thoughts'); *Alberts v California* (1957) 354 US 476. cf also *Chaplinsky v New Hampshire* 315 US 568, 315 US 571–72 (noting that the legal issue in Roth was the constitutionality of statutes which banned 'obscene, lawed, lascivious or filthy [...] or other publication of an indecent character', and involved also books such as the *Tropic of Cancer*).

[39] Miller v California 413 US 15 at 24–5 (1973), rejecting the 'utterly without redeeming social value' test (articulated in Memoirs v Massachusets 383 US 413 (1966) (regarding John Cleland's *Memoirs of a Woman of Pleasure*). See on this, Lockhart and McLure *supra* note 11 at 296.

[40] Miller v California at 24.

acceptance, which, albeit morally lower than that of the 'average person' does not reach the threshold of 'obscene content'. In a case regarding stand-up comedian George Carlin and his famous *seven dirty words*, for example, the US Supreme Court clarified the distinction between the two categories and found that contrary to obscene speech, indecent speech is protected by the First Amendment.[41] In this case, the Court, while not going as far as leaving indecent speech unregulated,[42] emphasized however that 'taking offence' is in fact a reason for according constitutional protection 'for it is a central tenet of the First Amendment that the government must remain neutral in the market-place of ideas'.[43] Only hardcore pornography seems to be clear-cut from the outset, and as Justice Steward famously wrote: 'I know it when I see it'.[44]

The European Court of Human Rights (ECtHR) on the contrary has never defined the criteria by which the 'average person' perceives obscenity. In cases related to public morality the Court typically defers the problem to Member States, via the margin of appreciation doctrine. The first judgement of the European Commission specifically on artistic freedom, delivered in 1983, concerned an 'obscenity trial' and the seizure of paintings that represented among other things sex and bestiality. One of the applicants' claim before the Commission was that in matters of artistic freedom obscenity cannot be defined with reference to the moral views of a person of 'normal sensitivity', as the Swiss Federal Court had done, because, as the applicants stated, 'the person of normal sensitivity is a legal fiction'.[45] The Commission did not specifically address this point. It did, however, agree with the applicants that their artistic freedom was violated and found that the confiscation of the paintings was disproportionate to the legitimate aim pursued. The Court, on the contrary, albeit not objecting to the nature of the disputed paintings as

41 *FCC v Pacifica* 438 US 726 (1978). cf South Korea Constitutional Court, *10-1 KCCR* 327, 95 *Hun-Ka* 16 (concerning press registration of 'Semi-Girl' photo binder and finding that contrary to obscenity, indecency is protected by free speech).

42 ibid at 743.

43 ibid at 726: '[t]he fact that society may find speech offensive is not a sufficient reason for suppressing it. Indeed, if it is the speaker's opinion that gives offense, that consequence is a reason for according it constitutional protection'.

44 *Jacobellis v Ohio* 378 US 184 (1964); for the US Supreme Court perspective, see generally Arnold Loewy, 'Obscenity, Pornography, and the First Amendment Theory' (1993) 2 *William & Mary Bill of Rights Journal* 474, fn 36 (arguing that 'freedom to advocate sexual promiscuity, does not necessarily imply freedom to engage in sexual promiscuity'); also Amy Adler, 'Post-modern Art and the Death of Obscenity Law' (1990) 99(6) *Yale Law Journal* 1360, 1361–62.

45 *Müller and Others v Switzerland* (Commission's decision), 22 July 1983, para 20, citing Article 204 of the Swiss Criminal Code that equally prohibited obscene material, including the representation of pornography and bestiophilia, and, additionally, provided for its destruction.

'artworks', ultimately found the restriction incidentally legitimate.[46] It agreed with the Swiss Federal Court that the paintings in question were 'morally offensive to a person of normal sensitivity' [sic],[47] without however providing its own definition of the 'normal person' standard. On the contrary, it remarked that it is not possible to find in the legal and social orders of the Contracting States a uniform European conception of morals.[48]

Artistic freedom cases touching upon public morality issues have been encompassed under the margin of appreciation doctrine also after *Müller*. The most pertinent occasion was *Human Earrings*, involving two small freeze-dried human foetuses displayed as a small sculpture at the Young Unknowns Gallery in London.[49] Following controversy, the work was removed under the common law offence of outraging public decency.[50] The Commission simply declared the case inadmissible with reference to the ECtHR's margin of appreciation doctrine and the 'express reference to their duties and responsibilities in Article 10',[51] ducking both the definition of obscenity and the 'average person' standard. Likewise, in pornography-related *Perrin*, whereby the applicants claimed an infringement on their 'artistic freedom', it dismissed the relevant claims for the simple reason that 'this is not art'.[52]

What appears to have been decisively agreed by the judges of the Court on the contrary is a bare minimum as to what should be, at the very least, excluded from the scope of obscenity. The European Court of Human Rights in *Akdaş* found that obscenity charges and the seizure of the publisher

46 *Müller and Others v Switzerland* (Court) App no 10737/84, 24 May 1988, para 35.

47 ibid at para 18. As the Swiss Federal Court noted in another passage of its judgment, 'they [we]re liable grossly to offend the sense of sexual propriety of persons of ordinary sensitivity', while 'the artistic license relied on by the appellant [could not have] in any way alter[ed] that conclusion in the instant case'.

48 ibid para 35 (referring to *Handyside*).

49 *S. and G. v United Kingdom* App no 17634/91, Commission Decision, 2 September 1991 (inadmissible). See also Section 6.2.2 of this chapter on cadaver art.

50 Analytically, Paul Kearns, 'Not a Question of Art: Regina v Gibson Regina v Sylveire' (1992) 1 *International Journal of Cultural Property* 383, 383–88; generally, Paul Kearns, *Freedom of Artistic Expression: Essays on Culture and Legal Censure* (Hart 2014).

51 *S. and G. supra* note 49 at 5 (noting that 'the applicants contended however' that 'the balanced protection of the Obscene Publications Act 1959 can now be circumvented by framing a prosecution on the basis that the article is offensive and disgusting rather than obscene, a distinction which, in their view, is impossible in reality to make').

52 *Perrin v United Kingdom* App no 5446/03, Admissibility, 18 October 2005 (inadmissible); *Pay v United Kingdom* App no 32792/05, Admissibility, 16 September 2008 (inadmissible) (regarding a case on sexual BDSM advertising on the Internet, in which the applicant also submitted that 'it is well-established that artistic expression, including that of an erotic nature, fell within the scope of Article 10'). See, however, *Pryanishnikov v Russia* no 25047/05, 10 December 2019 (and discussion in Chapter 1).

of the Turkish version of Apollinaire's novel *Eleven Thousand Virgins* (*Les onze mille vierges*) were in breach of artistic freedom,[53] because this work was part of the European literary heritage to which the Council of Europe attributes 'major importance'.[54] This judgment has been celebrated as 'clearly marking the beginning of a new era in the protection of artistic freedom'.[55] This is not necessarily the case – in fact, it is fairly evident that the Court could not have possibly envisaged the option to 'prevent public access to a particular language … to a work contained in the European literary heritage'.[56] In addition, the *Virgins*, despite being undisputedly scandalous when first published a century ago, was not the work of a marginal artist, but rather a work written by a classic author. This still allows the Court to apply large State discretion in all other cases.

6.1.3 *Artistic Value as an Oxymoron*

6.1.3.1 To Pronounce or Not to Pronounce on Artistic Value?

What remains to be seen therefore is whether, eventually, the question of *artistic value* could function as a defence against obscenity charges levelled against artistic and creative expression. This was in fact one of the points raised by the applicants before the European Court in the cases of both *Müller and S. and G.*, yet, neither the Commission nor the Court has analysed this further.[57] The ECtHR generally exhibits a tendency to disregard value-based arguments with reference to the margin of appreciation. In a case concerning a decision of the French Commission de Classification regarding the French movie *Baise moi*,[58] the ECtHR, without any hesitation, agreed with the French Film Classification Board, which had defined the film as 'cinematography' rather than 'pornography' (finding however that it should be made unavailable to minors under sixteen years as a precautionary measure). The discussion, however, was relatively succinct, implying that the film had some

53 *Akdaş v Turkey* App no 41056/04, Merits, 16 February 2010, paras 29–33.

54 ibid at 33.

55 See for example, Jean-Pierre Marguénaud and Benjamin Dauchez, 'Les onze milles vierges fondatrices du patrimoine littéraire européen' (2010) 17 *Le Dalloz* 1051 at 1052. cf Paul Kearns, 'The Judicial Nemesis: Artistic Freedom and the European Court of Human Rights' (2012) 1 *Irish Law Journal* 56, 75, n 60 (arguing, prudently, that 'there is no assurance given by the Court that the decision has any more general implications for contemporary literary works').

56 *Akdaş* at para 30 (author's translation).

57 *Müller supra* note 46 at 178; *S. and G. supra* note 49 at 3.

58 *V.D. and C.G. v France* App no 68238/01, Admissibility, 22 June 2006 (inadmissible).

artistic merit, before observing that it was 'essentially constituted of explicit scenes of violence and sex'.[59] Even so, the Court's outcome is not necessarily favourable for artists. By failing to pronounce the essential characteristics of artistic merit, the Court effectively lends credence to domestic courts and endorses Member States' violation of article 10 ECHR.

Questions related to merit are inherently subjective and imprecise, based on ontological appreciations of what is morally acceptable. In human rights law, this gives rise to the following oxymoron: by failing to determine an artistic value, it is implied that all arts are worth protecting on an equal footing, not because of their value but rather because of their mere existence as a form of expression with which governments should not interfere. This in turn leaves ample space for the judge to make other distinctions in order to distinguish 'art' from 'obscenity'. Most likely, however, this will turn out to be a distinction between art and non-art. This outcome is even more dangerous, first because the same amount of subjectivity is involved, and second because anything that falls short of good aesthetics will be automatically rejected. As a result, authoritatively determining artistic value does not offer any real solution to the question of limitations to artistic freedom. This is illustrated by the inconsistency in invoking the value of the arts in various cases; yet, finding against artistic freedom. In *Strauß-Karicatur* (and the cartoons portraying the Bavarian minister and later German chancellor, discussed earlier in Chapter 1), the German Constitutional Court solemnly proclaimed that assessing the value of art is unconstitutional. It went on to say that

> What is allowed and necessary is simply a distinction between art and non-art; any standard, in the sense of distinguishing between "higher" or "lower" art and good or bad art (and therefore distinguishing also between art less or more worthy to protect), leads to controlling its content, something that is constitutionally prohibited.[60]

This case was also mentioned in the rationale of two dissenting judges in *Bildender*, whereby they rejected the legitimacy of finding value in that particular painting (and subsequently, to find no violation of article 10).[61] In essence, any assessment of value supports the distinction between art and non-art. By way of illustration, the qualification of something as non-art was precisely the reason why Judge Loucaides dismissed the impugned painting

59 ibid (in French, author's translation).

60 German Constitutional Court, BVerfGE 75, 369 (at C –I, para 2) (*Strauß-Karikatur*).

61 *Vereinigung Bildender Künstler v Austria* App no 68354/01, Merits and Just Satisfaction, 25 January 2007. See also Chapter 1 of this book, *in fine*.

at stake in *Bildender* (concerning a painting portraying members of the Austrian right-wing party in a disparaging way), denying the qualification 'art' to the artwork, because in his view 'the picture in question could not by any stretch of the imagination, be called satirical or artistic'.[62]

The opposite position, namely determining artistic value, is equally problematic. In domestic law, various legal systems have crystallized defences on the basis of artistic value, particularly in the common law. In the United Kingdom, for instance, the Obscene Publications Act 1959 grants the possibility to submit 'overriding artistic merit' as a defence to obscene publications (based on the defence of 'public good').[63] Likewise, in the United States, artistic value is generally used as a defence against liability – as well as in a variety of other contexts (Soucek, for example, argues that 'aesthetic judgment pervades the law').[64] Its application to the art world, however, remains ambiguous. The *Miller* test established that 'artistic value' (and more precisely, *serious* artistic value)[65] is a crucial factor in establishing whether protection should be granted. In theory this would provide better outcomes for artists than the original *Roth* test. Yet, *Miller* is widely criticized by American constitutional lawyers, as well as artists and the art world, for being too imprecise; for not resonating well with the evolution of contemporary art; and for implying a distinction between valuable and less valuable art.[66] Artistic value, and especially *serious* artistic value, should not be a decisive factor by which to distinguish art from obscenity or in assessing art freedom limitations. This is because of the nature of artworks and performances, and the variety of features overlapping with each other that makes it impossible to base any such definition on merit alone. For example, how should a court evaluate expressions that apply to the prurient interest, which are otherwise harmless and popular, such as striptease dancing?[67] In equal measure, how should a court evaluate an explicit cartoon that is badly drawn and yet is humoristic or conveys a political message? And how should one evaluate a work of

62 ibid, dissenting opinion of Judge Loucaides.
63 Kearns *supra* note 50 at 384–85; also *Shaw v the Director of Public Prosecutions* (1962).
64 Brian Soucek, 'Aesthetic Judgment in Law' (2017) 69 *Alabama Law Review* 381, 381.
65 Miller supra note 39 at 24.
66 Adler *supra* note 44 at 1365–67 (noting that the 'The *Miller* test presupposes a theory of art' and 1373 (noting that 'any post-modern artist who uses sexually explicit material could be at risk under *Miller*, and the potential chilling effect is incalculable').
67 cf June Ross, 'Nude Dancing and the Charter' (1994) 1(2) *Review of Constitutional Studies* 298, 305–06 (citing e.g. Supreme Court of Canada, *Johnson v The Queen* (1973) 13 C.C.C. (2d) 402 (S.C.C.) and *R v Verette* (1990); also Harry Clor, 'The Death of Public Morality' (2000) 45 *American Journal of Jurisprudence* 33.

marvellous aesthetic value that is nonetheless explicit and provocatory, deviating from the average common standard?

6.1.3.2 Art Value for Funding

Whether or not an artwork is deemed to possess artistic value impacts its chances for governmental funding. This is another problematic aspect of value-based assessments that may also lead to indirect censorship and structures of patronage. States are compelled to provide cultural activities and the arts, as part of their positive obligations accompanying article 15 of the ICESCR, as discussed earlier in Chapter 4. Yet, can these obligations extend also to artworks that go against States' interests, including morality considerations?

These dilemmas were at the heart of the so-called cultural wars that took place in the United States in the beginning of the 1990s,[68] whereby questions related to funding and taxpayers' money 'elevated the arts to an unaccustomed level of political visibility and controversy' as Neil notes.[69] The debate was sparked over controversial artists and film-makers of the American art scene who received subsidies from the US National Endowment for the Arts (NEA). Reactions to Mapplethorpe's photographs and Finley's performances, in particular, were so vehement that various public officials and members of the public called their art a 'tax-paid obscenity'.[70] The exhibition *Sensations* is especially worth mentioning here. *Sensations* consisted of works from Saatchi's collection (previously exhibited at the Hamburger Bahnhoff in Berlin and the Royal Academy in London, attracting a record number of visitors) made and displayed by a circle of artists known as the 'Young British Artists'. They included the most recognizable artists in contemporary art, including Tracey Emin's tent titled *Everyone I Have Ever Slept With*; Chapman brothers' *Great Deeds against the Dead* (a 'life-size fibreglass sculpture made of butcher-shop mannequins'[71] reminiscent of Francisco de

[68] See Adler *supra* note 44 at 1369ff; also Danielle Caminiti, 'City of New York: the Death of the Subsidy and the Birth of the Entitlement in Funding of the Arts' (2000) 10 *Fordham Intellectual property, Media & Entertainment Law Journal* 875, 875. Also generally, Svetlana Mintcheva, 'When Words and Images Cause Pain: The Price of Free Speech' (Robert Atkins and Svetlana Mintcheva eds, New York 2006) 251, 255.

[69] Robert O'Neil, 'Artistic Freedom and Academic Freedom' (1990) 53 *Law and Contemporary Problems* 187, 187.

[70] Kimberly Schmaltz, '*National Endowment for the Arts v. Finley*: Viewpoint Discrimination Masked as the Government's Foray into the Realm of Art Patron' (1999) 26 *Northern Kentucky Law Review* 337, 340.

[71] Jennifer Ramkalawon, 'Jake and Dinos Chapman's Disasters of War' (2001) 18 *Print Quarterly* 64, 65.

Goya's homonymous series of prints); and Damien Hirst's *Physical Impossibility of Death in the Mind of Someone Living* discussed earlier in Chapter 1. When mounted in London, the most shocking artwork was considered the portrait of Myra Hindley, a convicted serial killer of children (the Moors murders). Once displayed in New York, however, the artworks that provoked most indignation were ultimately the following two: Andres Serrano's *Piss Christ*, consisting of an image of a crucifixion immersed in urine[72] (which a spectator attempted to smash with a hammer),[73] and Chris Ofili's *Black Madonna*, representing a black version of Virgin Mary painted with acrylic mixed with other materials, including also elephant dung[74] (which another spectator attempted to reach behind the Plexiglas in order to keep the Virgin 'pure and clean').[75] Both works quickly became flagships of artistic freedom, flaring up the existing controversy over taxpayers' money and museum choices. The campaign over descent art was led by the then mayor of New York Giuliani, who allegedly called the works 'sick stuff'.[76]

Following these reactions, Congress amended the NEA statute according to the *Miller* test. In its new funding criteria it now incorporated a 'serious artistic value' criterion, considering also the 'general standards of decency of the American public'. The decisions of the NEA were challenged before US circuit courts. The outcomes of these trials, however, were not particularly favourable for artists and curators, as the courts were in favour of the constitutionality of the NEA decisions. It was only much later that the 'serious value' criterion was abolished as enhancing viewpoint discrimination.[77] Still today a 'call for expressions of interest' by artists in the United States for any type of undertakings is typically subject to a condition of 'artistic excellence',[78] which is also another term for 'merit'. Soucek rightly argues that 'nearly every

72 Aaron Rosen, *Art and Religion in the 21st Century* (Thames and Hudson 2015) at 15. Also Richard Rambuss, 'Sacred Subjects and the Aversive Metaphysical Conceit: Crashaw, Serrano, Ofili' (2004) 71(2) *ELH* 497, 517; Brent Plate, *Religion, Art and Visual Culture: A Cross-cultural Reader* (Palgrave 2002) 1–18; Julian Young, *Heidegger's Philosophy of Art* (Cambridge University Press 2001) 28–33; also Antony Julius, *Transgressions of the Arts: Art that Offends* (University of Chicago Press 2002) 15–21.

73 Plate *supra* note 72 at 15.

74 Rambuss *supra* note 72 at 517–18 (explaining that the elephant dung was used by the artist for its role as symbol of fertility in African cultures); Rosen *supra* note 72 at 15–16 (noting that the black colour also evoked according to the artist the murder of black teenager Stephen Laurence in London, in 1993).

75 Rosen *supra* note 72 at 16.

76 Plate *supra* note 72 at 3–9; Young *supra* note 72 at 38–41.

77 Indicatively, Adler *supra* note 44 at 1370–71; O'Neil *supra* note 69 at 187; Soucek *supra* note 64 at 385–86; Schmaltz *supra* note 70 at 339–40.

78 <www.arts.gov/grants-organizations/gap/visual-arts>.

decision by the government to grant funding to an artist or arts organization involves an evaluative aesthetic judgment'.[79]

This said, the prohibition of viewpoint discrimination in governmental structures is virtually non-existent in other parts of the world. In the developing world, in particular, where funding is limited, the discourse on 'artistic value' is profoundly different. Funding remains a constant battle for artists, especially those working in conservative countries or repressive environments, those in conflict zones and those engaging in human rights activism. The 2018 UNESCO Global Report notes in this respect that '[w]hile Parties reported on measures to provide financial support for artists and through other mechanisms, artists may fear not getting funding for work that tackles difficult issues, and government funders may include political considerations in their arts funding policies'.[80] Artists and cultural rights defenders may be indirectly inhibited in their work, if their ability to receive international funding is curtailed (e.g. by being labelled as 'foreign agents'). This point has also been raised by the former Rapporteur on cultural rights, in discussing limitations to artistic freedom.[81]

6.2 OBSCENITY, ARTISTIC DEFENCES AND THE HUMAN BODY

This section proceeds on the premise that in disputes involving obscenity a presumption of freedom should be applied in favour of art, particularly *fine arts*. It further explores particular types of art that raise more delicate questions, such as human dignity, sexual exploitation and the protection of children. In this regard it refers to *cadaver art* and arts involving child pornography as 'hard cases'.

6.2.1 *Defences against Obscenity for Fine Arts and Performance*

Exploring the distinct nature of the arts as 'fiction' would be useful at this point. Defences against obscenity and other morality-related offences have emerged in domestic laws with respect to literary freedom, as explained in Chapter 2. Due to the imprecise nature and scope of the very term 'art' such

79 Soucek *supra* note 64 at 389–90 and 392–93.

80 UNESCO, *Re|Shaping Cultural Policies* (UNESCO 2018) at 222 (referring to State obligations to 'support, not intervene').

81 UN General Assembly, *Universality, Cultural Diversity and Cultural Rights*, 25 July 2018, UN Doc A/73/227, paras 35 and 74 (calling all States to 'Continue to engage with and support human rights mechanisms at the international, regional and national levels, including through adequate funding, so that they can uphold universal human rights for all').

defences cannot be applied to the arts in general. They should, however, be applied specifically in relation to fine arts and, arguably, performance.

6.2.1.1 Painting, Sculpture and the Artistic Genre of Nude

The first type of arts that could benefit from an artistic defence grounded on their 'special nature' is traditional fine arts. Contrary to those arts using the medium of speech, traditional fine arts, such as painting and sculpture cannot be penalized for obscenity. Art is not reality – neither is it necessarily a representation of it. This is also the point of the *Treachery of Images* by the Belgian surrealist painter Magritte, who painted a pipe in an extremely realistic way, adding the inscription *Ceci n'est pas une pipe* (i.e. this is not a pipe).[82] Similar findings have been those of the German Federal Constitutional Court (GFCC), starting with *Mephisto*: 'Artistic activity involves both the conscious and the unconscious, in a manner not rationally separable. Intuition, imagination, and knowledge of the art all play a part in artistic creation'.[83]

The *nude* is arguably the bare minimum of what should no longer be considered immoral, nor obscene. An argument could be made from the history and practice of art, namely the familiarity of artists with the human body and specifically the artistic genre of the *nude*. Since the rediscovery of antiquity and the neo-Platonic movement, artists have acquired their skills 'by long hours of copying antique and Renaissance masterpieces and by drawing studio models'.[84] This is true not only of European artists but also artists trained in Europe. The nude has in this way survived the centuries all the way to modernity. As Greek antiquity is rediscovered in the late Middle Ages, the representation of nudity becomes more frequent and more explicit, especially in mythology representations and the Hellenistic image of *Eros*. Works as famous as Ingres' *Grande Odalisque* (1814) were perceived as scandalous at the time of their creation, yet became famous in later times.[85] Some works with *nudes* however could be perceived as scandalous in any medium

82 cf Marci Hamilton, 'Art Speech' (1996) 49 *Vanderbilt Law Review* 73, 88, 94.

83 *Mephisto* 1 BvR 435/68 (24 February 1971) at 49; Markezinis trnsl, German Law Archive, 1999, available at <https://germanlawarchive.iuscomp.org/?p=56>. See also Chapter 2 (on the legacy of the Weimar Constitution).

84 McSherry Fowble, 'Without a Blush: The Movement toward Acceptance of the Nude as an Art Form in America, 1800–1825' (1974) 9 *Winterthur Portfolio* 103–21; Thomas Thorne, 'America's Earliest Nude?' (1949) 6(4) *The William and Mary Quarterly* 565, 565.

85 cf Adler *supra* note 44 at 1375 ('Indeed, the history of art includes many examples of sexually explicit art works that society denounced as shocking and repulsive only later to deem them masterpieces').

other than painting or sculpture. An illustration of this is Bronzino's *Allegory of Venus and Cupid* (1545), depicting a semi-naked young woman in a sexual encounter with a child, currently exhibited at the British National Gallery.

The way that the fine arts have evolved today should be interpreted in a way that grants a defence against indecency and obscenity to all kinds of paintings and sculptures, including the most realistic – and 'crude' ones (i.e. those that 'depict sexual relations in a crude manner').[86] Unlike what is commonly thought, obscenity, indecency and other public morality trials, albeit rare, still occur in the domain of fine arts. This is especially true for vivid and expressive artistic works, or art installations. For example, in 2001, a French first instance tribunal terminated the exhibition *Présumés Innocents* curated by the director of the Paris Ecole des Beaux Arts as 'child-porn'.[87] The exhibition contained about 200 artworks depicting among other things children naked or in sexualized poses (including, for example, Brook Shield's daughter 'naked and wearing make-up'),[88] but also realistic works (such as Elke Krystufek's installation showing her masturbating, previously at the Brooklyn Museum). Precautions such as zoning and warning signs for the protection of minors are sufficiently proportionate measures to protect childhood in these cases.

This element has also been taken into account by the ECtHR in virtually all cases concerning public morality that were brought before it. The outcome of *Müller* (or *S. and G.*) might have been different had the applicants taken better precautions to protect children from public viewing. In the former, the European Court and Commission respectively emphasized that 'the general public had free access to them, as the organisers had not imposed any admission charge or any age-limit'[89] and in the latter, that 'the sculpture was displayed in an exhibition which was open to, and which sought to attract the public'.[90]

6.2.1.2 Bodily Harm in Performance Art

The second type of arts that could eventually benefit from an artistic defence grounded on its 'special nature' and historic development is arguably performance. This, however, is not because of the nature of performance as 'fictitious', but rather because of its evolution as a sui generis theatrical activity.

86 *Müller supra* note 46 at 36.

87 Stéphanie Moisdon, 'Plainte contre l'exposition Présumés innocents, CAPC, Musée de Bordeaux' (2001) 42 *Chimères* 17 (in French). See also *infra* the next section on child pornography in the arts.

88 ibid at 21–22.

89 *Müller supra* note 46 at para 36.

90 *S. and G. supra* note 49 at 5 (*in fine*).

Performance in fact consists of particularly expressive, and typically provocative, conduct. Extreme performances may involve bodily harm, suffering, nude, S/M practices and trauma – occasionally causing bodily harm or damage. US-based artists' performance of the 1970s and 1980s played a pioneering role in establishing performance as an 'unparalleled exploration of the myriad ways in which performance has been interpreted, its importance to disciplines from anthropology to linguistics, and how it underpins essential concepts of human society'.[91] Chris Burden is arguably the author of the most notorious artistic performance of early postmodern art – *Shoot* (1971):

> 'Shoot' (1971) [performed in a gallery in California, at the presence of few friends] consisted of the 25-year-old Burden being shot in the arm at close range by a friend wielding a rifle. A few inches off, and Burden would have probably died. Instead, as we see in the original piece above, he walks off very quickly, more in shock than pain. His intention was to be grazed by the bullet. It went a little deeper [. . .].[92]

The legal interest of performance, however, is in reality minimal. In the context of criminal law, minor bodily harm is typically not prosecuted *ex officio*, while self-harm (and even suicide) is also left unpunished. Moreover, performers typically harm themselves but not others (with the occasional exception – *Piss Action*, for example, a 1969 performance where the performer urinated in front of the audience, eventually, harming those in the front rows).[93] This applies even to extreme forms of performance, such as of Italian Franko B who explores the 'ritual violation' of his own body[94] and Chinese performer Yang Zhichao, who planted grass on his back during a live performance.[95]

Things appear to be more complex in those cases where artistic performance coincides with vandalism and political activism. These cases are generally tackled under public order provisions, rather than public morality. As a general rule, however, symbolic speech has better chances of being protected

91 Indicatively, Marvin Carlson, *Performance* (3rd ed, Routledge) *A Critical Introduction* (2nd ed, Routledge 2016).

92 ibid at 171; Dominic Johnson, *Unlimited Action: The Performance of Extremity in the 1970s* (Manchester University Press 2019). See also Eric Kutner, 'Watch Chris Burden Get Shot for the Sake of Art' (1971), 28 May 2015 <www.openculture.com/2015/05/watch-chris-burden-get-shot-for-the-sake-of-art-1971.html>.

93 See e.g. <www.artsy.net/article/artsy-editorial-body-issues-artists-fought-erotic-readings-work>.

94 Patrick Campbell and Helen Spackman, 'With/out An-Aesthetic: The Terrible Beauty of Franko B' (1988) 42 *Theatre and Drama Review* 56–74 (on FranKo B's radical live art).

95 Thomas Berghuis, 'Considering Huanjing: Positioning Experimental Art in China' (2004) 12 *Positions: East Asia cultures critique* 711–31.

if it shows evidence of at least some degree of 'creativity', particularly when conveying a political message. By way of example, in a case against Hungary, the ECtHR accepted that exposing dirty clothing on the fence surrounding the Hungarian parliament 'qualif[ied] as an artistic and political' type of expression, since the purpose was to complain about the political crisis in the country.[96] The latest case law of the European Court shows a trend valuing activism even in cases of (minor) vandalism. In a case against Moldova, the Court found that condemning an applicant who protested before the Moldovan parliament by displaying sculptures 'represent[ing] an erect penis with a picture of the face of a high-ranking politician attached to its head [. . .]' and another 'represent[ing] a large vulva with pictures of several high-ranking prosecutors between the labia'[97] was an unnecessary infringement with regard to the right to freedom of expression under article 10 of the European Convention.[98] It would have been interesting to see whether the 'artistic freedom' defence would be sustained in the case of Andreyevich Pavlenskiy, Russian performing artist and political activist, regarding his condemnation for setting the Russian Federal Security Service (the FSB) headquarters' door on fire in the context of his performance 'art action'. His case, however, was discontinued due to the applicant's loss of interest in pursuing the case, according to the information received by the Court's Registry.[99]

6.2.2 *Human Dignity and Cadaver Art*

6.2.2.1 The Exhibition *Body Worlds* (*Korpewelte*)

The exhibition *Body Worlds* (*Korpewelte*)[100] is worth mentioning at this point due to its impact on debates concerning morality, artistic (and scientific) freedom and public entertainment. *Body Worlds* is in simple terms an anatomical exhibition – a macabre version of Madame Tussauds. It was presented for the first time in Berlin in 1995, evolved over time and still ongoing in

96 *Tatár and Fáber v Hungary* no 26005/08 and 26160/08, Merits and Just Satisfaction, 12 June 2012, at para 41. cf *Eon v France* no 26118/10, 14 March 2013.

97 *Mătăsaru v the Republic of Moldova* App nos 69714/16 and 71685/16, 15 April 2019, para 7 (noting also that the installation included also 'inflated balloons in the form of male genitals attached to nearby trees').

98 ibid para 36. The applicant was convicted for hooliganism under Moldavian law and sentenced to three years of imprisonment ('the domestic courts went beyond what would have amounted to a "necessary" restriction on the applicant's freedom of expression'). See also e.g. *Mandreigelya v Russia* App no 34310/13, 23 June 2020 (concerning a 'static demonstration').

99 *Petr Andreyevich Pavlenskiy v Russia* App no 18965/16, 3 September 2020 (Struck out of the list).

100 <https://bodyworlds.com/>.

various parts of the world. It consists of assembled human parts and cadavers put on display in various poses as well as body parts, organs, embryos and foetuses, preserved through the technique of plastination. Plastination is a technique invented in 1977 by German anatomist Gunther von Hagens, who is also the main exhibition organizer. It is considered a 'major breakthrough in the teaching of anatomy' and 'a remarkably useful research tool'.[101] As noted by Jones and Whitaker, while the first type of plastinates (the body parts – or 'body regions') is 'familiar territory to anatomists', the second type (the whole-body plastinates) 'are from another realm entirely'.[102] Hence, while immensely successful in terms of box office,[103] *Body Worlds* has triggered mixed reactions by anatomists[104] and the art worlds.[105] Criticism has been based on two counts. First, the fact that the entertainment rationale has replaced the scientific and educational one, particularly since the entrance fee and overall atmosphere is equivalent to that of a cultural event. Second, the origin of the bodies and the associated moral concerns and allegations of the International Coalition to End Transplant Abuse in China (ETAC) that the bodies may belong to 'executed Chinese political prisoners'.[106] This said, various official medical entities have expressed their support, including the American Association of Anatomy, 'on condition that the body donors had given informed consent'.[107] In Australia, on the contrary, following the latest *Body Worlds* exhibition, a Committee of Inquiry into Human Organ Trafficking and Organ Transplant Tourism was set up. This committee issued a report, questioning the procedures on the basis of which consent is given.[108]

101 Gareth Jones and Maja Whitaker, 'Engaging with Plastination and the Body Worlds Phenomenon: A Cultural and Intellectual Challenge for Anatomists' (2009) 22 *Clinical Anatomy* 770, 273.

102 ibid at 271.

103 ibid ('they have attracted more than 50 million visitors in over 140 cities across America, Africa, Asia, and Europe').

104 ibid at 771 and 277ff. See also J. T. H. Connor, 'Exhibit Essay Review: "Faux Reality" Show? The "Body Worlds" Phenomenon and Its Reinvention of Anatomical Spectacle' (2007) 81(4) *Bulletin of the History of Medicine* 848.

105 Nicky Falkof, 'The Exhibited Corpse: Spectacle and Display in Body Worlds Johannesburg' (2018) 32(1) *Critical Arts* 1.

106 See in particular, Madeleine Bridgett, *China's Plastinated Bodies and Specimen Industry – What Is Australia's Responsibility?* Presented at Parliament House, Canberra, Australia, 17 September 2018; Also Bodies on display: the risks in trading in human remains from China, report, available at <http://laogai.org/blog/bodies-display-risks-trading-human-remains.

107 Jones and Whitaker *supra* note 101 at 772 (citing Morriss-Kay 2002 and Burr 2008).

108 Australian report on Human Organ Trafficking, at <www.aph.gov.au/Parliamentary_Business/Committees/Joint/Foreign_Affairs_Defence_and_Trade/HumanOrganTrafficking/Tabled_Reports>. *Case Study on Alleged Human Tissue Trafficking*, 97–104.

6.2.2.2 Human Rights Concerns in Relation to Cadaver Art

Regardless of the accusations against human trafficking and transplant abuse, the human rights approach to *cadaver art* is likely to be less enthusiastic. Two legal issues appear to be pertinent. The first is the essentially scientific nature of such events. This places them in a substantially different position than any other purely artistic exhibition. This is because art, except for broadcasting and audiovisual, remains unregulated. Scientific exhibitions, on the contrary, abide by strict processes of approval by anatomy and bioethics boards. Some of these boards have not been particularly favourable to *Body Worlds*. For instance, the Florida Anatomical Board disapproved the event and called legislators to 'carefully consider the tolerable ranges within our *society of the use of human bodies for* science, study and exhibition'.[109] The exhibition, however, opened as an artistic event.

The applicable criterion in balancing the legitimacy of such events is equally important. Clearly maintaining the principle of harm as a criterion of legitimacy of this type of art would absolve the artists of these expressions from liability. International law appears to privilege a stricter criterion based on human dignity. This is not only because of emerging customary law on the display of human tissues,[110] but more so because it conflicts with the spirit of the Universal Declaration on Bioethics and Human Rights (2005), which underlines that the 'ethical issues raised by the rapid advances in science [...] should be examined with due respect to the dignity of the human person and universal respect for, and observance of, human rights and fundamental freedoms'.[111] In the context of the Council of Europe, in addition, the Convention on Human Rights and Biomedicine (1997) clearly prohibits organ and tissue removal from persons who are not able to consent (with the sole exception of regenerative tissue),[112] and specifically bans the display of parts of

[109] Orlando Sentinel, 'Cadaver Art Show Opens in Florida Despite Board's Objection' (*LA Times*, 19 August 2005) <www.latimes.com/archives/la-xpm-2005-aug-19-na-cadavers19-story.html>.

[110] Displaying human remains or tissues without consent is in violation of various domestic laws, such as, for example, the 2004 British Human Tissue Act.

[111] UNESCO Declaration on 19 October 2005.

[112] Convention for the Protection of Human Rights and Dignity of the Human Being with regard to the Application of Biology and Medicine: Convention on Human Rights and Biomedicine, Oviedo, 4.IV.1997, art 20, para 1.

the human body for financial gain, as in the case at hand.[113] Although this convention enjoys a particularly low number of ratifications,[114] it is still an important text to be taken into account in the balancing of the freedom to display artistic (or scientific) work against human dignity. The originality of this convention, however, is that for the first time, a legally binding international text does not simply refer to dignity as a principle applying to all rights, but rather as one, unique and justiciable right.[115] Moreover, it is cited increasingly as 'the ethical and legal frame of reference for the decision-making process [concerning] the principle of autonomy'.[116]

A far stretched view on the unlawfulness of *cadaver art* under human rights law is that espoused by the First Instance Court of Paris. In a 2009 provisional order, the court decided to ban the exhibition *Bodies* as a matter of urgency. This was not only because of the commercial nature of the exhibition and possible 'illicit origins' of the bodies, but also because *Bodies* was deemed disrespectful towards the dead. Interestingly, the court referred to Sophocles' tragedy *Antigone* (422 BC), and the fact that 'the treatment of human corpses is at the heart of the democratic debate since the triangle of Thebes: *Antigone, Creon, Polynice*'.[117] This could be taken as implying that respect for the dead is also a fundamental principle under natural law; chiefly on account of the fact that the particular passage (in which Oedipus' daughter decides to bury the corpse of her brother Polynices despite the opposing edict of her uncle and King of Thebes Creon) underlines the importance of burying the dead not only by 'the laws set among men' but also 'the unwritten and unfailing statutes of heaven' that mortals cannot override.[118]

[113] ibid art 21 (Prohibition of financial gain): 'The human body and its parts shall not, as such, give rise to financial gain'.

[114] As of today, only few States have ratified it (Croatia, France, Norway, Switzerland, Turkey), list available at <www.coe.int/en/web/conventions/full-list/-/conventions/treaty/164/signatures?p_auth=yK5hPe9u>.

[115] Details of Treaty no 164, Convention for the Protection of Human Rights and Dignity of the Human Being with regard to the Application of Biology and Medicine: Convention on Human Rights and Biomedicine, <www.coe.int/en/web/conventions/full-list/-/conventions/treaty/164>.

[116] E.g. *Lambert and Others v France* App no 46043/14, Judgment (Merits and Just Satisfaction) 5 June 2015, para 60.

[117] Tribunal de Grande Instance de Paris, Referees' order, 21 April 2009 (in favour of the Associations 'Solidarité Chine' and 'ensemble contre la peine de mort').

[118] See Sophocles, *Antigone* (Jebb transl.), verses 386–580 <http://classics.mit.edu/Sophocles/antigone.html>, Antigone reasons on the basis of the laws of God that are not written and 'immutable'.

6.2.3 *Paedophilia and Child Pornography as a Hard Case*

6.2.3.1 The Problem of Child Pornography in Fine Arts and Photography

One of the best known controversies in the United States arose in the early 1990s, when photographer Sally Mann took pictures of her three children at their summer home, in Virginia, United States, including in naked and semi-naked poses. The photographs were assembled in a project called *Immediate Family* and exposed since then in various galleries and museums.[119] The pictures could be interpreted by viewers as child pornography – yet, Mann wrote:

> These are not my children; they are figures on a silvery paper slivered out of time [. . .] I believe my morality should have no bearing on the discussion of the pictures I made.[120]

In the United Kingdom and the United States controversy has sparked over the work of several artists, including Balthus, Gauguin and Eric Gill. In 2019 the Metropolitan Museum of New York received a petition signed by over 8,700 persons to remove one particular work, Balthus' *Thérèse Dreaming* (1938), depicting a naked eleven-year old girl in a provocative pose.[121] Likewise, the British National Gallery has received requests to take down Gauguin's works, especially his painting *Tehamana Has Many Parents* (1893), which depicts a thirteen-year old girl (presumably Gauguin's lover).[122] In Gauguin's case, it has been further argued that the acts of persons behind the art are 'so egregious' that choosing to expose and perform as such would be difficult.[123] Other recent scandals concern Eric Gill's work, and paintings, particularly *Girl in Bath II* (1923), which is currently on display at the Ditchling Museum of Art + Craft in Sussex, United Kingdom.[124] In 2015, a

[119] Alina Cohen, 'Why Sally Mann's Photographs of Her Children Can Still Make Viewers Uncomfortable' (4 January 2018) <www.artsy.net/article/artsy-editorial-sally-mann-s-photographs-children-viewers-uncomfortable>.

[120] ibid.

[121] Eileen Kinsella, 'The Met Says "Suggestive" Balthus Painting Will Stay after Petition for Its Removal Is Signed by Thousands' (5 December 2017) <https://news.artnet.com/art-world/met-museum-responds-to-petition-calling-for-removal-of-balthus-painting-1169105>.

[122] Farah Nayeri, 'Is It Time Gauguin Got Canceled?' (*New York Times*, 28 November 2019) <www.nytimes.com/2019/11/18/arts/design/gauguin-national-gallery-london.html> (discussing Gauguin's notoriety for having a 'pray for young girls').

[123] ibid.

[124] Rachel Cooke, 'Eric Gill: Can We Separate the Artist from the Abuser?' (*The Guardian*, 7 April 2017) <www.theguardian.com/artanddesign/2017/apr/09/eric-gill-the-body-ditchling-exhibition-rachel-cooke>.

similar controversy erupted over artist and collector Graham Ovenden (incarcerated two years for paedophilia in 2013), when a district judge ordered that 'his personal collection of paintings and photographs be destroyed'.[125] One of the paintings showed a young girl's buttocks, which had been commissioned by Princess Diana, in order to raise money for a charitable cause.[126]

A difference should be drawn here between works considered well-established cultural heritage and contemporary productions. Realistically, the law cannot hinder in retrospect the display of controversial art produced prior to World War II, not even by concealing a certain paedophile 'gaze'. The slippery slope is evident and could wreak havoc on a great deal of art, music and poetry. Bans could be used to censor, adjust and even destroy paintings of Cupids in Renaissance and Baroque art, as well as passionate poetry and folk songs narrating the love for underage girls and boys. Ultimately, this solution could lead to the seizure and destruction not only of Gauguin, Balthus and Gill, but also Degas' *Dancing girls*, Sappho's poems, *Lolita* (the infamous novel in which Nabokov narrates the love of a literature professor for his underage stepdaughter) and numerous tales of the Greek mythology. Such arguments can have far-reaching implications, as clearly not all cultural heritage has been created with human rights ideals in mind. In fact, much of classical art promotes racist, segregationist, sexist or colonial notions and ideas.[127] Gauguin himself was not only attracted to young Tahitian girls; he was also the impersonation of the civilized Parisian artist vis-à-vis the exotic and primitive 'otherness'. The law clearly cannot play the role of the moralistic ruler, especially not in the sphere of fine arts. Cancelling what is already recognized as valuable is not only absurd and implausible, but also an outright attack against UNESCO principles and declarations on the preservation of cultural heritage (including intangible heritage). And yet, as the *Ovenden* case evinces, the question needs to be tackled not only with respect to the works of the past, but also contemporary artistic production. The impact of the works on the public should also be considered. The problem becomes more acute as the public is in fact naturally intrigued by such controversies, which causes the artworks to become extremely popular. By way of example, following the *New York Times*' cover story on *Immediate Family*, Sally Mann's photo-book sold about 10,000 copies. This, however,

[125] Brian Boucher, 'London Judge Rules Artworks by Graham Ovenden Must Be Destroyed' (*Art News*, 14 October 2015) <https://news.artnet.com/art-world/graham-ovenden-photos-destroyed-339976>.

[126] ibid.

[127] cf George Steiner, *Bluebeard's Castle: Some Notes towards the Redefinition of Culture* is a 1971. As Steiner notes in the *Bluebeard's Castle*, 'great art of the centuries has been created in conditions of racial discrimination, apartheid and total disregard for any human value'.

resulted in 'Mann's children becoming ever more visible',[128] which is precisely what the law, presumably, would disdain.

As discussed earlier in Chapter 2, the right to artistic freedom needs to be balanced not only against public morality considerations, but also the 'rights of others', particularly children's rights and their right to privacy.[129] Additional guidance or indications as to where exactly one draws the line are not provided in the text of any human rights treaty or the UDHR. The aforementioned 'defence of fiction' could be used, on the one hand, to absolve visual artists from liability. On the other hand, international human rights law and the protection of artistic freedom cannot operate in a vacuum. Child pornography has risen[130] to a matter of utmost concern for governments, international and regional bodies, regulatory entities, UN agencies and human rights bodies,[131] particularly in relation to virtual and online pornography and the increasing sexual exploitation of children. It is difficult to see how the artistic defence could be applicable in relation to artworks of photo-realism, for example.

An interesting analogy is the human rights approach towards racist attitudes accepted in the past. Slavery and colonialism are arguably the best illustrations. In the area of freedom of speech, hate speech may be viewed as emblematic of the various opposing forces. Incitement to racial hatred for instance may justify bans on expression today, even though people found this type of speech acceptable in the past.[132] By the same token, morality cannot serve as a perpetual ban. Limitations related to offences of sensibilities or trauma could provide another interesting parallel. The Israel Philharmonic Orchestra from 1938 onwards (at the time known as the 'Palestine orchestra') maintains an unofficial ban on Wagner's symphonies in light of the Holocaust national trauma.[133] The ban was confirmed in the mid-1980s by the Israeli Supreme Court,[134] which found that this was a lawful type of prior restraint.

[128] ibid.

[129] See e.g. Article 19, paragraph 3; Article 10, paragraph 2.

[130] Jonathan Clough, 'Lawful Acts, Unlawful Images: The Problematic Definition of Child Pornography' (2012) 38 *Monash University Law Review* 213, 216.

[131] Including the UN office of drugs and crime, the WHO, the UNESCO and the UN Committee of the Rights of the Child.

[132] cf *Stephen Hagan v Australia*, Communication no 26/2002, UN Doc CERD/C/62/D/26/2002 (2003), discussed also in Chapter 5.

[133] Moshe Brilliant, 'Playing of Wagner in Israel Provokes Disturbance' (*New York Times*, 17 October 1981) (reprint) <www.nytimes.com/1981/10/17/arts/playing-of-wagner-in-israel-provokes-disturbance.html>.

[134] Israeli Supreme Court, *Noah Films v Censorship Council of Films and Theatre* 549/75, PD 30 (1), 757, cited by Raphael Cohen-Almagor, *The Scope of Tolerance: Studies on the Costs of Free Expression and Freedom of the Press* (2006) at 84–85.

This approach is justified by a variety of reasons that are time-specific – for example, the association between that music with Nazi ideology, the memories of concentration camps and the fact that Holocaust survivors may be included among musicians and the public. Today, however, similar bans may no longer be self-evident. Indeed, in early 2011 members of the Orchestra decided to 'break the tradition' and 'play a work by Hitler's favourite composer'.[135]

6.2.3.2 Japanese Manga and *Lolicons*

The question that arises at this stage is whether a specific defence *pro artis* can apply against child pornography. An interesting example is offered by the Japanese tradition in comics (*manga*) and animation (*anime*). Contrary to American cartoons, as developed by Disney in the 1930s, manga has never been a child-specific type of entertainment. Takeuchi, for example, explains how the tradition of comics and anime are mainstream art forms in Japan, well rooted in Japanese history and artistic heritage.[136] *Manga* and *anime*, despite their popularity, have generally been outside the reach of legal regulation. In the 1960s and 1970s, in particular, during the era of 'censorship' in Japan, *manga* creators became extremely imaginative in finding ways to circumvent the prohibition of regulation (which generally prohibited the depiction of male genitalia and male orgasms, contrary to say, women's breasts, women's orgasms and non-human genitalia).[137]

This said, both *manga* and *anime*, and arguably also cyberpunk movies such as *Te-Tsuo* have been more open in the representation of sex, including sexualized versions of children. A particular type of *manga*, the so-called *Lolicons* has been at the centre of public debate on the limits of artistic freedom, cross-border child pornography and virtual pornography. *Lolicons* are manga-style representations of pre-pubescent girls drawn in a highly sexualized way,[138] which typically appear online or in 'erotic magazines' for adults such as *Manga Lo* (*Lolicons* only). *Lolicons* are generally perceived in

[135] Jane Biran, 'Richard Wagner's Troublesome History in Israel' (*The Jerusalem Post*, 28 January 2020) <www.jpost.com/israel-news/culture/richard-wagners-troublesome-history-in-israel-615645>.

[136] Susan Napier, *Anime from Akira to Princess Mononoke: Experiencing Contemporary Japanese Animation* (Palgrave 2001); Cory Lyn Takeuchi, 'Regulating Lolicon: Toward Japanese Compliance with Its International Legal Obligations to Ban Virtual Child Pornography' (2015) 44 *Georgia Journal of International and Comparative Law* 195, 198.

[137] Takeuchi *supra* note 136 at 79–80 and 165–66.

[138] ibid at 198.

the West as a shortcut for *Lolita*. This perception has been enforced by the omnipresence of child sex and sex-trafficking, as well as the photographic equivalent of *Lolicons*: the so-called junior idols, girls that pose for pornographic magazines, 'wearing bikinis or lingerie in highly suggestive poses'.[139] From the perspective of authors and cartoonists, however, it is widely perceived that the term 'Lolita complex' is 'an inappropriate rendering of *rorikon* [*lolicon*] given the Western popular representation of Lolita'.[140]

Lolicons have been recently the subject of criticism, especially among Western authors, as the Japanese legislator granted them artistic 'immunity'. The first time that Japan passed a relevant statute was in 1999, substantially amended to include child pornography in 2014. This amendment, however, while criminalizing child pornography provides an artistic defence for *Lolicons*.[141] For example, under Japanese criminal law, *manga* and *anime* constitute explicit exceptions to the relevant Japanese law.[142] This exception allows Japanese *manga* and *anime* 'containing depictions of pre-pubescent boys and girls engaging in sexual and oftentimes violent acts' to be free from restraints on the basis of such laws.[143] While the amendment has been passed largely thanks to the advocacy of the Japan Cartoonists Association, the debate on the impact of *manga* on the youth remains open. With few exceptions including the 'Otaku Murderer', harm to society is considered minimal.[144] In the United States popular sentiment has been that *manga* and *lolicons* are virtually equivalent to child pornography. An illustration is the prosecution of a manga lover in Iowa under the American 2003 PROTECT Act on virtual

[139] Takeuchi *supra* note 136 at 196; also Patrick Galbraith, 'Lolicon: The Reality of "Virtual Child Pornography" in Japan' (2011) 12 *Image & Narrative* at 83 and generally Patrick Galbraith, *Otaku and the Struggle for Imagination in Japan* (Duke University Press 2019).

[140] Deb Aoki, 'Is Translating "Lolicon" as "Pedophile" Accurate?' (9 August 2019) <www.animenewsnetwork.com/answerman/2019-08-09>.

[141] Takeuchi *supra* note 136 at 198.

[142] ibid, referring to the Japanese law 'Punishing Acts Related to Child Prostitution and Child Pornography'. Similar defences were accepted in the past in some jurisdictions (e.g. excluding works with artistic or educational merit from the definition of pornography), yet not without controversy, see. e.g. Supreme Court of Canada of 26 January 2001, *R. v Sharpe* [2001] 1 SCR 45 (reversed in 2011). On this, Marcin Górski, 'Freedom of Artistic Expression: Constitutional Lessons from Canada' (2017) 2 *Eötvös Loránd University Law Journal* 1.

[143] ibid at 197.

[144] ibid (reporting however that in the early 1980s, a horrific crime involving a manga-adept ('*Otaku*') shocked the Japanese society, when twenty-seven-year old Tsutomo Miyazaki (known as 'the *Otaku* Murderer') kidnapped, murdered and molested four preschool girls. His home collection contained, as reports, almost 6,000 videos, many of which were 'Lolicons').

child pornography, whose collection of about 1,200 manga books and publications were seized, including from the anthology *Comic Lo.*[145]

6.2.3.3 Raising Awareness about Child Pornography

A scenario explored last under this section is that involving child pornography photographs and videos that are part of a broader project of conceptual art. Under international human rights law, depictions of sexual or indecent material involving children are not justified, even when done for 'good cause'. The European Court of Human Rights has had the chance to deal with a similar case involving contemporary arts, in which it did not find artistic freedom relevant. A Finnish artist (and university lecturer) exhibited child-pornographic material downloaded from the Internet on the occasion of an exhibition titled *Virgin-Whore Church*. Kartunnen clearly did not aim at encouraging paedophilia, but rather at 'rais[ing] awareness of how widespread and easily accessible child pornography was'.[146] In the *cas d'espèce* the authorities seized Kartunnen's photographs and closed the exhibition on grounds of anti-obscenity criminal laws criminalizing, inter alia, the manufacturing and distribution of sexually obscene pictures or visual recordings depicting children, violence or bestiality.[147] Acknowledging 'the applicant's good intentions' and admitting that 'conceptions of sexual morality have changed in recent years',[148] the Court did not go as far as affirming that the specific works in question were protected as a form of artistic expression, as claimed by the applicant.[149] In this, obscenity offences could be juxtaposed with art that promotes hate speech, given one of those grounds that may legitimize prior restraints to free speech.

The main legal challenge in this respect is the definition of child pornography. The Convention on the Rights of the Child (CRC) establishes an obligation for States to take 'all appropriate measures' to combat 'the exploitative use of children in pornographic performances and materials',[150] and is complemented by an Optional Protocol to the CRC on the sale of children, child prostitution and child pornography.[151] Neither the convention nor the protocol, however, define what child pornography is. The Budapest Convention on

[145] Galbraith *supra* note 139 at 96.

[146] *Karttunen v Finland* App no 1685/10, Admissibility, 10 May 2011 (inadmissible).

[147] Act no 39/1889, as amended by Act no 650/2004, cited in para 13 of the decision.

[148] ibid at paras 23–24.

[149] In her submissions the applicant argued that 'it was well-established that artistic expression, including that of an erotic nature, fell within the scope of Article 10'.

[150] CRC, art. 34 (1) (c).

[151] A/RES/54/263, 25 May 2000.

Cybercrime on the contrary, that was negotiated in the context of the Council of Europe, defines child pornography as any pornographic material that visually depicts minors (or persons appearing to be minors) engaged in sexually explicit conduct.[152] This convention, in addition, appears to include a defence for 'abstract' art, as the definition of child pornography includes also 'realistic images' of child pornography.[153] Under this convention, therefore, painting, sculptures and *manga* may be excluded from the definition of child pornography. Photographs, on the other hand, and extremely 'realistic' depictions, even when they are illustrations or part of a conceptual art project, can legitimately be considered a crime under this convention. The argument on the 'representation of reality' as an artistic defence therefore does not and cannot go as far as to cover visual arts that use child pornography to raise awareness about it and a State that encourages this type of exhibitions can legitimately be held to be breaching human rights law standards.

CONCLUDING REMARKS

This chapter discussed the way that public morality considerations impact the arts, attempting to disentangle the concepts of 'indecency', 'obscenity' and 'pornography'. Public morality standards are constantly evolving and changing. This makes the concepts of decency and morality highly subjective and dependant on local standards. The absence of a universal agreement on defining morality (let alone 'obscenity') is also characteristic of the contextuality of the relevant offences.

Domestic courts occasionally attempt to define public morality, with reference to the 'average person's morality'. In US jurisprudence, for example, the *Miller* test defines obscenity, suggesting that a work that 'taken as a whole, lacks serious literary, artistic, political, or scientific value' falls outside the protection of the First Amendment. 'Indecent expressions' on the contrary may still be constitutionally protected – even if they are subject to regulation for the protection of children and other public interests.

The key question that arises with respect to artworks therefore is whether artistic value can eventually override these public morality considerations. And in practice too, criteria including value and merit impact creative practitioners' work and chances to receive funding (as it has been seen in the case of the US cultural wars).

[152] Council of Europe, Budapest Convention, 23 November 2001, ETS no 185, art 9 (2) (a) and (b) (entered into force in 2004).

[153] ibid at 9 (2)(c).

There is no one-size-fits-all solution. The case law of the ECtHR has never defined what public morality is or should be within Council of Europe Member States. Save for few exceptions (where decisively the Court set a minimum standard of what should be acceptable, as in the instance of a case regarding censorship of Apollinaire's *Les onze mille vierges* in Turkey), the Court's views largely revolve around the margin of appreciation doctrine. This means a wide discretion for States to decide on what is and what is not acceptable within a given society at a given time.

This chapter went on discussing possible minimum thresholds in considering artistic freedom vis-à-vis public morality offences. The artistic genre of *nude* in painting and sculpture is arguably the bare minimum of what should no longer be considered immoral, nor obscene. Furthermore, the special nature and historic development of performance, including those involving bodily harm, could possibly give rise to 'defences' for creative practitioners and performers. Depictions of child pornography on the contrary, even when part of a creative project, arguably do not fall in either of these categories. Child pornography is in fact increasingly outlawed by States around the world, impacting galleries and institutions' freedom to display art that was once acceptable. Arguments in favour of preservation could be advanced sparingly, and only with respect to works that are part of States well-established cultural heritage (such as Bronzino's *Allegory of Venus and Cupid* (1545) or Gauguin's paintings). Contemporary art involving depictions of child pornography however should never be legitimate under international standards, not even as actions of art activism and to raise awareness about paedophilia (as the European Court has also found in *Kartunnen*). The main issue in this respect is whether the depictions at stake are sufficiently 'realistic' – the Budapest Convention on Cybercrime, for instance, compels States parties to adopt measures in order to criminalize all expressions of child pornography, defining the latter not only as 'visual depictions' of sexually explicit conduct involving minors, but also 'realistic images' representing minors in such conduct. This clearly covers arts such as photography and illustration, and less clearly *manga*, cartoons and other types of non-realistic visual material. The case of *Lolicons* in the Japanese tradition of *anime*, in particular, including when created or transferred digitally, is a hard case, given that it involves highly sexualized depictions of pre-pubescent boys and girls engaging in sexual acts, without, however, being sufficiently realistic.

7

Blasphemous Paintings, Cartoons and Other Religiously Offensive Art

Close to five centuries have passed since 1573, when Paolo Veronese was tried by the Holy Inquisition for his version of *The Last Supper*. What was the Venetian painter's crime? According to the transcript of the trial,[1] he had failed to show appropriate reverence to divine figures, by painting, for example, Saint Peter 'carving a lamb in order to pass it to the other end of the Table', and another Apostle with a 'toothpick [cleaning] his teeth'.[2] This surely did not go down well with the Holy Inquisition, which enforced the rules of the Roman Catholic Church on artists' exercise of 'faithful diligence' when drawing religious themes.[3] Veronese finally got away with the punishment – anecdotally he merely changed the name of the painting to the *Feast in the House of Levi*, claiming that it was not meant to represent the Last Supper after all. Today, the theme of the Last Supper is quite routinely depicted in advertisements (as well as in LGBT activism in western European states)[4] (despite the divided stance of the

1 John-Henry Merryman and Albert Elsen (eds), *Law, Ethics and the Visual Arts* (5th ed, Kluwer Law International 2007) at 250. For a commentary also Daniel McClean and Armen Avanessian, 'Trials of the Title: The Trials of Brancusi and Veronese' in Daniel McClean (ed), *The Trials of Art* (Ridinghouse 2007) 37, 49–55.

2 Merryman and Elsen *supra* note 1 at 250–51 (In his defence, Veronese pointed to the precedent that his 'superiors' had set – in particular Michelangelo '[who painted] in Rome in the Pontifical Chapel our Lord, Jesus Christ, His mother, Saint John, St Peter and the Heavenly Host [. . .] all represented in the nude – even the virgin Mary – and in different poses with little reverence'.

3 James Waterworth, *The Canons and Decrees of the Sacred and Oecumenical Council of Trent* (Dolman 1848) 232–89 <history.hanover.edu> (especially the agenda 'on the invocation, veneration, and relics of saints, and on sacred images', and noting that religious art had to be the 'servant of the Church').

4 'Bronwyn Lundberg's Lesbian "The Last Supper" Painting Features Ellen DeGeneres and Other Gay Icons' <www.huffpost.com/entry/bronwyn-lundberg-lesbian-last-supper_n_2432348>; also 'LGBT Group Defends Gay Sex Version of The Last Supper' (Pink News, 13 April 2017) <www.pinknews.co.uk/2017/04/13/lgbt-group-defends-gay-sex-version-of-the-last-supper>.

Catholic Church on the matter).[5] Identifying artists and artworks as 'transgressive' surely in some contexts may have commercial benefits: the best illustration of this is arguably Madonna's 'Like a Prayer', which enabled her to gain artistic leverage and become a pop legend. In other cases, however, blasphemy in the sense of 'showing disrespect for God or a religion'[6] gives rise to extremely serious implications. At the time of writing, UN experts were making an appeal to Nigeria to release Yahaya Sharif-Aminu, an Islamic gospel musician from Kano, Northern Nigeria, awaiting execution on charges of blasphemy for a song he circulated on WhatsApp.[7]

Extrajudicial killings and terrorist attacks perpetrated by non-state actors have in fact, sadly, become a substantial part of the politics of blasphemy. In February 1989, a fatwa (i.e. a legal opinion on the interpretation of Islamic law) was issued by the late Ayatollah Khomeini against Salman Rushdie for his novel *The Satanic Verses*. The fatwa was in reality a death edict, setting a price of 100,000 USD on the British author's head.[8] Following publication, protests sparked not only in Iran but around the world, causing a number of injuries as well as deaths. The Iranian ambassador to the Holy See declared that 'he would kill Salman Rushdie with his own hands',[9] and various translators of the *Verses* were injured or murdered.[10]

Rushdie spent years in hiding, yet eventually got back to the literature scene.[11] The controversy over the *Verses* however left a permanent black mark against Western liberal understanding of freedom of speech. The liberty enjoyed by artists, novelists and performers in mocking religious beliefs has never been the same after 1989. This was confirmed in September 2005, when

5 Jason Horowitz, 'Pope Sends More Mixed Messages on L.G.B.T.Q. Rights' (27 June 2021) <www.nytimes.com/2021/06/27/world/europe/pope-sends-more-mixed-messages-on-lgbtq-rights.html>.

6 <https://dictionary.cambridge.org/dictionary/english/blasphemy?topic=swearing-and-blasphemy>.

7 UN Press Release, 'UN Rights Experts Urge Nigeria to Overturn Death Sentence for Singer Who Shared Song on WhatsApp' (28 September 2020) <www.ohchr.org/EN/NewsEvents/Pages/DisplayNews.aspx?NewsID=26302&LangID=E>.

8 Association for World Education, 'Written statement submitted to the UN Human Rights Council', 19 February 2004, E/CN.4/2004/NGO/252, at 2 (on The 'Rushdie Affair'/Rushdie syndrome: the right to life and the human rights mechanisms); also M. M. Slaughter, 'Salman Rushdie Affair: Apostasy, Honor, and Freedom of Speech' (1993) 1(79) *Virginia Law Review* 153, 159.

9 ibid at 15.

10 ibid at 15; Slaughter *supra* note 8 at 156.

11 Charlotte Higgins, 'Salman Rushdie: Living in Hiding Felt Like Comedy Routine at Times' (*The Guardian*, 11 August 2013) <www.theguardian.com/books/2013/aug/11/salman-rushdie-hiding-comedy-routine>. See generally also Kenan Malik, *From Fatwa to Jihad: The Rushdie Affair and its Legacy* (Atlantic 2009).

the Danish newspaper *Jyllands-Posten* published the twelve well-known controversial cartoons that produced a 'global crisis' (which culminated in attacks against embassies, death threats against cartoonists, severance of diplomatic relations and boycotts against Danish products). The crisis was repeated in 2015, when eight gunmen entered the *Charlie Hebdo* satirical magazine office in Paris, shooting at point-blank range twelve well-known French journalists, editors and political cartoonists. At that point, the world was split into two camps: those who were *Charlies*, shouting the slogan '*Je suis Charlie*', printing it on T-Shirts and posting it on Facebook pages, and those who were not.[12] The repercussions for Muslim minorities have immediately also become visible, perpetuating Islamophobic stereotypes on the one hand, and testing the foundational ideas of liberalism on the other.[13]

This chapter cannot possibly address the array of extremely complex issues raised by this new type of 'globalized controversies' – which has been, by now, the object of extensive and at times heated discussion.[14] It therefore confines itself to the human rights approach, emphasizing the need for a better, cross-cultural understanding of both religious and artistic traditions, while also pointing to the need to avoid undermining the value of free speech in the human rights edifice. The first section of this chapter therefore discusses blasphemous offences in the arts from both the 'local' and 'global' perspective, questioning the divide between secular and religious traditions. The second section examines the stance of the various human rights bodies towards blasphemous arts, attempting to identify the human rights principles applicable in controversies over creative freedom when incitement to religious hatred is involved.

[12] Mukul Devichand, 'How the World Was Changed by the Slogan "Je Suis Charlie"' (*BBC News*, 3 January 2016) <www.bbc.com/news/blogs-trending-35108339>. cf Neville Cox, 'Irreligious Beliefs' (2016) 16 *Human Rights Law Review* 195, 203; Neville Cox, 'Blasphemy and Defamation of Religion Following Charlie Hebdo' in Joel Temperman and András Koltay (eds), *Blasphemy and Freedom of Expression: Comparative, Theoretical and Historical Reflections after the Charlie Hebdo Massacre* (Cambridge University Press 2017) 53–86.

[13] For a discussion, see indicatively, Geoffrey Brahm Levey and Tariq Modood, 'The Muhammad Cartoons and Multicultural Democracies' (2009) 9(3) *Ethnicities* 427.

[14] Indicatively, Jytte Klausen, 'The Danish Cartoons and Modern Iconoclasm in the Cosmopolitan Muslim Diaspora' (2009) 8 *Harvard Middle Eastern and Islamic Review* 86–118; Jytte Klausen, *The Cartoons that Shook the World* (Yale University Press 2009); Anver Emon, 'On the Pope, Cartoons, and Apostates: Shari'a' (2006) 22 *Journal of Law & Religion* 303, 308–09; Neville Cox, 'Justifying Blasphemy Laws: Freedom of Expression, Public Morals, and International Human Rights Law' (2020) 35(1) *Journal of Law and Religion* 33–60; David Keane, 'Cartoon Violence and Freedom of Expression' (2008) 30 *Human Rights Quarterly* 845, 845–46. Also Jeanne Favret-Saada, *Comment produire une crise mondiale avec douze petits dessins* (Les Prairies ordinaires 2007).

7.1 LOCAL AND GLOBAL CONTROVERSIES

7.1.1 A *Divide between Religious and Secular States?*

7.1.1.1 The Decline of Purely Religious Arts

Looking at the history and practice of visual arts in the West, one may easily observe the decline of purely religious art. This is accompanied by a gradual openness to questions of sexuality and nudity.[15] Anti-religious art is increasingly well accepted as religious art in the Western tradition,[16] including as an avant-garde contribution to a 'theologically informed art tradition'.[17] Art critics such as Gablik have suggested even the full separation of art with the divine.[18] Installations and performances arguably more provocative than *Piss Christ* have been well-recognized as exploring questions on spirituality and faith, and sacred themes are routinely depicted in profane ways in international exhibitions and biennales. Illustrative and well-known examples in the contemporary art scene include Gober's *Virgin Mary* pierced by a six-foot long bronze-cast steel culvert pipe;[19] Kiki Smith's nude bronze sculpture with a shaved head representing the *Virgin Mary*;[20] and playful works such as *Kamera Skura* and Kunst-Fu's *Superstart* (featuring a Christ figure in a gym suit).[21]

Public morality considerations are generally wide enough to encompass controversies on religiously offensive art. In practice, the more conservative the milieu of display, the more intense reactions will be elicited. This is regardless of the characterization of the works as either blasphemous or immoral. Exhibitions featuring nudity, for example, are often targeted not only by religious extremists but also nationalist groups – as in the case of the

[15] Indicatively, see Kishore Singh, *The Naked and the Nude : The Body in Indian Modern Art* (Delhi Art Gallery 2013); also Priscilla Frank, 'Muslim Artist's Dreamy Nude Self-Portraits Show the Power of Self-Love' (*Huffington Post*, 18 April 2018) <www.huffpost.com/entry/muslim-artists-dreamy-nude-self-portraits-show-the-power-of-self-love_n_58c84fdfe4b09e52f55436d8>.

[16] James Elkins, *The Strange Place of Religion in Contemporary Art* (Routledge 2004) 39–49.

[17] Antony Julius, *Transgressions of the Arts: Art That Offends* (University of Chicago Press 2002) 27 (discussing Serrano's work).

[18] Erika Doss, 'Robert Gober's *Virgin* Installation: Issues of Spirituality in Contemporary American Art' in David Morgan and Sally Promey (eds), *Visual Culture of American Religions* (University of California Press 2001) at 136 (referring to Gibler's the 're-enchantment of Art').

[19] ibid 144–45 (on public responses).

[20] ibid at 130.

[21] Brent Plate, *Religion, Art and Visual Culture: A Cross-cultural Reader* (Palgrave 2002) 46. The artwork is currently located in the Art Institute of Chicago <www.artnet.com/magazine/people/robinson/robinson6-16-23.asp>.

Delhi Arts Gallery *Naked and the Nude* exhibition (featuring nudes painted in the 1900s) which was attacked by Hindu nationalists.[22] In other words, artists offending religious beliefs or sensibilities may still be slapped with obscenity charges, or another offences related to public morality.[23] In the case concerning Maqbool Fida Husain's version of *Bharat Mata* (Mother India), in which India was depicted as a naked woman, the High Court of Delhi found that the blasphemy provision in Section 298 of the Indian Penal Code was not applicable because there was no 'deliberate intent to wound the religious feelings of any person'.[24] The judgment therefore focused on Section 294, which dealt with obscene acts and songs, celebrating artistic freedom over moral considerations. The Court had recourse not only to pertinent judgments issued by other domestic courts but also to the Kama Sutra:

> We have been called as the land of the Kama Sutra then why is it that in the land of the Kama Sutra, we shy away from its very name? Beauty lies in the eyes of the beholder and so does obscenity.... It is most unfortunate that India's new '*puritanism*' is being carried out in the name of cultural purity and a host of ignorant people are vandalizing art and pushing us towards a pre-renaissance era.[25]

7.1.1.2 Persistence of Religious Offences

Albeit inactive in many cases, pure blasphemy offences persist in States with a constitutionally recognized religion, or in which religion holds a powerful status in the public sphere. According to the US Commission on International Religious Freedom (USCIRF) the act of blasphemy may trigger criminal prosecution in over seventy countries worldwide.[26] Blasphemy laws are also endorsed by a third of European countries, according to the Venice

[22] Mohammad Ali, 'Art Show Goes on Amid Tight Security, Protest' (*The Hindu*, 7 February 2013) <www.thehindu.com/news/national/art-show-goes-on-amid-tight-security-protest/article4386870.ece>; Singh *supra* note 15. On the Hindutva, see Sathianathan Clarke, 'Hindutva, Religious and Ethnocultural Minorities, and Indian-Christian Theology' (2002) 95 (2) *The Harvard Theological Review* 2002) 197, 200.

[23] cf Cox *supra* note 14 at 35ff.

[24] *Maqbool Fida Husain v Raj Kumar Pandey and Others*, Revision Petition nos 282/07, 114/2007 & 280/2007, 8 May 2008 (High Court of Delhi).

[25] ibid at para 110.

[26] Joelle Fiss and Jocelyn Getgen Kestenbaum, 'Respecting Rights?, Measuring the World's Blasphemy Laws' (US Commission on International Religious Freedom, July 2017) <www.uscirf.gov>.

Commission of the Council of Europe as of 2009.[27] In Poland, for instance, the controversy over blasphemous artists revived in 2015 after the Polish Constitutional Court held in favour of the constitutionality of the relevant Polish law,[28] in a case brought by an anti-establishment art collective and the pop singer Dorota Rabczewska.[29] Other blasphemy prosecutions are ongoing – for example, the prosecution of a metal band singer convicted after posting an image on social media showing him stamping on a picture of the Virgin Mary.[30]

In religious States and States where religion enjoys an important role in public life blasphemy offences are overall treated in a way harsher than in secular States. The case of Egypt has acquired publicity after the assassination of eminent intellectual and writer Farag Foda in 1992,[31] and the assassination bid on Nobel laureate Naguib Mahfouz in 1994, who, albeit 'a cultural light who brought Arab literature to the world',[32] was considered an apostate by

[27] European Commission for Democracy Through Law (Venice Commission), 'On the Relationship between Freedom of Expression and Freedom of Religion: The Issue of Regulation and Prosecution of Blasphemy, Religious Insult and Incitement to Religious Hatred', Strasbourg, 23 October 2008, CDL-AD(2008) 026 (hereafter 'Venice Commission Report') 273ff; also, indicatively, Ian Cram, 'Blasphemy, the Public Sphere and Democratic Self-Government' in *Blasphemy and Freedom of Expression supra* note 12 at 87, 96–97.

[28] Polish Constitutional Court, SK 54/13, 6 October 2015 <https://sip.lex.pl/orzeczenia-i-pisma-urzedowe/orzeczenia-sadow/sk-54-13-wyrok-trybunalu-konstytucyjnego-521903084>, and with reference to under article 196 of the Polish Criminal Code, which punishes whoever publicly offends the religious feelings of other persons with imprisonment of up to two years. See also <www.article19.org/resources/poland-blasphemy-conviction-pop-star-violates-free-expression>.

[29] ECtHR, *Dorota Rabczewska against Poland* App no 8257/13, 21 January 2013 (pending) (the singer was condemned to a criminal fine for religious insult for comments she made about the Bible on a news portal). See for instance, Joanna Kulesza and Jan Kulesza, 'Blasphemy Law in Poland' in *Blasphemy and Freedom of Expression supra* note 12 at 411, 415; Marcin Górski, 'Freedom of Artistic Expression: Constitutional Lessons from Canada' (2017) 2 *Eötvös Loránd University Law Journal* 1; 'Blatant Censorship': Polish Government Issues Artists with Fines – Then Withdraws Them' (*The Art Newspaper*, 28 May 2020) <www.theartnewspaper.com/2020/05/28/blatant-censorship-polish-government-issues-artists-with-finesthen-withdraws-them>.

[30] 'Nergal: Polish Metal Singer Accused of Blasphemy Appeals for Legal Funds' (*BBC News*, 25 February 2021) <www.bbc.com/news/world-europe-56195919>; also on this, Kulesza and Kulesza *supra* note 29 at 424–25.

[31] Slaughter *supra* note 8 at 171–72; Declan O'Sullivan, 'Egyptian Cases of Blasphemy and Apostasy against Islam: *Takfir al-Muslim*' (2003) 7(2) *The International Journal of Human Rights* 97, 105–07; also Maurits Berger, 'Apostasy and Public Policy in Contemporary Egypt: An Evaluation of Recent Cases from Egypt's Highest Courts' (2003) *Human Rights Quarterly* 720, 730. For an overview after 2011, Lowell H. Schwartz, Dalia Dassa Kaye and Jeffrey Martini, *Artists and the Arab Uprisings* (RAND Corporation 2012) 15–32 (discussing the impact of the Arab uprisings on artistic freedom in Egypt, especially the involvement of Muslim brotherhood and the influence of the Salafists in media regulation).

[32] Anon, 'President Pays Tribute to Mahfouz' (*BBC News*, 30 August 2006) <http://news.bbc.co.uk/2/hi/entertainment/5297470.stm>.

official authorities. In addition, in many Muslim and Sharia-compliant States, where Islamic law is recognized as the primary source of law,[33] the Sharia may, at least in theory, set aside any other conflicting rules (this is also reflected in the Declaration of Human Rights in Islam, which states that 'every man has a right to freely express his opinion, provided it does not conflict with the principles of Sharia').[34] The exact contours of the Sharia however vary, as will be discussed in the next section. This largely also allows States to use religion for political purposes, and misuse blasphemy offences, especially with the aim of prosecuting religious minorities.

The Rushdie affair has served to certain extent as a backdrop to legitimize death edicts for similar types of blasphemy accusations targeting artists, performers and writers – especially those educated or living in the 'West'.[35] The consistent abuse of blasphemy laws in Pakistan (articles 295 and 298 of the Pakistan Penal Code) became widely known following the highly mediatized case of Aasia Bibi,[36] and more recently Mashal Khan.[37] The chilling effect of these laws has also been impacting local artists and the film industry. An illustration is the edict issued by a Pakistani minister against the US-based producer of *The Innocence of Muslims*, setting a one million USD price on

33 This is the case, for example, of the constitutions of Gulf States. Also, references to the Sharia are pervasive in the new constitutions of Muslim States designed after the Arab Spring, see e.g. Intisar Rabb, 'Negotiating Speech in Islamic Law' in Anver Emon, Mark Ellis, and Benjamin Glahn (eds), *Islamic Law and International Human Rights Law* (Oxford University Press 2012) 144, 145; Clark Lombardi, 'Designing Islamic Constitutions: Past Trends and Options for a Democratic Future' (2013) 11 *International Journal of Constitutional Law* 615, 615–17 (discussing what he calls '*Sharia* Guarantee Clauses (SGCs)' in Muslim States' constitutions and noting that the principle that 'state law should be consistent with sharia' has a long pedigree in Islamic political thought).

34 Cairo Declaration on Human Rights in Islam, adopted by the Organisation of Islamic Cooperation (OIC), 9 June 1993, A/CONF.157/PC/62/Add.18.

35 cf Klausen *supra* note 14 at 91–92; Lorenz Langer, *Religious Offence and Human Rights: The Implications of Defamation of Religions* (Cambridge University Press 2012) 82–83 (with examples of prosecutions for blasphemy of the Danish Cartoons editors from Algeria, Yemen and Jordan).

36 UN Human Rights Council, 'Report of the Special Rapporteur on the Promotion and Protection of the Right to Freedom of Opinion and Expression', para 1753, UN Doc A/HRC/17/27/Add.1 (27 May 2011) (prepared by Frank La Rue); see Javaid Rehman and Eleni Polymenopoulou, 'Blasphemy Laws, Religious Minorities and the Case of Aasia Bibi' (2010) 6 *Asian Yearbook of International Law* 129–51.

37 UN Human Rights Committee, 'Concluding Observations: Pakistan', 23 August 2017, CCPR/C/PAK/CO/1, para 33 (freedom of religion and belief). See Arif A. Jamal, 'Making Islamic Penal Clauses: Translation, Transformation and Transmogrification' in Thio Li-ann and Jaclyn L. Neo (eds), *Religious Offences in Common Law Asia: Colonial Legacies, Constitutional Rights and Contemporary Practice* (Hart 2021) 103.

his head.[38] There are, however, other noteworthy examples, most notably the case of the Bangladeshi-Swedish feminist writer Tasleema Nasrin, and her novel *Dwikhandito*. Shortly after publication in West Bengal, India, in 2004, the local authorities in Kolkata issued an order of forfeiture of the book, and the author was prosecuted under Section 295A of the Indian Penal Code for 'deliberate and malicious intention of outraging the religious feelings of any class of citizens of India' (allegedly for passages in the book insulting the Prophet Muhammad).[39] Subsequently, various death threats were issued by local Imams and Muslim councils, offering a certain amount (500,000 rupees in one instance) to behead her.[40] This was regardless of the actual court judgment handed down in 2005 that lifted the ban, celebrating the literary value of the book as a critique of the 'hapless condition of women in [the] country'.[41]

It does seem, however, that there is a general trend to repeal *stricto sensu* blasphemy laws in European States, especially those that privilege the State religion over others (as was the case in the United Kingdom prior to the abolition of the common law offence of blasphemy in 2008,[42] in Greece prior to 2019[43] and in Ireland between 2009 and 2019).[44] In other European States, blasphemy laws tend to be replaced by legislation that aims to criminalize

38 Javaid Rehman, 'The Sharī'ah, International Human Rights Law and the Right to Hold Opinions and Free Expression: After Bilour's Fatwā' in Hossein Esmaeili et al (eds), *Islam and International Law* (Hart 2017) 244, 244.

39 *Sujato Bhadra v State of West Bengal*, 22 September 2005, 2005 (4) CHN 601, CriLJ 368, paras 79–80 (reiterating the local decision of forfeiture) at <https://indiankanoon.org/doc/79421>.

40 Laurent Gayer, Christophe Jaffrelot and Malvika Maheshwari, 'Cultural Policing in South Asia: An Anti-Globalization Backlash against Freedom of Expression?' in Helmut Anheier et al (eds), *Cultures and Globalization: Cultural Expression, Creativity and Innovation* (Sage 2010) 150–51.

41 *Sujato Bhadra supra* note 39 at paras 70–71 and 105. See also at para 49, referring to the Gazette of India, 1 September 1927 (i.e. the original report of the Indian Committee that drafted Section 295A of the Penal Code in 1927) which states: 'harsh and even somewhat abusive language used by an author is permissible if it is done in good faith with the sole and primary object of facilitating some measures of social reform by administering literary shock to the followers of that particular religion as would ensure notice being taken of, any such criticism so made through the literary work'.

42 See e.g. House of Lords, Reports, Session 2002–03, Religious Offences in England and Wales, First Report, Chapter 4, <https://publications.parliament.uk/pa/ld200203/ldselect/ldrelof/95/9506.htm>; Cram *supra* note 27 at 94–96.

43 Greek Criminal Code (revised), Law no 4619/2019. For an overview until 2017, see Eleni Polymenopoulou, 'Arts, Censorship and the Greek Law: Blasphemy v Hate Speech' (2017) 6 *International Human Rights Law Review* 1, 6–8; Efi Fokas, 'God's Advocates' in *Blasphemy and Freedom of Expression supra* note 12 at 389, 389–410.

44 Irish Defamation Act 1961, no 40, abolished in 2019, see generally, Tarlach McGonagle, 'A Draft Obituary for the Offence of Blasphemy in Ireland' in *Blasphemy and Freedom of*

incitement to religious hatred. This change evinces a shift of focus from religion per se to the good functioning of public order.[45] As Hill and Sandberg remark, the exact contours of these laws remain unclear – and it may also be the case that 'what was previously prohibited is not implicitly permitted'.[46] The idleness of criminal blasphemy laws, however, should not be used as justification for their legitimacy. Blasphemy laws, even when dormant, may be misused at any point, as in the case of a man prosecuted under article 140 of the Danish Criminal Code for burning a copy of the Qur'an, shortly after the *Jyllands-Posten* controversy.[47] A parallel could be drawn at this point with laws criminalizing private manifestations of homosexuality. The argument of idleness was brought by the respondent government in *Modinos*, which was submitted to the European Commission of Human Rights in the 1990s. The Cypriot government maintained that the applicant could not claim to be the victim of a violation of the European Convention inter alia because the challenged provisions of the Criminal Code were in practice no longer in force, and because no actual prosecutions were initiated, nor was there an intention to prosecute.[48] The Court however (akin to the UN Human Rights Committee in *Toonen* a few years later)[49] dismissed these arguments. It found that the mere existence of the prohibition in the law 'continuously and directly' was sufficient to demonstrate an unjustified interference with the applicant's private life.

7.1.1.3 The Unique Approach of the US Supreme Court to Religious Offences

The US Supreme Court has consistently dissociated between law and religion, by virtue of the 'establishment' and 'free exercise' clauses of the US Constitution[50] in

Expression supra note 12; also Joel Temperman, 'Blasphemy, Defamation of Religions and Human Rights Law' (2008) 26 *Netherlands Quarterly of Human Rights* 517.

45 Indicatively, Mark Hill and Russell Sandberg, 'The Right to Blaspheme' in *Blasphemy and Freedom of Expression supra* note 12 at 114, 128; Richard Moon, 'Religion and Hate speech in Canada' in *Blasphemy and Freedom of Expression supra* note 12 at 487–89 (discussing 'the challenge of religious hate speech').

46 ibid at 132.

47 Lars Grassmè Binderup and Eva Maria Lassen, 'The Blasphemy Ban in Denmark' in *Blasphemy and Freedom of Expression supra* note 12 at 431, 450; also Kimiko de Freytas-Tamura, 'Danish Man Who Burned Quran Is Prosecuted for Blasphemy' (New York Times, 23 February 2017) <www.nytimes.com/2017/02/23/world/europe/denmark-quran-burning.html>.

48 *Modinos v Cyprus*, 15070/89, Decision, Commission, 6 December 1990 *in fine*.

49 *Toonen v Australia* 488/1992, UN Doc CCPR/C/50/D/488/1992 (1994) para 8.2.

50 First Amendment to the US Constitution: 'Congress shall make no law respecting an establishment of religion, or prohibiting the free exercise thereof'.

all cases related to blasphemous and offensive arts. The Court has found unconstitutional a New York statute allowing motion pictures censorship, which led to the banning of Rossellini's film *The Miracle.* Drawing on the long tradition of free speech protections, the Supreme Court also noted in this case that the broad and all-inclusive definition of 'sacrilegious' is unconstitutionally vague,[51] precisely because

> it is not the business of government in [the American] nation to suppress real or imagined attacks upon a particular religious doctrine, whether they appear in publications, speeches, or motion pictures.[52]

This position has not been substantially altered since. Various authors have pointed to the 'the great divide' between the United States and the rest of the world in free speech matters.[53] A much discussed case is *Hustler and Falwell,* concerning a parody advertisement that appeared in Miloš Forman's satirical magazine *Hustler.*[54] This was in reality a privacy case: Falwell, a well-known Christian minister and televangelist, who was also the host of a nationally syndicated television show, sought to recover damages from *Hustler* magazine before local courts in Virginia, for breach of privacy, libel and 'intentional infliction of emotional distress'.[55] The Court examined thoroughly *Hustler* magazine's arguments on the nature of political cartoons as 'weapons of attack, scorn, ridicule and satire', by referring to the prominent role of cartoons and graphic depictions in the public and political debate of American life, 'from the early cartoon portraying George Washington as an ass because the speech in question is outrageous and may have an adverse emotional impact on the audience'.[56]

This is not to say, however, that freedom of creation in the United States is necessarily free from religious and moral concerns. American public life is still to a large extent influenced by the presence of religion, accompanied by

51 ibid at 505.

52 *Joseph Burstyn, Inc. v Wilson* 343 US 495 (1952) (concerning Rossellini's film, which recites the story of a shepherdess who gets pregnant by a vagabond, mistakenly taking him for Jesus).

53 John Bellinger III and Murad Hussain, 'Freedom of Speech: The Great Divide and the Common Ground between the United States and the Rest of the World' in *Islamic Law and International Human Rights Law supra* note 33 at 168–80. Also indicatively, Kirsty Hughes and Neil Richards, 'The Atlantic divide on privacy and free speech' in Andrew Kenyon (ed), *Comparative Defamation and Privacy Law* (Cambridge University Press 2015) 164–98. See also Chapter 3 of this book (on hate speech).

54 *Hustler Magazine, Inc. v Falwell* 485 US 46 (1988); see also Hughes and Richards *supra* note 53 at 172–73.

55 ibid at 46–47.

56 ibid referring to *NAACP v Claiborne Hardware Co.* 458 US 886, 458 US 910 (1982).

certain lack of proactivity in protecting religious minority rights and group rights,[57] evident also in the general lack of criminalization of hate speech (compared to say, European standards).[58] The presence of public morality considerations, as well as general bans against showing, or promoting content that is morally inappropriate or profane, is especially visible in media content regulation, and falls under the authority of the Federal Communications Commission (FCC). The present guidelines of the FCC, drafted in accordance with this standard, equally admit exceptions in regulating 'obscene, indecent, profane, violent, or otherwise objectionable programming'[59] as per US federal law and *FCC v Pacifica*, discussed earlier in Chapter 6.[60] This is an entirely different standard from the industry-driven regulation of the film industry[61] (Motion Picture Association of America Production), in which the large producers have a say.[62]

7.1.2 *The Rise of Globalized Cultural Conflicts*

7.1.2.1 Blasphemous Arts and Cartoons across Religious Traditions

Artistic depictions (icons) in Christendom have been deeply loved and cherished (to the point of belief in their miraculous capacities)[63] as well as loathed, polemized, damaged and destroyed. The offences of blasphemy and idolatry are also rooted in the Judeo-Christian tradition. The myth of the *Golden Calf*, in particular, narrated in the first book of the Old Testament, has served throughout the centuries as a basis to justify prohibitions against idol-

57 See Cram *supra* note 27 at 106–09.

58 E.g. *R.A.V. v St Paul* cited *supra* Chapter 2; also *Snyder v Phelps* 562 (2011) (upholding the right of a church congregation proclaiming slogans such as 'Pope in Hell' and 'Priests rape boys' in the public sideway next to the funeral of a former US marine soldier sent to Iraq). Indicatively, Bellinger and Hussain *supra* note 53 at 171–72; Hughes and Richards *supra* note 53 at 173–74.

59 Title 47 of the Code of Federal Regulations (CFR), Parts 73 and 74 (Radio broadcast services); see e.g. *CBS Corp. v FCC* no 06-3575 (3d Cir. 2 November 2011) (fine imposed on CBS for exposing Janet Jackson's breast during Super Bowl).

60 US Code, 2006 Edition, Supplement 5, Title 18 – Crimes and Criminal procedure, section 1464. See also *FCC v Pacifica* 438 US 726, discussed in Chapter 6 (on George Carlin's '7 Dirty words').

61 Claire Piepenburg, 'Not Yet Rated: Self-Regulation and Censorship Issues in the U.S. Film Industry' (2018) 25 *UCLA Entertainment Law Review* 97, 106–18.

62 MPAA board members represent Disney, Paramount, Sony Pictures, Universal, Warner Bros, and since 2019, also Netflix. See however Piepenburg *supra* note 61 (noting that 'it remains contested whether movies are truly a public art or a commercial product subject to regulation').

63 Hava Lazarus-Yafeh, 'Some Neglected Aspects of Medieval Muslim Polemics against Christianity' (1996) 89(1) *The Harvard Theological Review* 61–84 (noting how Muslim authors have also been fascinated by the belief in 'fraudulent images').

worshipping and art-making.[64] History is abundant with examples demonstrating the iconoclastic power of the *Calf*. The most pertinent is arguably Byzantine iconoclasm, which was transformed into the official doctrine of the empire under the emperors Leo III and Constantine.[65] Largely targeting 'pagan' antiquities and works of art iconoclasm culminated in large-scale destruction of cultural treasures and monuments.[66] During the early iconoclast Byzantine period, even artists and iconographers – clergymen and monks in their majority – convinced themselves that images were evil.[67]

It would seem therefore reasonable to focus on that tradition in order to understand contemporary iconoclastic practices. In addition, the doctrine of iconoclasm, while extending also to the Semitic and Caucasian worlds,[68] does not seem to have had an equivalent in the Muslim world. Historical research suggests on the contrary that, at least until the fall of the Umayyads, there were hardly any iconoclastic incidents outside Arabia, save for Yazid II's edict to destroy churches,[69] and that the only problematic symbol for Muslims was the Christian symbol of the cross.[70] Why is it therefore that the Islamic tradition is commonly regarded as the one that is inherently iconoclastic, hostile to visual arts and strictly punitive of blasphemous expressions? Several reasons can be advanced for this.

First, artists who are active in the Muslim world are likely to receive artistic education in a way that is deemed compatible with the teachings of the Sharia,

64 *Exodus*, 20: 5; 32: 4; 32:10; 34: 14. For an analytical discussion see Langer *supra* note 35 at 320–51; also, generally, Danièle Menozzi, *Les images ; les églises et les arts visual* (Cerf 1991) 73–77 [in French].

65 Jaś Elsner, 'Iconoclasm as Discourse: From Antiquity to Byzantium' (2012) 94(3) *The Art Bulletin* 368–94; Cyril Mango, *The Art of the Byzantine Empire 312-1453; Sources and Documents* (1972) and David Freedberg, *The Structure of Byzantine and European Iconoclasm* (1977), reprinted in Merryman and Elsen *supra* note 1 at 244–48.

66 Mango *supra* note 65 at 244–45; Gustave Edmund von Grunebaum 'Byzantine Iconoclasm and the Influence of the Islamic Environment' (1962) 2(1) *History of Religions* 1, 2–3.

67 Freedberg *supra* note 65 at 248.

68 Katrin Kogman-Appel, 'Christianity, Idolatry, and the Question of Jewish Figural Painting in the Middle Ages' (2009) 84(1) *Speculum* 73, 87–88 (noting also that it could be also read as reaction to it); Grunebaum *supra* note 66 at 3–4. For a general historical perspective, see also Gamboni (ed), *The Destruction of Art: Iconoclasm and Vandalism since the French Revolution* (Reaktion 1997).

69 G. R. D. King, 'Islam, Iconoclasm, and the Declaration of Doctrine' (1985) 48(2) *Bulletin of the School of Oriental and African Studies* 267, 274–75 (noting that this was so widely discussed precisely because it must have been an exception to the general rule of tolerance towards Christian heritage); also Elsner *supra* note 65 at 375 (noting that 'doubt has been cast on whether this edict really happened').

70 ibid at 269 (with respect to objections to Christian icons and representations).

and conversely, exercise their artistic freedom in a way that does not contradict it. Professor Grunebaum, writing in 1962, sees the Muslim artist as follows:

> The Muslim artist is confronted by a warning. On Judgment Day he will be challenged to breathe life into his figures and on his failure to animate the humans and the animals he has formed he will be consigned to the eternal fire as a blasphemous rival of the one and only Creator.[71]

Surely, not all artists will be afraid of Judgement Day. Still today, however, anxiety in conforming with religious rules and the permissibility of drawing, performing, music, filming (as well as specifically their approach to nudity and sexuality) is reflected in Muslim artists' inquiries. Questions such as 'Is it okay if I draw nude models, or is it *haram* in Islam?' or 'Is the painting of human faces prohibited in Islam?' and even 'Does Islam prohibit art?' are commonly posed to various web-imams in web forums as well as live Q&A sessions, raising the question of the compatibility of their practice with the Sharia,[72] in the same way that some Christians might wonder whether it is a sin 'to look at a naked woman for art'.[73]

Second, contrary to other legal traditions that are necessarily applied within the context of a legal system, the pure classical version of the Sharia is theoretically not confined within the territorial boundaries of a State. As a result, it may be argued that offences under Sharia law are of universal nature, and therefore extraditable beyond the territory of Muslim States. The effect of this logic would not be solely restricted in the area of media regulation – and the risk associated with either publishing or republishing offensive artworks.[74] States applying strict versions of Islamic law could go as far as asserting their jurisdiction on criminal matters extraterritorially for Sharia-related offences that took place outside their territory – even if the latter have been committed in States that do not penalize or criminalize them. This approach to jurisdiction sounds extremely far-stretched. Yet, this is precisely what happened in the case of Khomeini's fatwa, which arbitrarily sentenced a British author to be

71 Grunebaum *supra* note 66 at 5–6.

72 See indicatively, <www.youtube.com/watch?v=zmWEwcoziLo> (featuring an interview with Shabir Ally, President of the Islamic Information & Dawah Centre International in Toronto); also <www.quora.com/Is-painting-of-human-face-is-prohibited-in-Islam>.

73 Indicatively, <www.christianforums.com/threads/is-it-a-sin-to-look-at-a-naked-woman-for-art.7592246>.

74 Norimitsu Onishi, 'Charlie Hebdo Republishes Cartoons That Prompted Deadly 2015 Attack' (*New York Times* 1 September 2020) <www.nytimes.com/2020/09/01/world/europe/charlie-hebdo-cartoons-trial-france.html>.

executed.[75] This approach to criminal jurisdiction has been criticized by the UN Human Rights Committee. In its concluding observations on Iran, the committee stated that 'States parties violate the right to security of person if they purport to exercise jurisdiction over a person outside their territory by issuing a fatwa or similar death sentence authorizing the killing of the victim'.[76] And further, in General Comment no 9 on liberty of the person, it equally found that 'States parties must not arbitrarily or unlawfully arrest or detain individuals outside their territory'.[77]

It follows that the implications of these controversies on 'art and religion' are much broader than a mere 'conflict' of rights (whereby the right to artistic freedom would be conflicting with the right, say, to religious freedom, or even, the right of Muslim minorities to be free from discrimination). They extend in the sphere of both international politics and international security, as indicated by the notorious 'defamation of religions' debate within the political bodies of the United Nations,[78] and the recent involvement of the UN Security Council in cultural heritage controversies.[79] This is especially true as far as the discourse on the permissibility of arts and representation in the appropriation of the Islamic legal tradition by terrorist organizations and extremists is concerned. The deliberate and systematic destruction of cultural heritage in many parts of the world and especially the Middle East is arguably part of the same narrative,[80] raising the question of individual criminal responsibility for perpetrators of crimes related to the destruction of heritage

[75] cf Slaughter *supra* note 8 at 156–73 (noting, however, that charges were also brought in the United Kingdom for racial vilification in violation of the Public Order Act – at 158).

[76] UN Human Rights Committee, Concluding observations: Islamic Republic of Iran CCPR/C/79/Add.25, 1993, para 9.

[77] UN Human Rights Committee, 'General Comment no 35, Liberty and Security of Person' (art 9), CCPR/C/GC/35, 16 December 2014, para 63.

[78] Indicatively, Langer *supra* note 35 at 160–255 and 352–80; Marc Limon, Nazila Ghanea, and Hilary Power, 'Freedom of Expression and Religions, the United Nations and the '16/18 Process' in *Blasphemy and Freedom of Expression supra* note 12 at 645–80; Christian Green, 'Between Blasphemy and Critique: Freedom of Religion and Speech' (2014) 29 *Journal of Law and Religion* 176.

[79] UN Security Council, Resolution 2347 (24 March 2017) (condemning the 'destruction and smuggling of Cultural Heritage by Terrorist Groups'); see also Resolution 2199 (12 February 2015) (aiming at blocking ISIS, ISIL, ANF and Al-Qaeda's financial resources).

[80] Indicatively, Matthew Clapperton, David Martin Jones, M. L. R. Smith, *Iconoclasm and Strategic Thought: Islamic State and Cultural Heritage in Iraq and Syria* (2017) 93 International Affairs 1205–31; Benjamin Isakhan, 'How to Interpret ISIS's Heritage Destruction' (2018) *Current History* 344; On the legal framework, see Kristin Hausler, 'Culture under Attack: The Destruction of Cultural Heritage by Non-State Armed Groups' (2015) 2 *Santander Art and Culture Law Review* 117.

under international criminal law.[81] The fatwa against Rushdie was curiously issued exactly a year after Osama bin Laden had issued another fatwa against US nationals,[82] and in the aftermath of the Soviet forces' withdrawal from Afghanistan that signalled the end of the Cold War.[83] Moreover, neither *The Satanic Verses* nor the cartoons controversies were isolated incidents. Various other, smaller-size controversies followed, including attempts to blow up San Petronio Church in Bologna in 2008, where Giovanni da Modena had centuries ago painted *Mohammed in Hell*.[84]

7.1.2.2 What Does the Sharia Actually Say?

Most authors agree that an equivalent of the word blasphemy is not mentioned in the Qur'an. Rabb, for example, mentions that Abu Hanifa, that is, the leader of one of the four major schools of thought in Sunni Islam that is prevalent in the Middle East and South Asia, viewed blasphemy as the refusal of the oneness of God,[85] and therefore also the first pillar of Islam, the *shahada*. For Saeed and Hashemi, blasphemy seems to be equivalent to an offence named '*sabb*',[86] which generally means to express irreverent speech or more generally to 'insult'.[87] *Sabb* was initially conceived as an offence against either God (*sabb-Allah*) or the Prophet (*sabb-al-Rasoul*) – later extended also to the Messengers of God (i.e. the Angels) and the companions of the Prophet.[88] It appears that defamation charges, or other offences against public order have prevailed over blasphemy during the life of the Prophet and shortly

[81] *Situation in the Republic of Mali in the Case of the Prosecutor v Ahmad Al Faqi Al Mahdi*, Pre-Trial Chamber I, ICC-01/12-01/15-84-Red, 24 March 2016, and ICC-01/12-01/15, 27 September 2016, Public Judgment and Sentence.

[82] UN Security Council, 'Sixteenth Report of the Analytical Support and Sanctions Monitoring Team submitted pursuant to resolution 2161 (2014) concerning Al-Qaida and associated individuals and entities', 29 October 2014, S/2014/770, at 14, para 38.

[83] Gilles Kepel, *Beyond Terror and Martyrdom: The Future of the Middle East* (Harvard University Press 2008) 221ff.

[84] Philip Willan, 'Al-Qaida Plot to Blow up Bologna Church Fresco' (*The Guardian*, 24 June 2002).

[85] Rabb *supra* note 33 at 144; Abdullahi Ahmed An-Na'im, *Islam and the Secular State: Negotiating the Future of Shari'a* (Harvard University Press 2009) at 121; Kamran Hashemi, *Religious Legal Traditions, International Human Rights Law and Muslim States* (Martinus Nijhoff 2008) 31; Generally also Abdullah Saeed and Hassan Saeed, *Freedom of Religion, Apostasy and Islam* (Ashgate 2004) 37–38.

[86] Saeed and Saeed *supra* note 85 at 37–38; Hashemi *supra* note 85 at 31–33.

[87] Hashemi *supra* note 85 at 31.

[88] See Hashemi *supra* note 85 at 36 – citing Qur'an, Surat Al-Baqarah (the Cow) II, verse 256; 'Āli `Imran (Family of Imran) III, verses 72–90; An-Nisa IV verses 48 and 137; Surat Al-Mā'idah (The Table Spread) V verse 54.

after his death. Rabb, for example, refers to the case of poet Imran Hittan, whose poem in praise of Ibn Muljam (known for assassinating Ali) was considered political dissent rather than blasphemy and it is for this reason that it attracted criminal sanction.[89] Also, according to some narrations, the Prophet pardoned Jewish poet Ka'b bin Al-Ashraf who had composed poetry insulting the Prophet and his companions.[90]

There is no agreement as to the exact legal consequences of either *sabb* or blasphemy.[91] It is generally accepted that blasphemy is a *tazir* offence for which punishment is discretionary.[92] Soon after the Prophet's death, however, blasphemy and offences related to religious defamation were conflated with apostasy (*irtidad* or *ridda*), in the sense of rejection of Islam.[93] This is also because utterances contrary to theological consensus constitute implicit rejection of Islam[94] and a 'signal of departure from the community of Muslims and the laws governing them'[95] as noted by Seed and Rabb, respectively. The status of apostasy is generally considered to be among the crimes entailing *hadd* punishment, that is, the most serious crimes in Islamic criminal law.[96] The Qur'an does not contain specific sanctions for apostasy – which is also

89 Rabb *supra* note 33 at 161.

90 Hashemi *supra* note 85 at 31–32.

91 Rabb *supra* note 33 at 41 (noting that apostasy and blasphemy remain of 'disputed status'); Hashemi *supra* note 85 at 31–32 (suggesting that the Prophet himself and his immediate successors were rather tolerant towards divergent opinions expressed in public – provided only that this speech did not defame the Caliphs; also Slaughter *supra* note 8 at 199 (referring to a minority of authors who believed that those liable for *sabb* should be executed).

92 On crimes under Islamic law, see generally, Cherif Bassiouni, *The Shari'a and Islamic Criminal Justice in Time of War and Peace* (Cambridge University Press 2013) 118–19 and 132–33 (noting that the Sharia contains three categories of crimes: *hudud*, *qisas* and *tazir* and that 'the *Sunni* and *Shia* jurisprudential schools all give different interpretations as to the exact elements required for crimes in each of these three categories'). For examples in State practice, see e.g. Ujala Akram, 'Freedom of Speech, Freedom of Religion and Islam' (2014) 2 *European Journal of Law Reform* 363, 364 (especially fn 71–73 and 82–84) (Pakistan); Berger *supra* note 31 at 722 (Egypt); Amr Shalakany, 'Islamic Legal Histories' (2008) 1(1) *Berkeley Journal of Middle Eastern & Islamic Law* 2, 26 (Ottoman empire).

93 Rabb *supra* note 33 at 146 (arguing that 'over time, jurists . . . drew on the *hadith* in times of war to authorize the Head of State generally to use his discretion to impose the death penalty on one-time Muslims who manifested their disbelief'); Abdullah Saeed, 'Pre-modern Islamic Legal Restrictions on Freedom of Religion, with Particular Reference to Apostasy and Its Punishment' in *Islamic Law and International Human Rights Law supra* note 33 at 228; Slaughter *supra* note 8 at 177–78.

94 ibid 147–48 and 158; cf Berger *supra* note 31 at 731 (discussing the case of academic Nasr Abu Zayd before the Egyptian Court of Cassation, in which the latter allowed *takfir*).

95 Saeed *supra* note 93 at 228.

96 Bassiouni *supra* note 92 at 188–89.

why a multiplicity of authors have been opposing its severe punishment.[97] The law of apostasy is in fact relatively complex – for example, while apostates remain legally entitled to possession of property, as noted by Saeed, their rights are suspended pending repentance,[98] and they 'lack the capacity to inherit, even from those within another religion'.[99] Over time juristic opinion developed on the legal nature of apostasy drawing on the extremely powerful condemnation of disbelief (*kufr*) in the theological sense. Indeed, throughout the Qur'an, the word 'disbelief' is used numerous times with extremely negative connotation.[100] Hence, while 'early Islamic scholars distinguished between a *kafir* (i.e. unbeliever, infidel) and *murtadd* (i.e. apostate)', the preeminent Islamic scholars of the main Sunni schools failed to separate the two concepts.

Furthermore, classical Islamic law tolerates visual arts and architecture – albeit primarily 'for the purpose of *ibra* (learning in order to avoid the errors of others)'.[101] To be sure, extraordinary collections of illuminated manuscripts that include the image of the Prophet are exhibited presently in collections around the world. Among the most impressive are works from the early years of Islamic art, including arguably variations of the so-called *Shāh-namā* (the Book of Kings) and the *Fāl-namā* (the Book of Omens), which features also episodes from *Qisas an anbiya* (tales of the Prophets, whose initial texts date from AD 732).[102] The tradition of figurative art is also well maintained in Shia Islam, including contemporary Iran. This is visible, for example, in the streets of Tehran, whereby graffiti encompasses not only representations of

[97] Saeed *supra* note 93 at 231–32; Hashemi *supra* note 85 at 36–38; Rabb *supra* note 33 at 147; Saeed and Saeed *supra* note 85 at 28; also Slaughter *supra* note 8 at 179ff; also Abdullahi A. An-Na'im 'Religious Minorities under Islamic Law and the Limits of Cultural Relativism' (1987) 9 *Human Rights Quarterly* 1–18, and generally, Abdullahi An'Naim, 'Human Rights in the Muslim World' (1990) 3 *Harvard Human Rights Journal* 13, 17 (arguing for a 'constructivist approach to human rights, through a reinterpretation of the Sharia').

[98] Saeed *supra* note 93 at 228.

[99] ibid 230–31.

[100] E.g. *Surat Al-Baqarah* (the Cow) II, verse 88 (reiterating the Biblical story of the Golden Calf). Indicatively, Saeed *supra* note 93 at 233–34.

[101] See Anis Ahmad, 'Islam and Cultural Heritage' in *Proceedings of the Doha Conference of 'Ulamâ on Islam and Cultural Heritage* (UNESCO, 2005) 51.

[102] Eva Hoffman, *The Beginnings of the Illustrated Arabic Book: An Intersection between Art and Scholarship* (2000) 17 *Muqarnas* 37, 37–52; see generally Rachel Milstein et al, *Stories of The Prophets: Illustrated Manuscripts of Qiṣaṣal-Anbiyā'* (Mazda Publishers 1999) and Ernst Grube, 'Islamic Iconography' in Robert Hillenbrand (ed), *Image and Meaning in Islamic Art* (Altajir Trust 2005) 13–33. See also cf also Klausen *supra* note 14 at 97. Also Eleni Polymenopoulou, 'Caliphs, Jinns and Sufi Shrines: The Protection of Cultural Heritage and Cultural Rights under Islamic Law' (2022) 36 *Emory International Law Review* 743, 760–61.

martyrs (*shahids*),[103] but in some cases also scenes from the life of Prophet Muhammad.[104] In all of these representations nonetheless the image of the Prophet appears in a respectful way, and generally with the aim 'to provide a spiritual blueprint for commemorating and visualizing the Prophet after his Death'.[105] The head of the Prophet, like other prophets that appear in Islamic iconography, is often intentionally blurred.[106] This could be, according to art historians, an additional indication of the divine beauty of the Prophet that is inaccessible to artists, who are confined to a physical representation of a figure that exists only in collective consciousness.[107] Furthermore, the issue of figuration is extremely contested. Finbarr Flood, for example, refers to an incident that took place in Eastern Anatolia in 1655, concerning a merchant punished for defacing a *Shāh-namā* containing pictures of the Prophet that he thought were offensive.[108]

Aesthetic limitations will in fact always come into play in Islamic iconography as in any type of religious art (including, for instance, Byzantine art, in which religious persons will need to be represented in a particular manner and on the basis of archetypes).[109] In a fatwa concerning the legitimacy of the image of Prophet Muhammad on the fringe of the US Supreme Court, Taha al-Alwani (Professor of *fiqh* and *usul* at Imam Muhammad bin Sa'ud University in Riyadh, Saudi Arabia and former member of the OIC Islamic Fiqh Academy in Jaddah) discusses these limitations, and concludes that representations of the Prophet espousing the message of the Prophet as part of universal cultural heritage are warranted, and in fact, desired as signs of appreciation towards the

103 Christiane Gruber, 'Images of the Prophet Muhammad in and out of Modernity: The Curious Case of a 2008 Mural in Teheran' in Christiane Gruber and Sune Haugbolle (eds), *Visual Culture in the Modern Middle East: Rhetoric of the Image* (Indiana University Press 2013) 5–8, 63, 87ff

104 ibid at 63–113 (especially image 1.1 and Plate 1).

105 Christiane Gruber, 'Between Logos (*Kalima*) and Light (*Nūr*): Representations of the Prophet Muhammad in Islamic Painting' (2009) 26 *Muqarnas* 229, 234.

106 On Islamic iconography, Grube *supra* note 102 at 16; Richard Ettinghausen and Oleg Grabar, *The Art and Architecture of Islam* (Yale University Press 1987) 119–25. Also Gruber *supra* note 102 at 65ff and 205–08.

107 Gruber *supra* note 88 at 235; Priscilla Soucek, 'The Theory and Practice of Portraiture in the Persian Tradition' (2000) 17 *Muqarnas* 97, 106; for a discussion, see also Polymenopoulou *supra* note 102 at 760, fn 101 and accompanying text.

108 Finbarr Barry Flood, 'Between Cult and Culture: Bamiyan, Islamic Iconoclasm, and the Museum Art' (2002) 134 *Art Bulletin* 641, 645.

109 Waterworth *supra* note 3 (on the trial of Veronese); also Averil Cameron, 'The Language of Images: The Rise of Icons and Christian Representation' (1992) 28 *Studies in Church History* [vol 6 on the Church and the Arts] 1–42; Grunebaum *supra* note 66 at 6 ('. . . the prototype, above all the Christ in his humanity and divinity, is really, although not materially, identical with his image').

Islamic tradition.[110] Similarly, Dr Al-Ansari, dean of the College of Sharia and Islamic Studies at Qatar University, on the occasion of the Doha Conference of the Ulamas that was organized in Doha shortly after the bombing of the two Buddhas of Bamiyan, detailed the accommodation of the cultural heritage of different nations and peoples,[111] pointing to the fact that

> in numerous verses of the Qur'an, attention is … drawn to the act of meditating on the antiquities and heritage of those from the past in order to learn lessons and derive benefit from them, since human history is a chain of interrelated events, regardless of religion, nation or culture.[112]

These arguments are significant with respect to the preservation of heritage, and to oppose cultural crimes committed by extremists against cultural property. Offensive and blasphemous expressions, however, those that aim at ridiculing, or even worse, rejecting Islam, will arguably not fall within this category of permissibility and even desirable expressions. In other words, taken by the standards of classical versions of Islamic law, cartoons such as that portraying Muhammad as a terrorist are undoubtedly offensive (and, according to most Muslims unacceptable).[113] In those handful of States that still resist human rights scrutiny and maintain harsh apostasy laws, the *Jyllands-Posten* cartoonists would arguably 'stand guilty as charged' – to paraphrase Slaughter.[114] Reform of these laws nonetheless remains a topic of heated debate even within the Muslim world.

7.2 THE APPROACH OF HUMAN RIGHTS BODIES

7.2.1 *Key Elements of Religious Offences in the Arts*

7.2.1.1 What Are Intentional Offences?

A central question prior to assessing the legitimacy of laws regulating religious offences is to consider whether they require intent. In fact, about one third of

[110] Taha Jaberal-Alwani, 'Fatwa concerning the US Supreme Courtroom Frieze' (2013) *Law and Religion* 1, 27–28.

[111] Hamid Al-Ansari, 'Islam and the Preservation of the Human Heritage' in *Doha Conference supra* note 101 at 27, 28–29.

[112] ibid 28.

[113] cf Suzan Harkness, Mohamed Magid, Jameka Roberts and Michael Richardson, 'Crossing the Line? Freedom of Speech and Religious Sensibilities' (2007) 40 *Political Science and Politics* 275, 276.

[114] Slaughter *supra* note 8 at 177–79.

blasphemy laws around the world require *mens rea* as an element of the crime.[115] This is surely a better solution than the maintenance of impersonal blasphemy laws, lacking the element of intent. From the perspective of artists, the decision to make or display a transgressive work does not necessarily involve an intention to outrage religious beliefs, and in fact, more often than not is an unwitting one. The appreciation of offences as gratuitous or not is in fact a *non-lieu* in the case of artworks – for the mere reason that art is not required to have a particular purpose – political, aesthetic or other. 'The transgressive inhibits', writes Julius, 'represents a boundary that today's artist must transgress'.[116] Offensive, unconventional and otherwise inappropriate artworks and performances are seldom manifestations of pure disrespect for the divine per se. They may be statements of criticism (towards social standards, attitudes, public order, or even, political power), or simply 'assertions of artistic authority'.[117] Pussy Riot's performance of 'Punk Prayer: Virgin Mary Drive Putin Away' (filmed inside a cathedral), for example, is a form of protest and political activism,[118] in the same way that Renée Cox's *Yo Mama's Last Supper* (featuring a standing naked woman in the middle surrounded by 'an all black cast save a white Judas')[119] is a feminist and pro-equality statement rather than sacrilege. Is there an intent to sacrilege, in, say, the surrealists' 'Our collaborator Benjamin Peret insulting a priest';[120] or, in Kippenberger's 'Crucified Frog with Egg and Beer', which managed to outrage the Pope?[121] Our world would be less rich in representations without these visual representations. An intention to sacrilege, even if present, is hardly direct, and even if direct, is intertwined with a statement of artistic authority.

[115] US Commission on Religious freedom *supra* note 27 at 3.

[116] Julius *supra* note 17 at 53.

[117] ibid at 16.

[118] cf Jeroen Temperman, '"Mother of God, Drive Putin Away": On Blasphemy and Activist Art in the Jurisprudence of the European Court of Human Rights' in *Blasphemy and Freedom of Expression supra* note 12 at 294, 304 and 310 (noting that 'through its lyrics, Pussy Riot conveys above anything a profoundly political message'). Also Anna Baranchuk, 'Balaclavas and Putin: Pussy Riot, Carnivalesque Protest, and Political Culture Jamming' in Marilyn DeLaure and Moritz Fink (eds), *Culture Jamming: Activism and the Art of Cultural Resistance* (New York University Press 2017) 365–90; Eleni Polymenopoulou, 'La liberté d'expression en Russie : journalistes, artistes et écrivains persecutés' (2012) 3 *Lettre de la Ligue des Droits de l'Homme pour l'Europe de l'Est* 9–12.

[119] Plate *supra* note 21 at 44–45.

[120] Ian Chilvers and John Glaves-Smith, *A Dictionary of Modern and Contemporary Art* (3rd ed, Oxford University Press 2009) 688–89.

[121] ibid at 365–67; Haroon Siddique, 'Pope Labels Crucified Frog Sculpture Blasphemous' (*The Guardian*, 28 August 2008) <www.theguardian.com/world/2008/aug/28/italy>.

The extent to which artists may be held unreasonably accountable for their artistic and aesthetic choices even without demonstrating intention may equally be seen in cultural decision-making. An illustrative example is the decision of the local cultural authorities of Segovia, Spain, to place a controversial statute in one of the tourist spots of the old town (which is part of the World Heritage List).[122] The sculpture consisted of a small smiling devil perched on a wall, longing the city and taking selfies with his bronze mobile phone,[123] inspired by a similar 'Devil' sitting on the stairs of St Mary's Church in Lübeck, Germany. The popularity of the sculpture quickly became evident,[124] yet the members of the Christian association *San Miguel y san Frutas* saw in it a 'diabolic iconography', and sponsored a petition to take it down.[125] An injunction was also filed under the Spanish Criminal Code that, despite the abolition of the blasphemy law in 1988, continues to criminalize insults against members of a religious congregation, and the public disparagement of their feelings.[126] Regardless of the fate of the complaint, which is pending at local level, an interesting aspect of this debate is that the purpose of the work has been entirely misinterpreted and taken out of context. As both the sculptor himself, José Antonio Abella, and the City Council explained, the devil commemorated a local legend associated with the construction of a Roman-era aqueduct 'by the devil himself in just a single night'.[127] In other words, in most scenarios it may be easily assumed that the intent of the artist is a political statement (as in the case, say, of Pussy Riot), and if not, it could be also a purely symbolic statement (as in the case, say, of the Segovia devil).

7.2.1.2 The Impact of the Work

Under current human rights standards, effect-based distinctions of speech categories are generally acceptable. Artistic expressions are not an exception

[122] <https://whc.unesco.org/en/list/311/>.

[123] Palko Karasz, 'Statue of a Friendly, Selfie-Taking Devil Divides a Town' (*New York Times*, 18 January 2019) and 'Spain: The Devil from Segovia' <www.dw.com/en/spain-the-devil-from-segovia/av-55868979>.

[124] See e.g. Nicolás Pan-Montojo, 'How a Selfie-Snapping Statue of the Devil Has Raised the Ire of Segovia Locals' (*El Pais*, 15 January 2019) <https://english.elpais.com/elpais/2019/01/14/inenglish/1547483270_385288.html>.

[125] <www.change.org/p/ayuntamiento-segovia-que-no-pongan-la-estatua-del-diablo-en-segovia>. Up to the date of closure the petition had obtained over 5,651 signatures (which is over 10 per cent of Segovia's population).

[126] Spanish Criminal Code, art 525.

[127] Francesca Street, 'Friendly' Satan Statue Causes Anger in Segovia, Spain' (*CNN News*, 18 January 2019) <https://edition.cnn.com/travel/article/friendly-satan-statue-segovia-spain/index.html>.

to this. Yet, the standard is clear-cut in the case of racism and expressions inciting to discrimination,[128] and less clear-cut in the context of intolerant expressions. Under article 4 of the International Convention on the Elimination of Racial Discrimination (ICERD), and article 20 of the International Covenant on Civil and Political Rights (ICCPR) what is clearly prohibited is first, *incitement* (i.e. advocacy of racial or religious hatred that constitutes incitement to discrimination, hostility or violence, under article 20 of the ICCPR), and second, *discrimination* (and even, incitement to discrimination against a specific racial or ethnic group).[129] Both are different thresholds from the mere fact of taking offence.

Hate speech, in particular, as defined by the UN Committee on the Elimination of Racial Discrimination (CERD) and UN experts is well-distinguished from purely discriminatory speech, or inflammatory speech that does not target communities (and therefore does not constitute incitement).[130] Subsequently, the truly problematic question is, as Ghanea points out, 'speech that is aimed at the victim(s) and which has *not* had the effect of inspiring its audience to harm the victim(s) concerned'.[131] In the arts, this would be translated into the following question: what happens in the case of artists (or performers, or cartoonists) who intentionally target religious communities (individuals or members of a religious minority), yet without reaching the appropriate level of harm? These are encompassed with the range of expressions constituting simply 'offensive style'.[132]

7.2.2 *Where Would UN Human Rights Bodies Draw the Line?*

A right 'not being offended' in one's religious beliefs is in principle not included in the scope of the right to religious freedom. The general approach of international human rights bodies is not to criminalize blasphemy, unless it reaches the threshold of hate speech (or incitement to discrimination). In General Comment no 34 concerning freedom of expression, in particular, the UN Human Rights Committee took the view that blasphemy laws are contrary

[128] E.g. *Mohammed Hassan Gelle v Denmark*, Communication no 34/2004, UN Doc CERD/C/68/D/34/2004 (2006).

[129] See Chapter 3 (on hate speech and incitement).

[130] Nazila Ghanea, 'Intersectionality and the Spectrum of Racist Hate Speech: Proposals to the UN Committee on the Elimination of Racial Discrimination' (2013) 35 *Human Rights Quarterly* 935, 938–39 (with reference to Susan Benesch and thematic discussion on Racist Hate Speech, held on 28 August 2012 in Geneva).

[131] ibid at 940.

[132] Ilias Trispiotis, 'The Duty to Respect Religious Feelings: Insights from European Human Rights Law' (2013) 19(3) *Columbia Journal of European Law* 499, 529–37.

to international human rights standards, 'except in the specific circumstances envisaged in article 20, paragraph 2, of the covenant',[133] and also 'that it would not be permissible for such prohibitions to be used to prevent or punish criticism of religious leaders or commentary on religious doctrine and tenets of faith'.[134] Furthermore, article 4 of the ICERD compels States to legislate in order to criminalize hate speech, namely, to declare an offence punishable by law all dissemination of ideas based on racial superiority or hatred. Both provisions therefore (article 4 of the ICERD and article 20 of the ICCPR) are applicable in hate speech contexts, and indeed the exact relationship between them has been the subject of extensive discussions both at UN level and beyond.[135]

A hard case scenario arises therefore in respect of States that opt not to criminalize artistic expressions or performances giving rise to religious critique, yet at the same time disseminate religious stereotypes. *Charlie Hebdo* cartoons republished in wide-circulation magazines portraying the Prophet as a terrorist therefore would most likely be considered as breaching ICCPR standards, not because they were derogatory or blasphemous (in terms of international human rights law this would obviously be an invalid point),[136] but rather, because they could be seen as publicly advancing the view that all Muslims are related in one way or another to terrorism, and therefore inciting the public to 'discrimination, hostility or violence' against them. Similarly, they would be most likely considered in breach of hate speech standards under the ICERD, and because of dissemination speech inciting to religious discrimination.[137] In fact, despite the fact that the ICERD was in principle conceived to protect racial minorities alone, the CERD accepts that religious minorities and cultural groups are protected, especially when intersectionality is proved[138] – recompensing in a way for the absence of a treaty that protects

[133] UN Human Rights Committee, 'General Comment no 34, Freedoms of Opinion and Expression', (art 19), CCPR/C/GC/34, 12 September 2011, para 48.

[134] ibid at paras 48–50.

[135] See especially the OHCHR Expert meeting on the 'Links between Articles 19 and 20 of the ICCPR: Freedom of Expression and Advocacy of Religious Hatred that Constitutes Incitement to Discrimination, Hostility or Violence'. On international law standards in relation to the Danish cartoons, see analytically, Langer *supra* note 35 at 91–142.

[136] ARTICLE 19, 'Response to publication of Charlie Hebdo Cartoons and Distribution of Innocence of Muslims video', 20 September 2012.

[137] Analytically, Langer *supra* note 35 at 88–90.

[138] David Keane, 'Addressing the Aggravated Meeting Points of Race and Religion' (2006) 6 *University of Maryland Law Journal of Race, Religion, Gender and Class* 367, 367 (fn 2), and 370. Indicatively also Patrick Thornberry, 'Confronting Racial Discrimination: A CERD Perspective' (2005) 5 *Human Rights Law Review* 239, 258–59; cf Cox *supra* note 14 at 69–72.

against religious intolerance.[139] The CERD, in particular, in General Recommendation 30, concerning non-nationals, expressly recommends that States parties take 'resolute action to counter any tendency to target, stigmatize, stereotype or profile, on the basis of race, colour, descent, and national or ethnic origin, members of "non-citizen" population groups, especially by politicians [...]'.[140] And in General Recommendation 34, it instructs media to 'avoid referring unnecessarily to race, ethnicity, religion and other group characteristics in a manner that may promote intolerance'.[141] Furthermore, contribution to public debate is generally of little relevance to the ICERD when racial discrimination is at stake, as the jurisprudence of the committee aptly demonstrates. For example, the CERD has found Germany liable under the ICERD for failing to prosecute effectively a politician who commented on the integration of Turkish minorities in Germany (in a way that used denigrating stereotypes),[142] and equally found Denmark liable for its lack of effective prosecution and punishment of a Danish politician who commented on the need to consult Somali associations on a bill concerning female genital mutilation equating them to 'paedophiles and rapists'.[143] In this last case, the committee specifically noted that the context of political debate does not absolve the State party from its obligation to investigate whether or not such statements amount to racial discrimination.[144]

7.2.3 *Where Would the European Court Draw the Line?*

The now defunct Commission of Human Rights has held views that are favourable to artistic freedom, as already discussed earlier (for instance, in *Müller* and *Naegeli*). Consistently with this approach, in all cases before it, it weighted artistic freedom more heavily than religious sensibilities. In *Dubowska and Skup*, for example, concerning a cartoon published in a national weekly magazine depicting Mary and Jesus wearing gas masks, it

139 ibid at 386ff (on the drafting history of the ICERD, the abandoning of the idea of the 'Religion' Convention – and the subsequent adoption of the UN Declaration on the Elimination of All Forms of Intolerance and of Discrimination Based on Religion or Belief in 1981).

140 CERD, 'General Recommendation no 30 on Discrimination against Non Citizens', 1 October 2002.

141 CERD, 'General Recommendation no. 35, Combatting Racist Hate Speech', CERD/C/GC/35, at 40.

142 E.g. *TBB-Turkish Union in Berlin/Brandenburg* no 48/2010, 4 April 2013, CERD/C/82/D/48/2010, paras 7.1–8.3.

143 *Mohammed Hassan Gelle v Denmark*, Communication no 34/2004, UN Doc CERD/C/68/D/34/2004 (2006) at 2.1.

144 ibid 2.4 and 7.4; cf *TBB-Turkish Union in Berlin/Brandenburg*, paras 12.7–12.9.

stated unequivocally that the 'members of a religious community must tolerate and accept the denial by others of their religious beliefs'.[145] In *Wingrove*, in which the United Kingdom refused to grant a cinematographic visa to a short (18-minute) video titled *Visions of Ecstasy*, the Commission agreed with the video artist that his work had been unduly censored.[146] Moreover, in the much discussed case of *Otto-Preminger-Institut*, it had decided that the seizure and forfeiture of Werner Schroeter's film *Das Liebeskonzil*, which was scheduled for a mere six screenings in a small cinema hall in Innsbruck, was in breach of the convention, highlighting that 'satirical texts or films can normally not be completely prohibited even if some restrictions ... may be possible'.[147] Consistent with its views, it equally dismissed the claim of a Muslim applicant, who brought blasphemy charges against Salman Rushdie under article 9 of the convention (on religious freedom).[148]

The Court on the other hand has virtually always showed itself significantly more conservative on this matter. Taking the opposite view from the Commission, it has consistently accepted that 'in the context of religious opinions and beliefs there may legitimately be included an obligation to avoid as far as possible expressions that are *gratuitously* offensive to others'.[149] This particular statement of the Court has been already widely commented upon and criticized (i.e. the view that expressions that are gratuitously offensive should be altogether avoided) and rightly so. Maintaining that States have a general obligation of diligence to be mindful that writers, artists and performers avoid *gratuitous* religious offences to others unnecessarily expands the legitimacy of restrictions against artistic freedom and goes against the very principle of the Court that restrictions should be considered narrowly. At the same time, the Court has considered inadmissible complaints that could have shed light on the relationship between religion and arts – for example, the complaint of Turkey's censorship of René Clément's *Forbidden Games* by TRT (in which the Court considered that the applicant had other ways to watch the film such as renting a video copy from the local video club).[150]

145 *Dubowska and Skup v Poland* App nos 33490/96 and 34055/96, Commission Report, 18 April 1997, at para 2 (law).

146 *Wingrove v United Kingdom* App no 17419/90, Commission Report, 10 January 1995, at para 67. See Eleni Polymenopoulou, 'Does One Swallow Make a Spring: Artistic and Literary Freedom at the European Court of Human Rights' (2016) 16(3) *Human Rights Law Review* 511, 522–23; Cram *supra* note 27 at 96–99.

147 *Otto Preminger* App no 13470/87, Commission Report, 14 January 1993, at para 77.

148 *Choudhury v United Kingdom* App no 17439/90, Admissibility, 5 March 1991 (inadmissible).

149 *Otto-Preminger-Institute v Austria* App no 13470/87, Judgment, 20 September 1994, para 49.

150 *Ozkan v Turkey* App no 23886/94, Admissibility, 5 April 1995 (the broadcast ended after TRT received threatening phone calls accusing the film of Christian propaganda).

There have indeed been few instances indicating a shift in the jurisprudence of the Court towards exclusion of offences to sensibilities from the protective scope of article 10 of the ECHR in artistic freedom cases. This first evidence of a shift was made explicit in cases decided shortly after the Danish cartoons controversy, concerning primarily scientific and academic freedom.[151] It makes sense therefore to presume that the parallel developments that took place in the context of both the Council of Europe and the EU shortly after the Danish cartoons controversy had an impact on the jurisprudence of the Court. Of particular importance at that time was the work of the Venice Commission on the matter, including the organization of various workshops and roundtables to discuss the question of 'Art and Religion'[152] and the subsequent report of the Commission which concluded that it 'must be possible to criticize religious ideas, even if such criticism may be perceived by some as hurting their religious feelings'.[153] Resolution 1510 of the Parliamentary Assembly of the Council of Europe (PACE) has also similarly highlighted that 'freedom of expression … should not be further restricted to meet increasing sensitivities of certain religious groups'.[154]

Even so, however, the jurisprudence of the Court remains to date relatively inconsistent,[155] and emerging 'defences' for artists, such as humour and satire for instance, are used rather sparingly.[156] A detailed discussion of the approach of the Court over its interpretation of religious pluralism in democratic societies (and the subsequent use of the margin of appreciation doctrine in such a way as *not* to accommodate minority religious beliefs to their full extent) goes beyond the scope of this study.[157] Suffice to say, however, for the

[151] *Aydin Tatlav v Turkey* App no 50692/99, Merits and Just Satisfaction, 2 May 2006; *Giniewski v France* 77 App no 64016/00, Merits, 31 January 2006; *Klein v Slovakia* 78 App no 72208/01, Merits and Just Satisfaction, 31 October 2006 (concerning the advertising poster for Miloš Forman's *The People vs. Larry Flynt*, see also *Hustler Magazine, Inc. v Falwell supra* note 54). cf Temperman *supra* note 118 at 294–314 (referring also to *Albert-Englemman v Austria* App no 46389/99, Merits, January 2006 and *Nur Radio*, 27 November 2007).

[152] Indicatively, 'Art and Sacred Beliefs: From Collision to Co-existence', (Athens, 31 January–1 February 2008).

[153] Venice Commission Report *supra* note 27 at 16, para 76.

[154] Adopted by the Parliamentary Assembly on 28 June 2006.

[155] Ian Leigh, 'Damned If They Do, Damned If They Don't: The European Court of Human Rights and the Protection of Religion from Attack' (2011) 2 *Res Publica* 55, at 67–70; Trispiotis *supra* note 132 at 546–47.

[156] Polymenopoulou *supra* note 146 at 530–38.

[157] Indicatively among the vast doctrine, see Nathwani, 'Religious Cartoons and Human Rights – A Critical Legal Analysis of the Case Law of the European Court of Human Rights on the Protection of Religious Feelings and its Implications in the Danish Affair Concerning Cartoons of the Prophet Muhammad' (2008) 13 *European Human Rights Law Review* 488

purposes of this chapter that questions living together in democratic societies, religious beliefs and matters of public order in European societies are extremely complex. As noted in the Parliamentary Assembly on freedom of religion and living together in a democratic society, many of the practices the Court has considered touch upon questions that are divisive even among communities.[158]

In addition, the judgments over artistic works, ultimately, are indicative of the extent to which the value of free speech is (or maybe not) truly accepted. To date, judgements over public morality and religious sensibilities have done little justice to the *Handyside* formula and the motto 'ideas that shock, offend, or disturb' – starting with *Handyside* itself.[159] As a result, even when in favour of artistic freedom, cases are decided with a very narrow margin, as in *Bildender Künstler v Austria*.[160] Hence, there is no indication that the Court will consider in the future those cases involving arts and religious sensibilities in a way different from the past. The Court is generally hesitant to affirm the prevalence of free speech at the cost of hurting or offending sensibilities. In the aforementioned case of Pussy Riot's Schliessmann Punk Prayer', for example, while ultimately condemning Russia for the extremely harsh treatment of the members of the group (which amounted to violations of article 3 of the convention), the Court did not go as far as discussing in detail the question of offence to religious beliefs.[161] This, however, could have been an essential part of the judgment, given that proceedings in Russia were based inter alia on religiously motivated hatred,[162] and indeed also 'the disparagement of the spiritual foundation of the Russian State'.[163] Other cases that could have eventually shed more light on these questions have been considered inadmissible in accordance with article 27 of the convention, including for instance the case concerning the Danish cartoons (dismissed *ratione*

at 504; generally, Nathan Lerner, *Religion, Secular Beliefs and Human Rights: 25 Years after the 1981 Declaration* (2006) 81–117.

158 PACE, *Freedom of Religion and Living Together in a Democratic Society*, Resolution 2076 (2015), paras 6–8.

159 *Handyside v United Kingdom* no 5493/72, 7 December 1976, para 49 (concerning the ban of the *Little Red Book*). See also Chapter 3.

160 *Vereinigung Bildender Künstler v Austria* no 68354/01 25 January 2007. See Chapter 1.

161 cf Temperman *supra* note 118 at 312 (noting that the Court 'should overrule once and for all the judgment in Otto-Preminger').

162 *Alekhina and Others* App no 38004/12, 11 September 2018, paras 87–95 (noting that the members of the band were prosecuted inter alia for incitement to religious hatred and insult of religious feelings).

163 Baranchuk *supra* note 118 at 376.

loci for lack of jurisdictional link between the applicants and the respondent State),[164] and the case concerning the closing down of exhibition *Caution, Religion!* in the Sakharov Museum and Public Center in Moscow (exhibiting among other things a Coca-Cola advertisement with the image of Christ as 'the Blood of Christ').[165] In addition, in the more recent case of *E.S.* decided in 2018 (concerning the prosecution of a journalist for derogatory comments about the Prophet Muhammad), the Court relied on the *Otto-Preminger* jurisprudence and reiterated once more that States may legitimately take restrictive measures to prevent 'expressions [that] go beyond the limits of a critical denial of other people's religious beliefs and are likely to incite religious intolerance, for example in the event of an improper or even abusive attack on an object of religious veneration'.[166] It further found a wide margin of appreciation of the State, finding that Austrian courts were 'in better position to evaluate which statements were likely to disturb the religious peace in their country'.[167]

CONCLUDING REMARKS

This chapter addressed controversies over religious offences involving artworks. It did not address in detail the extremely complex issues raised by 'globalized controversies', neither that of extrajudicial killings, and terrorist attacks perpetrated by non-state actors on the grounds of blasphemy. Rather, it confined itself in the human rights approach, and the examination of the ways that the human rights system and international bodies address the question of controversies over blasphemous and otherwise 'transgressive' artworks. Due to the global ramifications of terrorist incidents such as the *Charlie Hebdo* attacks, however, the chapter does briefly refer to the position of the Sharia on blasphemy and apostasy offences, pointing to the lack of agreement among Muslim scholars as to the exact scope and legal consequences of these offences.

164 *Ben El Mahi and Others v Denmark* App no 5853/06, Admissibility, 11 December 2006.

165 *Samodurov and Vasilovskaya* App no 3007/06, 15 December 2009 (inadmissible) at paras 4–5 (describing the destruction of the exhibits). Also Plate *supra* note 21 at 55–57.

166 *E.S. v Austria* App no 38450/12, Merits, 25 October 2018, at para 43 (referring to *Otto-Preminger supra* note 1 at para 47 and *İ.A. v Turkey* App no 42571/98, Merits and Just Satisfaction, 13 September 2005, para 29). For a critique, see Stijn Smet, 'Free Speech versus Religious Feelings, the Sequel: Defamation of the Prophet Muhammad in E.S. v Austria' (2019) 15 *European Constitutional Law Review*; Eva Hauksdóttir, 'Restricting Freedom of Expression for Religious Peace: On the ECHR's Approach to Blasphemy' (2021) 2 *European Convention on Human Rights Law Review* 75.

167 ibid at para 50.

The question of the potential criminalization of offences related to the publication of offensive cartoons under human rights law standards is an extremely hard and complex one. Controversies over religiously offensive cartoons in particular test the limits of international human rights law as a way to safeguard freedoms, pluralism and tolerance in a global world. As discussed above, according to human rights bodies, States should find ways to effectively prosecute journalists and creatives when inciting to hatred and racism, or simply discrimination – including in the sense of diminishing stereotypes about religious beliefs. Yet in the recent case of *E.S.*, the ECtHR introduced an additional factor to measure the effect, based on a likelihood to intolerance.[168]

This parameter, however, introduces an extremely low standard of protection for creative speech, impacting artists and cartoonists' freedom in multifold ways. First, the contribution of cartoons to the public debate and their status as political speech cannot be disregarded. The significant parameter therefore is this: if the impugned expression can be taken out of context, the offence is likely to be a gratuitous one, aiming solely at harming and offending (an example would be the racist cartoons depicting Serena Williams, in the relevant controversial case before the Australian Press Council).[169] Controversial cartoons however such as *c'est dur d'être aimé par des cons* (which cost the life of the illustrator) cannot be read out of their context: they were part of a substantial public debate on the spread of radicalization and the multiplication of terrorist attacks in the name of religion. For this reason alone they cannot be interpreted as inciting to hatred against religious minorities, or gratuitously aiming at stirring up religious intolerance. The globally widespread controversy over their nature and publication is precisely the proof of the contribution of these cartoons to the public debate. Second, the causal link between the cartoons and the exact impact on religious minority rights is extremely weak. The fact that many of those who felt offended had not actually seen the cartoons is also not one to be taken lightly. As one of the ECtHR judges had already pointed in 2005, in his dissenting view in and *İ.A.*, it is one thing for individuals (or minority groups) to feel offended, and another to allow the criminalization of authors:

> nobody is ever obliged to buy or read a novel, and those who do so are entitled to seek redress in the courts for anything they consider blasphemous

[168] *E.S. supra* note 168 at para 43.

[169] Damien Cave, 'Serena Williams Cartoon "Not About Race," Artist Says. Experts Strongly Disagree' (*New York Times*, 11 September 2018) <www.nytimes.com/2018/09/11/world/australia/serena-williams-cartoon-herald-sun-racist.html>.

and repugnant to their faith ... But it is quite a different matter for the prosecuting authorities to institute criminal proceedings against a publisher of their own motion....[170]

Last, the extended approach to protection against intolerance is effectively 'chilling' all possible humorous reactions to serious issues, ignoring the contribution of this particular artistic genre to public life whose very *raison d'être* is to be scornful. The US Supreme Court case law, despite its fallacies, provides a useful benchmark in this case. This is because, first, this court generally bans content-based restrictions, and requires State neutrality even in the 'free exercise raison d'être' clause.[171] Second, because even in the case of offences that could, potentially, qualify as 'libel of groups' they would be prohibited only if rising to a level of breach of the peace,[172] or imminent lawless action that is likely to produce such action.[173] Likelihood of intolerance, even considering the latest case law of the US Supreme Court,[174] is still a very far leap away.

Surely, free speech is accompanied by 'duties and responsibilities' as per the relevant provisions in human rights instruments, yet this is not something that 'go[es] easily with the profession' to paraphrase Keane.[175] Overemphasizing the need for tolerance in a way inverses the problem: it is in the name of tolerance that free speech is ultimately restricted, producing even more intolerance. Finding that free speech should legitimately be curtailed even in the event of potential rise to religious intolerance overshadows the threats faced by artists – and cartoonists –around the world.[176] Sadly these threats include also both intolerance and religious fundamentalism.

170 *İ.A. v Turkey supra* note 168 at Joint Dissenting Opinion of Judges Costa, Cabral Barreto and Jungwiert, para 5 (concerning a novel that addressed philosophical and theological issues on Islam).

171 See Chapter 2.

172 *Beauharnais v Illinois* 343 US 250 (1952).

173 *Brandenburg v Ohio* 395 US 444 (1969).

174 E.g. *Walker v Sons of Confederate Veterans* (2015) (regarding legislation that would allow licence plates bearing the image of the Confederate flag) and generally George Wright, 'A Variable Number of Cheers for Viewpoint-Based Regulations of Speech' (2021) 96(2) *Notre Dame Law Review Reflection* 82–106.

175 Keane *supra* note 14 at 875.

176 Committee to Protect Journalists (CPJ), *Drawing the Line: Cartoonists under Threat*, Report prepare by Shawn Crispin, <https://cpj.org/reports/2015/05/drawing-the-line-cartoonists-under-threat-free-expression-zunar-charlie-hebdo/>; Also Keane *supra* note 14 at 848–57.

Index

For EU product safety concerns, contact us at Calle de José Abascal, 56–1°,
28003 Madrid, Spain or eugpsr@cambridge.org.

www.ingramcontent.com/pod-product-compliance
Lightning Source LLC
LaVergne TN
LVHW011812200926
848484LV00005B/1167
* 9 7 8 1 1 0 8 8 4 4 2 0 8 *